METROPOLITAN SCHOOLS:

Administrative Decentralization
vs. Community Control

by

ALLAN C. ORNSTEIN

The Scarecrow Press, Inc.
Metuchen, N.J.   1974

Library of Congress Cataloging in Publication Data

Ornstein, Allan C
   Metropolitan schools.

    1. Education, Urban--United States. 2. Schools--
Centralization--United States. 3. Community and school
--United States. I. Title.
LC5131.076 1974   379'.1535   73-20487
ISBN 0-8108-0653-3

Dedicated to

Virgil Clift, Shelly Marcus, Gene Hedley ... in New York;
Barney Berlin and Harriet Talmage ... in Chicago;
Dan Levine and Russell Doll ... in Kansas City;
and Phil Vairo ... in Los Angeles

TABLE OF CONTENTS

FOREWORD

The literature of urban and metropolitan education has expanded exponentially over the past ten years. Unfortunately, much of the writing consists of opinion, conjecture, or one man's personal experience generalized to global proportions. In addition, sensitivity on all sides of racial issues, community control issues, and various administrative issues leads to a further clouding of the perceptions of those concerned with education in metropolitan areas.

While Dr. Ornstein can not (and did not) single-handedly unify and clarify all points of view relating to administrative/community perspectives of metropolitan education, it seems that this book provides much needed clarity of thought in a number of important areas. One need not agree with all of the author's interpretations and conclusions to recognize that the data presented require careful consideration by anyone concerned with metropolitan schools, either as a teacher or an administrator.

This book begins on a theoretical note, with a discussion of social systems, and presentation of several models which might enable the reader to develop a cohesive view of a school system with which he is familiar. The author then proceeds to analyze the policy reports which recommend varying degrees of decentralization of the five largest school systems.

While administrative decentralization and community control of schools (frequently both approaches are recommended) are not the only suggestions which have been advanced for improving urban schools, they are among those heard most frequently. Thus, the final two sections, analyzing 16 medium-sized systems with some degree of decentralization and community participation, and Detroit and New York as systems with significant community control, allow the reader to formulate a clearer picture of the

"blessings" of these changes. The data (sometimes controversial) are presented; the conclusions are up to the reader.

Dr. Barney M. Berlin
School of Education
Loyola University
of Chicago

INTRODUCTION

People change; the issues change. Writers and social scientists continue to be held accountable all their lives for something they said once that may no longer be true; authors are repeatedly quoted out of context. Perhaps I will regret someday what I say now in this book. Indeed, academic freedom is limited in many college classrooms. Yesterday, it was difficult to discuss frankly the war in Vietnam, and in another time it was evolution or questioning the existence of God that was difficult to speak of. Today, it is at best abstruse to discuss all the issues related to race and race relations.

For purpose of this book, it is important to define three terms:

1. ADMINISTRATIVE DECENTRALIZATION: decentralization is a common occurrence in most city and suburban school systems comprising 50,000 or more students. A particular school system may decentralize and stop at this point, or it may, as it usually does, then proceed to increase community participation. In only two cases, Detroit and New York (which we discuss in detail in Chapter 4), have the school systems proceeded to the stage of community control.

With administrative decentralization alone, the locus of political power remains with the single, central administration and board of education. The system is broken into administrative or smaller units, and sometimes these units are further subdivided. For example, the Chicago school system presently comprises three areas, and these areas are further divided into 27 districts. By breaking down the system, in theory, the administration is brought closer to the schools and community, and there is closer communication between the schools and central office. The central administrative span of control is reduced. There is a major shift of influence from the central office to the administrative or smaller unit. The decentralized field administrators, such as the district or area superintendents and school principals, attain the power to make some decisions which were formerly made at the central office. Accountability is still directed upwards, not toward the community. Since the professionals retain power and there is no radical change in the status of their positions, most school people prefer this kind of school reorganization.

2. COMMUNITY PARTICIPATION: although decentralization need not always lead to increased lay participation, there is often such an increase. With this policy, the decision-making powers still remain with the professionals, especially at the top of the hierarchy. Community participation usually results in the formation of advisory committees, truly only advisory in nature, comprising various combinations of representatives of parents, community residents without children attending the public schools, teachers, administrators, students, local business, political, religious, and social agencies. Committee members are usually appointed by the school principal, if the committee is operating on the school level, or by the field administrator and/or central office administrator, if the committee is operating on the decentralized or central level; however, a few school systems permit these committees to elect members from the above representative groups.

The committees that are formed may operate at any of the various levels of the school system--the school, administrative or decentralized unit, or central office--providing some kind of advisory input, making recommendations, and serving as a liaison between the schools and community. Community participation is accepted and encouraged by teachers, administrators, and school board officials, as well as by many minority parents and community leaders; it is, however, rejected by most liberal and militant groups for it does not transfer decision-making authority to the community.

3. COMMUNITY CONTROL: demand for community control is often heard from black communities (not only with regard to the schools but also with regard to other systems such as the political, the economic, and the social). They argue that the schools have been unresponsive to the needs and interests of black children. Since the professional educators have failed to educate their children, first the

militant part of the black community and now a growing segment of the rest of the black community argue for a chance to succeed, or at least to fail themselves.

The general procedure is to advocate the decentralization of the schools within the existing administrative framework, which in turn facilitates local control. But while community control can be created through some form of administrative decentralization, the decentralization process does not necessarily lead to community control. Community control connotes a legal provision for an elected local school board to function under specific guidelines in conjunction with the central school board. Carried to the fullest extent, it means decision-making power by the community (or so-called representatives from the community) over personnel (hiring, firing, and promoting), curriculum (course electives, ordering textbooks), student policy (student-teacher relations, discipline, testing and evaluation), and financing (federal funding, allocation of money, even determination of the budget). In short, the powers of the professional educators are abridged--an act most school personnel reject.

We can collapse the three organizational models into two options: administrative decentralization and community participation, or decentralization and community control. Most professionals advocate the first option because their power and authority remain intact, and they still make the major decisions. Many liberal and militant groups prefer the second option; this connotes a transferring of decision-making authority and political power to members of the community.

A Note on the Present Work

The reader should note that this book is divided into four chapters. The first examines the concepts and issues related to understanding social systems and how the schools can be viewed as a social system. The differences between centralization and decentralization, as well as systems-analysis and management-control approaches are also explored. In the next chapter, we are concerned with the research on administrative decentralization, community participation, and community control. Special emphasis is placed on the problems of the research and how it may be improved. Chapter three examines the administrative-community plans of 16 medium-sized school systems; the data are based on a survey for this book. The final chapter consists of a detailed case study of the Detroit and New York City school systems; these two school systems are the only ones where some form of community control has been legally enacted with specific guidelines.

Chapter 1

ADMINISTRATIVE ORGANIZATIONAL THEORY

This chapter examines various approaches to studying the school as an organization. First, all schools may be considered a social system which comprises a network of institutional and individual dimensions that produce various kinds of behavior. Second, we can view the school as a closed system which gives primary attention to its internal structures and then relate these internal structures to the concepts of debureaucratization and decentralization. Third, we can view the school in terms of an open system which gives primary attention to external forces and then relate this orientation to the concepts of community participation and community control. Finally, we can consider the school which utilizes the closed-system and open-system approaches, especially for methods of problem solving for planning educational change and reorganizing the schools--say, in the form of administrative decentralization or the provision of greater community participation or community control.

The School as a Social System

The use of the term "system" connotes a pattern of relationships. Systems have either biological or social relationships. The biological systems have a fixed physical boundary, whereas the social systems comprise a conceptual framework and a network of interpersonal and social patterns of behavior. As Linton (1936), in his classic text on The Study of Man, writes: "Each of the patterns which together compose a social system is made up of hypothetical attitudes and forms of behavior, the sum total of these constituting a social relationship" (p. 256). Similarly Parsons (1951), in his important text on The Social System, perceives it as "a plurality of individual actors interacting with each other in a situation which ... is defined and mediated in terms of a system of culturally structured and shared symbols" (p. 5-6). Baldridge (1972) envisions the social system

13

as a network of people organized for achieving "human goals,
values, and purposes," through internal or external processes (p. 4).

Most often the concept of the social system is applied
to a large and complex pattern of human relationships such
as the community, city, or metropolitan area--even up to
the level of society at large. But one of the advantages of
the concept of social system is that it is not limited by size
or magnitude of interaction. In one respect, these larger
entities (community, city, etc.) may be considered as a
social system, with the schools, churches, businesses,
houses, legal body, etc., as subsystems. For another purpose, the schools, churches, businesses, houses, and legal
body may be studied as social systems* with the classroom,
church auxiliary, personnel department, rental office, and
legal committee perceived as subsystems. For still other
purposes, the classroom, church auxiliary, personnel department, rental office, and legal committee may be considered as themselves social systems (Getzels, Lipham, &
Campbell, 1968; Havighurst and Levine, 1971). Thus, the
size of the interaction is not the major consideration: it
is the group interaction and mutual relationships which constitute the social system.

We can describe any formal organization, including
the schools, as a social system, then divide the organization
into basic parts or subsystems; this approach for examining
organizations has been developed by theorists in management, public administration, and sociology, and it has been
largely adopted by educational administrators for studying the
schools. Parsons (1960) describes three levels or subsystems to a formal organization: (1) technical, concerned
with transforming the input energies available so as to develop a new product or train people; (2) managerial, comprising the organized activities for controlling, coordinating,
and directing the various organizational functions; and
(3) institutional, referring to the fact that the organization
interacts with a social environment or larger segment of
society. For purposes of our book, the technical functions

_____
*Levine and Havighurst (1967) outline 14 of these social
systems which interact in a metropolitan area. Many social
scientists contend that the larger area, whether it is a
metropolitan complex, city, community, or even society in
general, may be viewed as the suprasystem.

belong largely to the teachers, the managerial functions deal mainly with the administrators, and the institutional functions deal with the way the school interacts with the community. In terms of the institutional subsystem, the organization (school) needs the support and legitimation of its activities by the social environment or larger social structure (community). Awareness of this facet or organizational functioning should be considered with regard to the way the schools today interact with the community, as well as the claim by advocates of community control that the schools are illegitimate unless controlled by the community. The argument goes that the only way the schools will be responsive to the needs of minority students is if the schools are controlled by the community, including the authority and power to hold accountable the technical and managerial personnel.

Udy (1965) describes five subsystems: (1) the technology that the system uses, (2) the individuals within the system, (3) the group processes that develop because of the individuals, (4) the administrative structure, and (5) the interaction between the organization and environment. In terms of the schools, the materials, media, and facilities represent the technology; the students and teachers represent the individuals, and their subsequent relationships connote the group processes; the chairman, supervisor, principal, etc. are the administrators; and the community connotes part of the environment.

Katz and Kahn (1966) also divide organizational functioning into five subsystems, and we will tend to use this approach later in the chapter. Their first two subsystems-- (1) technical and (2) managerial--are similar to Parsons' (1960) first two subsystems and Udy's (1965) first and fourth subsystems. Their three remaining subsystems are: (3) supportive, which carry on means of continuing the source of production inputs; (4) maintenance, activities which preserve the fabric of interrelationships through recruitment, indoctrination, rewards, and sanctions; and (5) adaptive, the way the organization responds to and adopts to the changing and demanding environment. With regard to the schools, we have already considered the technical and managerial subsystems. The supportive subsystem is linked to the organization and development of curricula and instructional activities, as well as to the socio-psychological services--all which aid in the process of developing the product, or in this case educating the

student; this subsystem is similar to Udy's (1965) technology
or first subsystem. The maintenance subsystem is concerned
with student admittance requirements and classroom grouping,
teacher recruitment and training, the way we exact conformity from students and teachers, or the way we fit people
into the system as functioning parts; this tends to correspond with Udy's (1965) second and third subsystems related
to individuals and group processes. The adaptive subsystem,
as with Parson's (1960) institutional component and Udy's
(1965) organizational-environmental interaction, considers the
environment. Whether the demands of the environment are
fair or legitimate is not our concern at this point; to refuse
to accede to the demands means that the maintenance structures as envisioned by Katz and Kahn (1966) become more
difficult. For example, because of political, economic,
and social factors of the environment some students are de-
fiant toward many of their teachers. Similarly, because of
the implications of politics and economics, some groups are
attempting to dethrone many school administrators. The
idea is for the organization (school) to sense the changes and
demands of the environment (community), and to translate
these energies into a viable relationship. The departments
affiliated with research and development should normally provide sufficient feedback from the external enivronment and
enable the system to improve its product or training and
correct any deviations from course. But when demands involve raw politics and political power, when opposing groups
become adamant and refuse to compromise, when one or
more groups intentionally seek conflict, when the gain of one
group means the loss of power for another, and when the
energy exchange involves race and ideology, then the regu-
latory adaptive mechanisms begin to break down.

     We can treat any formal organization as a social sys-
tem, and indeed many theorists have done just that. For
our purposes, we will assume that all formal organizations
can be considered a social system; then we will ask, just
what kind of social system? In this respect, we will divide
the organizations (schools) into the closed-system model and
open-system model.

The School as a Closed System

     While formal organizations may be considered as a
social system, they can also be classified as closed systems
or open systems. The closed system tends to represent

traditional organizational theory and gives primary attention to the internal structures of the organization, while the open system tends to be representative of contemporary organizational theory and recognizes the importance of environmental forces. The closed-system theory is perhaps best illustrated by Weber's (1946) description of the bureaucratic model and the principles of management by Taylor (1923) and the public administration account of Gulick and Urwick (1937).

The bureaucratic model. The American school, along with most large organizations connected with business, the service industry, and the government, is a bureaucracy. To many people, the word "bureaucracy" connotes rigidity and inefficiency; to others, it means the most rational and efficient form of organization. Weber's (1946) concept of bureaucracy consists of six basic characteristics, and they have been continuously analyzed in the literature.

1. Rules and regulations justify and govern official decisions and actions among people in specific positions.
2. The positions and offices are organized into a hierarchy with various levels of authority and subordination.
3. The management (administration) of the organization is based on written documents and files.
4. Administrators are expected to assume an impersonal orientation in contacts with workers or subordinates and clients; the clients are to be treated as cases.
5. The administrators are specifically trained and employment by the organization is considered a career for them.
6. The administrators follow a stable set of rules and policies.

In Weber's view, these organizing principles maximized rational decision-making and administrative efficiency; bureaucracy was considered the most efficient form of administrative organization, where trained experts were qualified to make decisions. The six characteristics of the bureaucracy were interrelated, and these interrelations maximized efficiency. Write Blau and Scott (1962):

A careful reading of Weber indicates that he tends to view elements as 'bureaucratic' to the extent that they

contribute to administrative efficiency. This contribu-
tion to efficiency appears to be the criterion of 'per-
fect' embodied in his ideal type [p. 34].

The bureaucratic structure is fragile, as Weber saw it; and
it needs, according to Etzioni (1964), to be protected "against
external pressures to safeguard the autonomy required if it
is to be kept closely geared to its goals and not others"
(p. 54). In this connection, the city school districts were
originally organized around political wards; in order to make
them less political and less ridden by nepotism and corruption, bureaucracies were formed to insulate them from politics and other external pressures.

Weber's description of the bureaucracy is pertinent to
schools and indicates the extent of school bureaucracy. The
corresponding characteristics of Weber's bureaucratic model
and the characteristics of the school's bureaucracy are listed
below; they are based on data from Blau and Scott (1962),
Faber and Shearron (1970), and Getzels et al. (1968).

1. Specialization: Tasks are distributed among people holding various positions; there is a clear-cut division
of labor based on rules and regulations that makes possible
a high degree of specialization. Specialization promotes the
need to recruit people on the basis of qualifications and expertise, to provide inservice training, and to pay them according to their paper qualifications. Hence, teachers,
supervisors, and administrators are paid different salaries
according to their position, education, and training.

2. Hierarchy: The hierarchical structure of the
school is usually in the form of a pyramid, where each official is responsible for his subordinates but delegates some
authority to them. Regardless of the size of the school, a
clear chain of command exists--from teacher to principal.
Another chain of command exists within the school system,
starting with the school principal at the bottom and finally
reaching the general superintendent at the apex.

3. Written Records: Teachers and administrators
are usually engulfed by records. Records must be complete,
accurate, and on time; often school personnel are rated by
how well they keep and turn them in to their superiors.
Each official has a file or a set of records on his subordinates which act as a basis for making such decisions regarding tenure, promotions, etc.

4. Impersonal Orientation: Teachers are expected
to maintain a social distance from their clients (students),
and administrators are expected to do the same with the
workers (teachers). The impersonal relationship between
professional and client is designed to maintain objectivity in
grading as well as good classroom management. The impersonal relationships within the hierarchical levels of the organization and between the administration and teachers are
designed to prevent personal feelings of the administrators
and teachers from distorting their judgments in carrying out
their duties.

5. Training and Career Patterns: The qualifications
of teachers and administrators are often proven by the attain-
ment of certificates and/or tested by examinations. Since
administrators are appointed and not elected, they are dependent on the good opinion of their superiors, which in turn
helps maintain the bureaucratic system. Employment by the
school, or at least by the school system, constitutes a life-
long career for administrators, and even for the teachers.
Tenure and pensions are provided; advancement is partially
based on seniority and on also "what you know." At the
higher levels of the administrative hierarchy, advancement
is often based on "who you know," thus creating an in-group
at the top echelons of the school system and subsequently a
certain amount of homogeneity and maintenance of the system.

6. Rules and Policies: Official decisions and actions
are regulated by the school's and system's rules and policies.
The idea is for the principal of the school and the superintendents of the system to apply the general rules and policies
to specific cases. These regulations ensure a certain amount
of uniformity and also eliminate some personal favors and
preferential treatment based on background or personalities.

The scientific management and public administration
approaches. The scientific management perspective is closely
related to the public administration theory, and both models
extend the basic assumptions of bureaucracy and are also
closed-system theories. Taylor (1923) is considered the
founder of the scientific management approach. In Taylor's
system:

> The work of every workman is fully planned out by
> the management ... and each man receives in most
> cases written instructions, describing in detail the
> task he is to accomplish, as well as the means to
> be used in doing the work [p. 39].

Taylor's theory stressed close supervision of workers and application of economic incentives. Supervision and planning became very detailed. Every aspect of behavior was standardized on the basis of time and motion studies. Performance control was provided by records of workers completed by supervisors at the end of the day and transmitted upward to the next office. Salaries were paid on the basis of output, as measured by the number of units produced in a specified time interval. (Although the reader might criticize this emphasis on breaking down tasks into minute specifications and maintaining rigid controls on performance, one should be aware that the recent trends in behavioral objectives also break down both curriculum and instructional practices into precise terms and measurable outcomes. Similarly, the notion of accountability emphasizes rigid controls of performance and economic incentives or penalities; units of achievement in given specified time periods are also calculated.)

The public administrative theories of Gulick and Urwick (1937) were introduced in their book of readings, Papers on the Science of Administration. Their basic orientation was to break down complex tasks into simpler components and thereby specify expectations associated with each person performing a task. In the book, Gulick (1937) contended that the main elements of departmentalization were purpose, process, person, and place. Tasks were to be assigned to departments on the basis of their general purpose, similarity in process, the people who performed them, or the place and clientele to be served. Urwick (1937) proposed the well-known elements of educational administration: planning, organizing, staffing, directing, coordinating, reporting, and budgeting, commonly referred to as POSDCORB. A large portion of waste and inefficiency in organizations could be traced to the problems associated with POSDCORB. Key organizational concepts were elaborated on such as: (1) "unity of control"--tasks broken down into smaller components by a central authority; (2) "division of labor"--work patterns are delineated with specific boundaries; (3) "span of control"-- the ratio between supervisors and workers; (4) "scalar chain"--the chains of command from the lowest to highest ranks; and (5) the "pyramid of control"--the center of authority leading up to the top executive. In the same book, Fayol (1937) listed 14 principles of management which were stated as hypotheses; the most important ones were concerned with: (1) "unity of command"--for every action an employee should receive orders from one supervisor;

(2) "subordination of individual interests to general interests"
--the interests of the organization prevail over the interests
of the individual or group; (3) "centralization"--everything
that increases the importance of the subordinate's role is
related to decentralization and everything that decreases it
is related to centralization; (4) "equity"--equal treatment
dealing with employees; and (5) "esprit de corps"--harmony
and good morale strengthens the organization.

Thus, the closed-system organization was considered
a way of optimizing rationality--or allocating all resources
and tasks to fit a specific goal. In this connection, Hague
(1965) developed a set of propositions and corollaries that
served as an index for considering the organization's means
and ends, or the extent of "closedness" of the organization.
Four variables were listed under the organization's means:
(1) complexity, which is measured by the division of labor
and the amount of specialities and the level of training required
for the job; (2) centralization, the proportion of people having decision-making positions and in the number of areas
they make these decisions; (3) formalization, concerned with
the number of codified jobs; and (4) stratification, which can
be measured by the difference in income and prestige among the
various jobs and the rate of mobility between low and high
ranking jobs. Four variables were also listed under ends:
(1) adaptiveness, measured by the different jobs and techniques annually adopted; (2) production, the number of units
produced per year and the rate of increased production per
year; (3) efficiency, the cost per unit of output per year
and the amount of idle resources; and (4) satisfaction, measured by working conditions and rate of annual turnover.
These means-ends variables are listed in Table 1.1; they
are derived from Hague (1965).

The combined eight variables are concerned with optimizing rationality within the organization, that is coordinating means and ends, and these variables largely reflect
the internal organization's methods for achieving maximum
output. The list of propositions and corollaries consider the
organization as a system by itself and are only minimally
concerned with external factors. In viewing this closed system approach, however, Thompson (1967) points out that in
order to be as rational as possible the organization will attempt to buffer itself from external conditions. When this
fails, the organization will ration their resources or attempt
to work out some kind of solution with the environment. We
will return to Thompson later in this chapter but in the

Table 1.1*

PROPOSITIONS AND COROLLARIES
OF CLOSED SYSTEM ORGANIZATIONS

Major Propositions
I. The higher the centralization, the higher the production.
II. The higher the formalization, the higher the efficiency.
III. The higher the centralization, the higher the formalization.
IV. The higher the stratification, the lower the job satisfaction.
V. The higher the stratification, the higher the production.
VI. The higher the stratification, the lower the adaptiveness.
VII. The higher the complexity, the lower the centralization.

Derived Corollaries
1. The higher the formalization, the higher the production.
2. The higher the centralization, the higher the efficiency.
3. The lower the job satisfaction, the higher the production.
4. The lower the job satisfaction, the lower the adaptiveness.
5. The higher the production, the lower the adaptiveness.
6. The higher the complexity, the lower the production.
7. The higher the complexity, the lower the formalization.
8. The higher the production, the higher the efficiency.
9. The higher the stratification, the higher the formalization.
10. The higher the efficiency, the lower the complexity.
11. The higher the centralization, the lower the job satisfaction.
12. The higher the centralization, the lower the adaptiveness.
13. The higher the stratification, the lower the complexity.
14. The higher the complexity, the higher the job satisfaction.
15. The lower the complexity, the lower the adaptiveness.
16. The higher the stratification, the higher the efficiency.
17. The higher the efficiency, the lower the job satisfaction.
18. The higher the efficiency, the lower the adaptiveness.
19. The higher the centralization, the higher the stratification.
20. The higher the formalization, the lower the job satisfaction.
21. The higher the formalization, the lower the adaptiveness.

*Jerald Hague. "An Axiomatic Theory of Organizations." Administrative Science Quarterly, 1965 10, p. 300. Reprinted by permission of the publisher.

meantime it is necessary to point out that the closed-system organization cannot totally be divorced from the environment; it must at least adapt to the changing environment or become dated or cease to be viable.

There are still other considerations about the closed system that need to be discussed. The research of Gouldner (1954), Merton (1940, 1957), and Selznick (1949) are important works that suggest dysfunctional or unintended consequences of the closed system. More recent theories by Hall (1972), Katz and Kahn (1966), and March and Simon (1958) are also considered important for summing up some of the weaknesses of closed systems.

Briefly, Gouldner (1954) points out that by defining unacceptable behavior, there is an increase of knowledge about minimum acceptable behavior which in turn increases the disparity between organizational goals and actual performance. Close supervision, whether it is a result of this disparity or a part of the organizational structure, increases the visibility of authority which subsequently increases the tension level. Merton (1940, 1957) contends that the reduction of personalized relationships, the increased internalization of rules, and the decreased search for alternatives combine to increase the predictability of the participants' behavior as well as their rigidity of behavior. An esprit de corps and commonly perceived goals increase the participants' defense mechanisms against outside pressure and also increases their rigid behavior. Selznick (1949) points out that specialization and departmentalization create conflict among the parts or subsystems of the organization, where each subunit develops its own ideology and subgoals, sometimes different from the common philosophy of the total organization. The needs of the subunits often dictate a commitment over and above the commitment to the organization. The weakness of the closed system, as purported by Hall (1972), Katz and Kahn (1966), and March and Simon (1958) can be summed up by pointing out that the authors all seem to agree that there are false assumptions about the participants' acting in accordance with the organization's goals, that the closed system ignores the wide range of roles (family member, union member, church member, etc.) which the participants simultaneously perform, and that sometimes their related values are different from those of the organization and have higher priorities. The above authors also state in various ways that the closed system too often treats humans as machine components and takes too little account of its external environment; this is, in fact, the crux of the Katz and Kahn (1966) thesis.

In considering the closed system, the principles of the bureaucratic model receive the widest attention, although they overlap with and include the principles of scientific management and public administration. The closed-system principles and some of their shortcomings have been referred to in the recent literature as "Theory X" (McGregor, 1960), "directive leadership" (Argyris, 1960), "mechanistic system" (Shepard and Blake, 1962), and "machine theory" (Worthy, 1950). These approaches have been developed for the purpose of efficiency and rationality at the expense of personal needs of humans and their greater willingness to cooperate under more flexible conditions.

The more ideal patterns of a closed system have been considered by theorists too, and they may be categorized as "adaptable," marking a system that is more flexible and relies on more cooperation among the participants of the organization. These ideas include what McGregor (1960) refers to as "Theory Y," Likert (1961) expresses as "linking patterns of management," Shepard and Blake (1962) call "organic system," and Mayo (1933) views as the "human approach."

In the same vein, Hague (1965) envisions two types of closed systems based on his propositions and corollaries, one with emphasis on production and the other with emphasis on adaptiveness--each with eight differentiating characteristics. The production model is characterized by: low complexity, high centralization, high formalization, high stratification, low adaptiveness, high production, high efficiency, and low job satisfaction. The adaptive model is characterized by the opposite relationships: high complexity, low centralization, low formalization, low stratification, high adaptiveness, low production, low efficiency, and high job satisfaction.

Adaptiveness becomes an essential concept. No matter how closed a system appears, some flexibility exists because of changes and variations from one situation to another; hence, there exists an intangible but real inflexible-flexible continuum. As we approach the right side of this continuum, or as the organization becomes flexible, it is in effect being adaptive. For example, Burns and Stalker (1961) note that organizations fluctuate from relative stability to change, depending on external conditions and the rate of change in society, even if the organization is concerned with its internal

structures. Lewin (1947) extends this theory and points out
that organizations go through change processes, from
(1) freezing to unfreezing, (2) moving to a new level, and
(3) refreezing. The second stage, or the unfreezing process
represents a shift toward greater adaptability. Blau and
Scott (1962) contend that even authoritarian bureaucrats modify their behavioral patterns by utilizing informal managerial
practices and feedback mechanisms; hence, some adaptability
usually takes place, but there is still a return to the traditional bureaucratic pattern. Merton (1957) notes that in a
bureaucracy there is a strong tendency for employees to use
rules and norms of impersonality in dealing with clients, but
the client in the private sector can also register an effective
complaint by transferring his business elsewhere. Likewise,
this author contends that the client in the public sector can
report the employee to his superiors or demand certain rights
as in the case of welfare recipients, prisoners, and students.
In both cases, the client's reaction serves as a change agent
or causes an adaptive shift. In the final analysis, however,
Burns and Stalker (1961) assert there is a drift within all organizations, including adaptive systems, toward bureaucratic
patterns. The reasons are numerous, including the fact that
administrators develop a vested interest in their positions
which tends to discourage internal variations in the organization. Even new administrators often perpetuate traditional
methods so as not to appear too visible or threatening.
Model 1.1 helps the reader summarize and picture the traditional closed system and the way it shifts and becomes
somewhat adaptive.

Schools are bureaucratic organizations; thus to some
degree they are closed systems. There is no escaping from
this fact. But we can try to make the schools more adaptable or, in effect, more flexible. The assumption is that an
adaptable school system is more responsive to change, so
long as the ranges are supported with sound reasoning or
preferably with empirical evidence, and more able to make
decisions closer to the source of action. In connection with
the traditional closed system and the adaptable closed system, we extend Model 1.1 and present three available sources
of data which use schools as a backdrop to help characterize
these two types of closed systems.

Griffiths et al. (1962) characterize two patterns of
school organizations; the first one closely resembles the
traditional closed system, comprising a: (1) complex organizational hierarchy, (2) tall organization, (3) central chain

Model 1.1.   TWO TYPES OF CLOSED SYSTEMS [CS]

Characteristics	Traditional CS	Adaptable CS
Interchangeable models	McGregor "theory X" Argyris "directive leadership" Shepard/Blake "mechanistic system" Worthy "machine theory"	McGregor "theory Y" Likert "linking patterns of mngmt" Shepard/Blake "organic system" Mayo "human approach
Hague's emphasis on production versus adaptiveness	Production low complexity high centralization high formalization high stratification low adaptiveness high production high efficiency low job satisfaction	Adaptiveness high complexity low centralization low formalization low stratification high adaptiveness low production low efficiency high job satisfaction

Inflexible-flexible continuum

Inflexible   Flexible
Traditional   Adaptable

Burns and Stalker's continuum, and their view of oscillations:
☐

relative stability ⟵   ⟶ relative change

☐ Lewin's view of change:
Level A   x_____
                    unfreezing | Moving to a
                            Level B   x| new level
        Level C   x____refreezing_____|

Blau and Scott's view of tendencies in managerial succession:
☐
    authoritarian bureaucrat   informal managerial practices

☐ Merton's analysis of employee-client relationships:

    bureaucrat's impersonality   client's protest
    ⟵   ⟶

☐ The general tendency for an organization to drift to a
    bureaucratic type noted by Burns and Stalker
    ⟵

of authority, (4) excessive span of control, (5) intense supervision, (6) vertical communication, (7) lack of alternative
proposals and (8) rigid roles and rules. For purposes of
quality education, the authors suggested a modification of
these organizational patterns which resembles our adaptable
system: (1) reduced hierarchy, (2) flat organization, (3) delegation of authority at lower levels, (4) reduced span of control, (5) less supervision and more cooperation, (6) vertical
and horizontal communication, (7) willingness to explore alternative proposals, and (8) more flexible but prudent roles and
rules.

Moeller and Charters (1965) measured the degree of
bureaucratization, ranging from bureaucratic alternatives to
nonbureaucratic alternatives, in 20 school systems in the
Midwest. The bureaucratic alternatives coincide with the
traditional closed system, and the nonbureaucratic alternatives coincide with our adaptive closed system. In all, eight
items were measured, and on a weighted scale, the following
are characteristics of bureaucratic schools: (1) a uniform
course of study is specified by the system for teachers to
follow; (2) school board members and the general superintendent communicate to employees only through established
channels; (3) procedures are established for hiring and dismissing teachers and are uniformly applied in all cases;
(4) it is next to impossible for administrators to lose their
jobs unless they violate a specific regulation; (5) decisions
are made by administrators based on wirtten school policies;
(6) the teachers' jobs are closely defined and they know exactly where their responsibilities begin and end; (7) each
member of the school system is directly responsible to someone in higher authority for his work; and (8) a standard
salary schedule determines where new teachers will be paid.
Nonbureaucratic schools, or what this author refers to as
adaptive schools, were characterized by the opposite alternatives: (1) teachers are permitted to depart from or alter
the course of study; (2) school board members and the general superintendent are likely to communicate directly to any
person in the school system about school matters; (3) procedures for hiring and dismissing teachers vary with individual situations; (4) administrators can be dismissed for several reasons other than violating specific regulations; (5) decisions are made by administrators on the basis of the issues
without strict reliance on established policy; (6) the teachers'
jobs are loosely defined; (7) the lines of authority are under-
emphasized; and (8) salary conditions vary with each case
and depend on needs.

Rogers (1969) outlined an authoritarian, monocratic school system and a professional model needed in order to reform the system. The authoritarian, monocractic system resembles the traditional closed system, and the professional model resembles our adaptable closed system. The authoritarian, monocratic system is exemplified by: (1) extensive centralization, (2) authoritarian leadership, (3) extensive hierarchy, (4) assumed omniscience of top administrators, (5) upward orientation of field employees, (6) discipline enforced by a central authority, (7) extensive specialization and parochialism, (8) extensive departmentalization and veto blocks and groups, (9) recruitment and promotion in relation to bureaucratic codes--causing inbreeding, (10) fragmentation of authority and power of top administrators, despite centralization, (11) extensive politicization, oriented toward extrinsic rewards, and (12) limited and short-range planning. The professional system is exemplified by the opposite: (1) flexible centralization, with some decentralization, (2) professional leadership, (3) limited hierarchy, (4) consultative relationships with top administrators, (5) lateral, collegial orientation of employees, (6) informal and professional standards, limited emphasis on authority, (7) limited specialization, (8) limited departmentalization and commitment to wider organizational goals, (9) flexible recruitment and promotions, willing to hire outsiders, (10) consolidation of authority and power of top administrators, (11) professional orientation, oriented toward intrinsic rewards, and (12) system-wide and long-range planning. Model 1.2 summarizes and conceptualizes these sources of data. In this respect, it is a continuation of Model 1.1.

In recent years, the schools have been criticized for their bureaucratic structures and expanding centralization. While both processes characterize a closed-system model, they are different processes which educators often fail to distinguish and therefore misinterpret. Indeed, there is confusion between debureaucratization and decentralization-- roughly speaking, between a shift towards adaptability and a shift toward greater delegation of powers and decision-making at the lower levels of the administrative hierarchy. Another way of describing this difference is to note that debureaucratization is concerned with rules and policies, administrative leadership, and employee-client relationships; decentralization is concerned with subdividing the organization, coordination of subunits, and dispersing subunits where specialization or local knowledge is important. Part of the confusion is linked to the fact that there is overlap between

the two processes; that is, when the organization decentral-
izes it also tends to reduce its bureaucratic structures.

But in practice, although the two processes are different, there is a tendency for organizations, including the
schools, to revert to more bureaucratic and centralized
structures after either or both types of change. This re-
versal coincides with Blau and Scott's (1962) "routinization
of tasks," Likert's (1961) belief that managers (administrators) are reluctant to relinquish power during and after organizational changes, Michels' (1949) "iron law of oligarchy,"
that administrators and leaders, tasting power, also do not
want to relinquish it, and Selznick's (1957) concept that new
delegation of powers return to an organizational maintenance.

While most educators agree that the bureaucratic
structures of the school system need to be reduced and that
the system often needs to be decentralized, these educators,
along with the harsh critics of the schools who advocate the
dethronement of bureaucracy and centralization, should know
that these two administrative processes will always be a part
of the school system. This is true even with the free school
movement, although these processes may exist on a smaller
scale because of the difference in organizational size. Educational critics and critics of educators must come to the
realization that the characteristics of the closed system--
such as files and records, standardized norms, efficiency
ratings, technically competent participants, division of labor,
chain of command, written communications, impersonal contacts, rational discipline, etc. --will continue to exist within
the school systems; likewise, they will exist at the school
level, too, regardless of which group controls the schools.
Simply put, the school systems and their respective schools
are closed models; the best we can do is to make them
more adaptable.

The School as an Open System

The distinction between the closed-system and open-
system models is somewhat rooted in the differences between
the "rational system" and "natural system" approaches to
analyzing organizations which roughly encompass a period
from Barnard (1938) to Gouldner (1959), followed by the elaboration of the natural system by Thompson (1967). The rational approach stresses the importance of goal-seeking behavior, whereas in the natural system the goals are one of

Model 1. 2

TWO TYPES OF CLOSED SYSTEMS FROM A SCHOOL PERSPECTIVE

Data Source	Traditional Closed System	Adaptable Closed System
Griffiths et al.	Complex organizational hierarchy Tall Organization Central chain of command Excessive span of control Intense supervision Vertical communication Lack of alternative proposals Rigid roles and rules	Reduced hierarchy Flat organization Delegation of authority at lower levels Reduced span of control Less supervision and more cooperation Vertical and horizontal communication Willingness to explore alternative proposals Flexible but prudent roles and rules
Moeller and Charters' patterns of school organization	A uniform course of study specified by the system for teachers to follow School board members and the general superintendent communicate to employees only through established channels Procedures are established for hiring and dismissing teachers, uniformly applied in all cases Next to impossible for administrators to lose their jobs unless they violate a specific regulation Decisions are made by administrators based on written school policies	Teachers are permitted to depart from or alter the course of study School board members and the general superintendent are likely to communicate directly to any person in the school system about school matters Procedures for hiring and dismissing teachers vary with the situation Administrators can be dismissed for several reasons other than violating specific regulations Decisions are made by administrators on the basis of the issues without strict reliance on established policy

Rogers' authoritarian, monocratic system and professional system	
The teachers' jobs are closely defined, and they have knowledge of exactly where their responsibilities begin and end	The teachers' jobs are loosely defined
Each member of the school system is directly responsible to someone in higher authority for his work	The lines of authority are underemphasized
A standard schedule determines where new teachers will be placed and paid	Conditions for employment vary with each case and also depend on needs
Extensive centralization	Flexible centralization with some decentralization
Authoritarian leadership	Professional leadership
Extensive hierarchy	Limited hierarchy
Assumed omniscience of top administrators	Consultative relationships with top administrators
Upward orientation of field employees	Lateral, collegial orientation of employees
Discipline enforced by a central authority	Informal and professional standards, limited emphasis on authority
Extensive specialization and parochialism	Limited specialization
Extensive departmentalization and veto blocks and groups	Limited departmentalization and commitment to wider organizational goals
Recruitment and promotion in relation to bureaucratic codes--causing inbreeding	Flexible recruitment and promotions, willing to hire outsiders
Fragmentation of authority and power of top administrators, despite centralization	Consolidation of authority and power of top administrators
Extensive politicalization, oriented toward extrinsic rewards	Professional orientation, oriented toward intrinsic rewards
Limited and short-range planning	System-wide and long-range planning

several important needs to which the organization is oriented. Both Barnard (1938) and Gouldner (1959) note the importance of the external environment but do not develop the conditions very far. Thompson (1967), however, stresses the importance of the environment and also ties the rational approach with the closed-system model and the natural approach with the open-system model. Describing the open system, he writes:

> ... instead of assuming closure, we assume that a system contains more variables than we can comprehend at one time, or that some of the variables are subject to influences we cannot control or predict....
>
> It is also clear that [this approach] regards interdependence of organization and environment as inevitable or natural, and as adaptive or functional [p. 6-7].

As indicated by the above reference to the interdependence of organizations, Thompson also pointed out the need for open systems to study other organizations within the external environment. This leads us to a discussion on differentiating intraorganizational analysis (parts or subunits within an organization) and interorganizational analysis (interactions among the various organizations with a specific organization). By making this intra/interorganizational distinction, the reader is sensitized both to internal factors that impinge on an organization closely related to our closed-system model and to external factors that impinge on an organization closely related to our open-system model.

In this connection, Litwak and Hylton (1962) distinguished between those organizations which were dependent versus those less dependent on other agencies within the immediate environment or local community. For example, by virtue of cultural norms (churches) or current interest (American Cancer Society), some organizations have a fixed market, either of clients or money available. These organizations could resist incorporation by other agencies or the general environment.

Clark (1965) argued that economic, demographic, and political forces made it impossible for school organizations to function independently from its external environment. The relevance of education made it necessary to move from an intraorganizational approach with bureaucratic processes toward an interorganizational approach with fewer bureaucratic processes. The first approach largely corresponds to our closed system and the second approach corresponds to our open system. Below is a model of these two organizational patterns, as they are distinguished from one another on the basis of a summary of a number of characteristics by Clark (1965).

Model 1.3

INTRAORGANIZATIONAL, BUREAUCRATIC AND
INTERORGANIZATIONAL, LESS BUREAUCRATIC
PATTERNS OF ORGANIZATION

Characteristic	Intraorganizational, Bureaucratic Patterns	Interorganizational, Less Bureaucratic Patterns
Authority and supervision	Inherent in the position	Less through formal structure and more shared by specific consent.
Accountability	Accountability directed upwards; supervision down the line	Less accountability and supervision; provided by general agreement, limited in scope and in time
Standards of work	Explicit rules, formalization, universal application	Less formal, more indirect; there is the manipulation of resources and incentives in a large market or economy of organizations
Personnel assignment	Periodic review of performance, replacement or reassignment where necessary	Other methods of strengthening weak sectors, including additional resources
Research and development	Usually provided for in organizational chart	Subsidizing private innovative groups by major agencies, facilitating dissemination of innovations to the field

Warren (1967) distinguished four types of organizations along an intra/interorganizational continuum: unitary, federative, coalitional, and social choice. The unitary organization had no contact with other organizations, and its locus of authority and the decision-making process corresponded to our closed system. The federative organization had limited contact with external organizations. The coalitional organization exemplified cooperation with other organizations and considered external factors, thus corresponding with our open-system model. Finally, the social-choice organization represented no goals and autonomous behavior within the organizational parts and subunits; its orientation to external organizations varied with the issues.

We now come to the open-system model. The law of the open-system concept is that the organization survives and maintains its internal order by importing environmental energies and that it understands and copes with the outside forces that impinge on it. Miles (1964) defined the open system (1) as a bounded collection of interdependent parts, (2) as devoted to accomplishing some goal or goals, and (3) as having the parts maintained in relationship to each other and to the environment by means of standard operational methods and feedback methods from the environment. Argyris (1964) developed a similar definition: (1) the open system consists of several parts; (2) they maintain themselves through inter-relatedness; (3) they accomplish objectives while (4) adapting to the environment; and (5) the interrelated state of the parts is thereby maintained.

The open-system perspective was fully developed by Katz and Kahn (1966), Schein (1965), and Thompson (1967). Some of the common characteristics of all open systems are listed below and based on Katz and Kahn (1966).

1. Importation of Energy: The open system imports some of the energies from the external environment; the organization recognizes that it is not self-sufficient and draws renewed supplies of energy from other institutions or the material environment.

2. Through-Put: The system transforms the energy available to them. Some work is accomplished.

3. Output: The open system exports a product or person into the external environment.

4. <u>Systems as Cycles of Events</u>: The product exported into the environment produces the sources of importation of energy for repetition of events. (In business, the monetary return of the product is used to obtain materials and labor to repeat the cycle and produce the product again. In school, the product or student has a need fulfilled so that energy renewal is directly related to the organization's activity itself.)

5. <u>Negative Entropy</u>: To survive, the open system acquires negative entropy; that is, it arrests the universal entropic process of disorganization or death. By importing more energies from the external environment than it needs, the organization can store energy and counteract the entropic process--or acquire a negative entropy.

6. <u>Information Input and Coding</u>: Information inputs furnish data to the open system about the environment. The simplest form of information input is negative feedback which enables the organization to correct deviations or keep it on target. The way the organization rejects and accepts--or assimilates--the information input refers to the coding process.

7. <u>Steady State or Dynamic Homeostasis</u>: The open system ideally imports a steady flow of energy from the external environment; this is the best way of arresting the entropy process. Actually, most open systems operate through a "quasi-stationary equilibrium"; that is, an adjustment in one direction yields a movement in the opposite direction. Thus a temporal chart of activity will indicate a series of ups and downs and not a smooth curve or linear progression.

8. <u>Differentiation</u>: The system moves toward multiplication and elaboration of structures and roles as it expands; in short, the organization creates a web of specialized functions.

9. <u>Equifinality</u>: The open system can reach the same state or condition through several different paths. Thus different responses can produce the same problem or solution.

The overriding characteristic of the open system is that it attempts to cope with external forces by assimilating them into its structure or acquiring control over them. The basic principle of the system is to preserve itself.

The social system will incorporate environmental energies essential for survival. In this vein, the adjustive process for the school system means that community participation would probably be more advantageous than community control. The latter option would incorporate the schools into the community and could reconstruct the organization to coincide with its norms and values. Although this analysis is highly suggestive, it must be restated that the concept of the open system does not clearly provide an answer on the differences between community participation and community control.

The idea that the organization can be conceptualized as a complex organization interlocking with the external environment was developed by Schein (1965). In Schein's view, the organization interacted with (1) society as a whole, (2) organizations on the same level as itself, and (3) parts or subsystems within the given organization such as formal and informal groups, which in turn were composed of individuals who also were influenced by society. The organization, according to Schein, was linked to the environment through key people who occupied positions in both the organization and the environmental systems or by people in the organization who had contact with people in the environmental systems. For example, the superintendent linked the school system with the board of education and the school board served as the link between the school and environment.

For Schein, not groups but role sets of individuals within the organization determined the relationships, and these role sets were also influenced by external factors. The organization as a whole could be conceived as a set of overlapping and interlocking role sets, some of which linked the organization with the environment. Schein (quoted below) suggested six important characteristics of the organization; they illustrate two concepts, that is, the organization is a social system as well as an open system.

1. The organization must be conceived of as an open system, which means that it is in constant interaction with its environment, taking in raw materials, human resources, energy, and information, and transforming these into products of services which are exported into the environment.
2. The organization must be conceived of as a system with multiple purposes or functions which involve multiple interactions with its environment. Many of the activities of subsystems cannot be understood without

considering these multiple interactions.
3. The organization consists of many subsystems which are in dynamic interaction with one another. Instead of analyzing organizational phenomena in terms of individual behavior, it is essential to analyze the behavior of such subsystems, whether they be conceived of in terms of groups, roles, or some other concept.
4. Because the subsystems are mutually dependent, changes in one subsystem are likely to affect the behavior of other subsystems.
5. The organization exists in a dynamic environment which consists of other systems, some larger, some smaller than the organization. The environment places demands and constraints upon the organization. The total functioning of the organization cannot be understood, therefore, without explicit study of these environmental demands and constraints.
6. The multiple links between the organization and its environment make it difficult to specify clearly the boundaries of any given organization [p. 95].

Understanding open systems involves more than defining characteristics and interlocking arrangements that are necessary for their functioning. Thompson (1967) postulated a set of propositions (paraphrased below) on how open systems act or should act, given the fact of internal and external constraints on rationality and their three major activities: input, technical, and output. He also established another set of propositions on how these organizations maintain a measure of self-control over competing external factors. For our purposes, we will describe only these two sets of propositions. The first set of five propositions deal with how an open system acts or should act, and the second set or next five propositions are related to retaining control over the environment.

1. Organizations seek to protect their technological activities from the environment.
2. Since complete closure is impossible, they attempt to buffer environmental factors by stockpiling inputs and outputs.
3. Because some environmental variations cannot be controlled or predicted, organizations smoothen input and output transactions.
4. Organizations also attempt early detection of

environmental changes, anticipating and adapting
to these variations which cannot be buffered or
smoothened.

5. Finally, when buffering, forecasting, and smoothen-
    ing fail to protect their technological activities,
    organizations resort to rationing [e.g., they es-
    tablish priorities--smaller student:teacher ratios,
    extra personnel in a given school, extra commu-
    nity input].

6. Organizations attempt to minimize the power of ex-
    ternal factors over them by maintaining alterna-
    tives and scattering dependence.

7. Organizations seek prestige; it is an easy way of
    acquiring power and gaining a measure of control
    over environmental elements without making any
    concession.

8. Organizations may have to resort to: (1) contracting
    (negotiation of an agreement, informal or formal),
    (2) co-opting (absorbing new elements of the external
    environment or altering them into a policy-determin-
    ing structure as a means of averting threats to its
    existence), or (3) coalescing (joint ventures with
    one or more organizations in the environment).

9. The more an organization is contrained in some as-
    pects of the environment, the more it will seek
    power over remaining elements of the environ-
    ment.

10. When such a balance is obtainable, it will seek to
    enlarge its power over the environment.

Thompson (1967) concludes that the more the organization compromises and the more maneuvering in defense of
domains it makes, the more disruptive and costly it is to the
organization. The idea is for the organization to "minimize
the necessity of maneuvering and compromise" (p. 38). This
statement by Thompson, coupled with his last set of propositions, is directly related to the conflict between the school
systems and the groups that advocate community control.
There is a point where absorption of energies from the external environment, even excessive maneuvering and compromises, have destructive effects on the organization or school
system. Demands from the external environment must be
controlled by buffers, forecasting trends, contracting, and
co-opting or coalescing. If this is impossible, the system
will attempt to cope with the external forces by digesting
them or acquiring control over them--in short, by assimilating

Figure 1.1

SCHEMATIC MODEL OF ORGANIZATION
FUNCTIONING AND CHANGE ENVIRONMENT

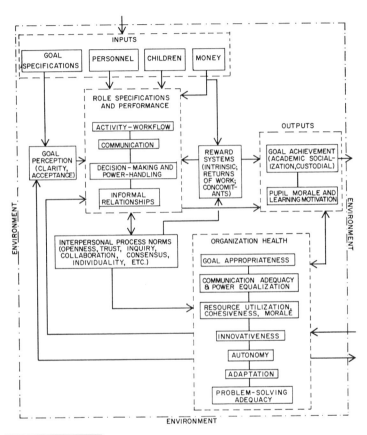

*This figure is taken directly from Richard O. Carlson et al., Change Processes in the Public Schools. Eugene: Center for the Study of Educational Administration, University of Oregon, 1965; p. 16. Reprinted by permission of the publisher.

these outside energies--or it will be replaced by these energies. Community control connotes the opposite: that the external forces have digested the system.

Carlson et al. (1965) have developed an "educational organization" in relation to the open-system concept, as illustrated by Figure 1.1. The reader should notice that the usual hierarchical arrangements are absent, since the parts of the system are viewed as socio-psychological and interrelated components, not as people or work groups. The diagram shows that the school exists within an environment from which it receives input: personnel, children, and money. The school releases outputs--student achievement and performance--in relationship to the input and goal specifications. The goal specifications are affected by various role specifications and performance of the people within the school. A system of rewards and penalties, as well as norms governing the school, regulates role performance. If all goes well, desired outputs are achieved.

The arrows in the figure indicate directions of influence between and among the various parts or subunits of the system, as well as a variety of feedback mechanisms which help maintain the system in a relatively steady state. Beyond the input-throughput-output network, there is a set of organizational health characteristics which helps the school continue adequate and improved functioning. These health characteristics help the school cope with its environment and plan short-term and long-term changes in relation to the environment and future events.

Ornstein's (1972) comparison between "traditional" and "ideal" schools closely resembles the difference between the closed-system and open-system organizations; it serves as a mechanism for associating some of the characteristics and propositions of the open system to the schools. Although Ornstein categorized 35 characteristics under three dimensions, we will list (Model 1.4) only seven characteristics under the one dimension of "organizational norms and structures." These items tend to elaborate some of the previously stated concepts of the open system.

Ornstein is arguing that schools are basically traditional; they constitute bureaucratic organizations and utilize management principles, and they treat their participants as machine components. The ideal school by way of contrast utilizes the concepts of the open system, especially recognizing the importance of the environment.

The focus of the environment is the key concept of the open system; it is a natural part of the organization,

Model 1.4*

ORGANIZATIONAL NORMS AND STRUCTURES OF
CLOSED-SYSTEM (TRADITIONAL) AND
OPEN-SYSTEM (IDEAL) SCHOOLS

Characteristics	Traditional School	Ideal School
Norms of Reciprocity	Individual is isolated	People are mutually dependent on each other
	Limited teamwork	Teamwork, people help each other
Energy	Disregards external environment	Continuous inflow of energy from external environment
	Fails to recognize that it is functional, in part, on external environment	Changes with or ahead of external environment
Information Input	Hides and ignores its problems	Recognizes and corrects its problems, small groups organized to solve problems
	Limited and ineffective procedures for solving problems	Variety of procedures used to find solutions
	Screens out new data, reluctant to change	Unenclosed, willing to accept new ideas and change
Research	Describes problems	Geared toward solutions
	Dissonance between researcher and practitioner	Communication and rapport between researcher and practitioner
	Research rejected by practitioner as impractical, practice considered anti-intellectual and mechanical by researcher	Researcher and practitioner see the value of each other's work
Innovation	Hit-or-miss, is based on hunches and sentiment	Scientific, based on feasibility and success factors
	Wasted cost, effort, and time	Cost-effectiveness criteria
Implementation	Based on mandates from higher authorities	Based on research findings and evaluation, revisions, and re-evaluation
Cycle of Entropy	Organization becomes outmoded, runs down, and moves toward disorganization and decline	Organization accepts and stores new input, thus acquiring a negative entropy.

*Allan C. Ornstein, Urban Education: Student Unrest, Teacher Behaviors, and Black Power. Columbus, Ohio: Merrill, 1972; p. 176-77. Reprinted by permission of the publisher.

from goal setting to production arrangements, from input to
output. Environmental factors have a great deal of influence
over the organization; they even influence the internal structures. Perhaps the best way to illustrate this approach is
to divide the environment into the general, immediate and
focal--and to explain their interaction with the school.

1. General Environment: The general environment
consists of four broad components: political, economic, social, and scientific trends. Each of these trends interacts in
multiple ways, in turn, affects the immediate environment.

2. Immediate Environment: This includes the various
social systems and their respective organizations.* For example, the school system consists of several organizations
such as the neighborhood school, college, and adult training
center. The public service system consists of such organizations as the police, fire, and sanitation departments. The
various social systems and their respective organizations
also interact in a multiple and complex way, in turn, affecting the focal environment.

3. Focal Environment: The focal environment consists of the specific social system and organization(s) under
examination. The organization, in turn, consists of several
parts or subunits. For example, we saw in the beginning of
this chapter that Katz and Kahn (1966) analyzed five subsystems: (1) supportive, (2) managerial, (3) technical, (4) maintenance, and (5) adaptive. Referring to these five subsystem
components and using the school as the focal organization,
the school must (1) procure students from the external environment and have insight into their characteristics and needs,
(2) organize, coordinate, and administer activities, (3) recruit and train personnel, (4) control and motivate the work
force through rewards and sanctions, and (5) ensure survival
in a changing environment, or at least make appropriate
changes in proportion to the external changes and pressures.

In short, the three environments--general, immediate,
and focal--interact from time to time, sometimes frequently,
occasionally, or infrequently; sometimes in cooperation, indifference, or conflict. The organization under consideration

---

*The following may be considered as social systems: local
government, public service, cultural, recreational, social
welfare, religious, civil, leisure, health maintenance, transportation, housing, communication, ecology, and educational.

manifests itself through an input-output cycle with the environments; the managerial subsystem (administrators) must preserve the organization and be aware of environmental factors.

Because of the input from and the output to the environment, it follows that organizations need to create units and departments and hire and train personnel to adjust to the changing world, to gauge its organizational needs, to devote full time to research and develop, to develop systems analysis and scientific management-control approaches which we will discuss below. For our purposes, we need only to mention one general environmental change (a social trend such as urbanization and its related problems), one related social system change (the housing system and an increase in the number of low-income projects within the school's jurisdictional boundaries), and one possible interorganizational change (a community action group that increases its militancy and seeks community control over the schools), and the internal parts or subsystems of the focal organization, in this case the school, is tilted out of balance--its input-output structures are upset. Many of the subsystems within the school will need to utilize their full resources to cope with the environmental changes and challenges.

Since schools are not competitive organizations, they have few systematic plans and policies for gathering data about the external environment. (At best, they project budget needs and construction needs for the future, and other such financial matters.) In short, they lack a staff who devote themselves to the type of systems analysis and management control needed to deal with the external environment; for example, the school system's research and development budget usually represents no more than one percent of their total budget, and most of the research funds are derived from federal and foundation sources. Similarly, only in recent years have some large-city school systems expanded their school-community internal subsystem into a group of experts or specific department.

The relationship of the focal organization such as the school, like all social relationships, takes a variety of forms--ranging, in simple terms, from conflict to cooperation. In general, advocates of community participation generally seek cooperation with the schools, while advocates of community control frequently seek conflict--and often conflict for the sake of conflict under the theory that this is the best way of changing the system.

While the maintenance function focuses inward, the adaptive function focuses outward. Katz and Kahn (1966) contend that both subsystems move in the direction of preserving constancy and predictability of organizational conditions, but the

> ... maintenance function moves toward a constant set of internal structures [and] the adaptive function tends to achieve environmental constancy by bringing the external world under control [p. 91].

Control may be too strong a word, and perhaps it is best to envision the organization as establishing "exchange" methods, as purported by Etzioni (1964) and Levine and White (1961), or "buffer" mechanisms, as reported by Thompson (1967). When these methods fail, the organization attempts to deal with the environment through "public relations," as cited by Hall (1972), "bargaining," as indicated by Etzioni (1964), or through "cooperative strategies," as reported by Thompson (1967), which include contracting, co-opting, and coalescing. As a last resort, the adaptive subsystem can move in the opposite direction; it then can either strive to control the environment or obtain some kind of rationality and predictability by modifying its internal structures--which some school systems and their schools are being forced to do in order to come to terms with minority communities. Guetzkow (1966), Katz and Kahn (1966), and Thompson (1967) all tend to agree, however, that the organization will attempt to seek some kind of dominance over the environment rather than modifying internal structures. The reason is that the first option is easier and affirms the power and legitimacy of the organization, while the latter is threatening to the organization. The latter option also connotes a radical change, especially for the maintenance subsystem, in what is considered legitimate and proper; the change implies new roles and the task of getting people to accept these new roles. It also means a threat to the job security of some of the personnel.

The demand for community control over the schools is not only likely to be antagonistic and antithetical to the organization, but it is also likely to violate the important "defense of domain." The concept of a viable domain is, in effect, a political problem. Writes Thompson (1967):

> It requires finding and holding a position which can be recognized by all the necessary 'sovereign'

organizations.... It requires establishing a position
in which diverse organizations in diverse situations
find overlapping interests. The management of interorganizational relations is just as political as the
management of a political party or of international
relationships....

And just as political parties and world powers move
toward their objectives through compromise, complex
purposive organizations find compromise inevitable.
The problem is to find the optimum point between the
realities of interdependence with the environment and
the norms of rationality [p. 36].

From the view of the defense of domain, community participation and interaction is rational and serves the school and
community; community control leads to conflict, polarizes
the conflicting organizations and people within the organizations. In the final analysis, the community as an organization or as part of the local environment, in its demand for
control over another organization (i. e. , the school), is violating the latter organization's defense of domain.

In addition, the advocates of community control are
criticizing the schools in relation to the closed-system
model, thus pointing out the nature of bureaucracy: centralized leadership, hierarchical structures, over-span of
control, chain of commands, standard procedures, rules
and regulations by the book, specialization of function, merit
promotions, appointments through objective examinations,
accountability upwards, etc. The community control advocates perceive these characteristics as instruments of maintaining the system and excluding the community (Fantini,
Gittell, & Magat, 1970; Gittell, 1970; Hamilton, 1968;
Levin, 1970; Miller & Wook, 1970; Rogers, 1969).

Their arguments are inapplicable to the situation;
these school patterns of behavior reflect a closed system,
but the critics' arguments should be used only to seek debureaucratization and decentralization--to make the system
more adaptable, but not to destroy it. Their arguments
have little, if anything, to do with the open-system approach,
and how the school as the focal organization interacts with
external forces, including the community. The critics of
the schools, if they are to legitimize their arguments about
community control, need also to direct their analysis in
terms of open-system structures and processes--and it

"appears," if we are to be kind to them, that they have not
done their homework. They are oversimplifying the schools
as a traditional closed system, ignoring or unaware of the
adaptable nature of the closed system. They are also over-
looking the concept of open systems--how the organization
(school) works with the environment (community) but needs
to maintain control over it--or else the school ceases to
exist as a viable and independent organization.

The School That Considers the Closed and Open Systems

Compared with the closed-system approach, the open-
system model is obviously broader in scope. However,
Etzioni (1964) points out that with the open system there is
usually "an over-allocation of resources," because the approach "explicitly recognizes that the organization solves
certain problems other than those directly involved in the
achievement of the goal ... " (p. 17). The indirect-goal
activities of the open system may result in the decline of
staff morale and decreased efficiency. At the present, the
open system is "constructed on a high level of abstraction"
and therefore it is difficult to apply "directly to the analysis
of actual organizations" (p. 18). Hall (1972) contends that
the various input-output variables of the open system have
not even been moderately developed, and the multiple factors
are still uncontrollable, thus perhaps making realistic utilization of the model nearly impossible. March and Simon
(1958) have stated that decision-making and organizational
functioning are based on "bounded rationality." When the
full implications of the bounds of rationality are considered,
the weaknesses of the open system become evident. The
questions are: Can the conflicts of the closed system and
open system be reconciled? Can the insights and advantages
of both systems be meshed into one theory? Only the future
will provide the answers.

One of the most widely known theories of educational
administration of the schools was developed by Getzels and
his colleagues at the University of Chicago. The theory ex-
emplifies the concept of the social system, which we introduced in the beginning of the chapter, and which developed
to its fullest combines the characteristics of the closed system and open system. In the first stage of development,
Getzels and Guba (1957) viewed administration as a hierarchy
of relationships for purposes of allocating roles and acting
out behaviors to coincide with the goals of the organization

which they referred to as the institution; this is a view similar to the closed-system model.

The social system consists of two main dimensions which interact. The first dimension is referred to as the nomothetic axis and is shown on the top of Figure 1.2. It consists of the institution and its roles and role expectations. The second dimension is referred to as the idiographic axis and is shown on the bottom of the figure; it consists of the individual and his personality and need disposition. Behavior within the system is a function of these two dimensions. In other words the nomothetic or the institution's dimension and the idiographic or the person's dimension interact to form social behavior within the social system. To understand the observed behavior of anyone in the system, it is necessary to know the nature of the institution's roles and role expectations, and the individual and his personality and need disposition. This relationship is represented pictorially in Figure 1.2

Figure 1.2*

THE NORMATIVE AND PERSONAL DIMENSIONS OF SOCIAL BEHAVIOR

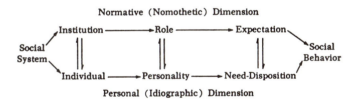

Normative (Nomothetic) Dimension

Personal (Idiographic) Dimension

---

*Jacob W. Getzels and Egon G. Guba. "Social Behavior and the Administrative Process," School Review 1957; 65, p. 429. Reprinted by permission of the University of Chicago Press.

According to Getzels and Guba, the administrator has delegated authority, similar to Weber's view of rational authority, in a bureaucracy. Administrators also have some earned influence; both authority and influence are viewed as power. An administrator who lacks influence can only use his authority to achieve desired behavior. The most effective administrator uses both authority and influence to manage his subordinates.

A certain amount of role personality conflict is inevitable. There are <u>alienating forces</u> which militate against the social system, as well as <u>integrating forces</u> which support it and hold it together. Both of these forces can evolve from within the social system or from without and both of these forces hinder or help the administration. Thus there is the beginning recognition of external factors associated with the open system. For example, teachers may be committed to external goals and values which militate against the school, or they may become seriously alienated by the school itself. On the other hand, the teachers can be committed to external goals and values which coincide with the school, or they can develop a dedication to teaching by working in the school. The idea is for the administrator of the social system, in this case the school, to deal with and smooth the alienating forces while enhancing the integrating forces, thus strengthening his authority and influence.

Getzels and Thelen (1960) extended the social system model by adding an anthropological dimension--factors such as ethos, mores, and values--to the nomothetic (top) axis and a biological dimension--factors such as the organism, constitution, and potentialities--to the idiographic (bottom) axis. The ideal balance of emphasis on actual behavior is now a function of interaction of these enlarged institutional and individual relationships. Putting all these dimensions together into a simple representation, the relationship appears as in Figure 1.3.

Figure 1.3*

INTERRELATIONSHIPS OF THE ANTHROPOLOGICAL DIMENSION AND THE BIOLOGICAL DIMENSION

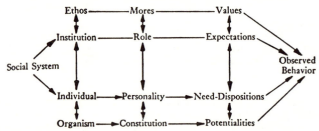

---

*Jacob W. Getzels and Herbert A. Thelen. "The Classroom Group as a Social System," in: N. B. Henry (ed.), <u>The Dynamics of Instructional Groups</u>. Part II. Fifty-ninth Yearbook of the National Society for the Study of Education. Chicago: University of Chicago Press, 1960; p. 73. Reprinted by permission of the National Society for the Study of Education.

In connection with Figure 1.3, the authors also identified three types of leaders: (1) the nomothetic, whose orientation emphasized the institution, its role and expectations,
and the anthropological factors; (2) the idiographic, whose
stress was on the individual, his personality and need dis-
positions, and the biological factors; and (3) the transac-
tional, one whose style recognized the resources and limits
of both the institution and individual and made intelligent application of the two for solving particular problems. The
authors favored the third leadership style and considered it
as the most productive type of behavior for the social system.

Getzels et al. (1968) extended the biological dimension
by adding the anthropological dimension, that the human organism was influenced by culture, his constitution was influenced by ethos, and his potentialities was influenced by
values. In addition, Getzels et al. concluded that the environment comprised the outer ring of all the interacting forces
of the social system and social behavior. All these variables,
when put into a pictorial representation would look like Figure 1.4.

Figure 1.4*

INTERRELATIONS OF THE MAJOR DIMENSIONS
OF BEHAVIOR IN A SOCIAL SYSTEM

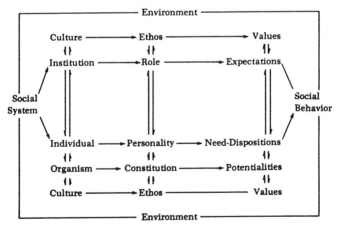

*Jacob W. Getzels, James M. Lipham, and Roald F. Camp-
bell. Educational Administration as a Social Process. New
York: Harper & Row, 1968; p. 105.

Thus what started out as a social system ended up
including biological system components, too. And what
started out as a closed social system ended up also including an open-system approach. Here, indeed, is a complete
system for viewing organizations, one which is also considered a classic model among many educators. Furthermore,
many of the assumptions, concepts, and variables of the above
figures have been verified by research, and the most complete
treatment of the research is summarized in Getzels et al. (1968).

Development of Strategies for Planning Educational Change.

Most of the basic models and technologies for planning
educational change and organizing the schools--which can be applied to administrative decentralization or to greater community
participation or community control--have been developed during
the last 30 years by government agencies and private businesses.
Many of these planning strategies have been adopted for use in
education; however, some of the important concepts have been
developed by educators themselves, and they are still relevant
today. For example, the National Council of Chief State School
Officers (1944) outlines the following policies and criteria for
planning educational change and organization.

1. The responsibility for leadership in planning the edu-
    cational program properly belongs to and should
    be assumed by the regularly constituted educa-
    tional agencies and authorities at the proper level.
2. The planning procedure and process should be care-
    fully formulated, unified, and systematically car-
    ried out.
3. Educational planning should be recognized and carried
    out as an integral aspect of community, state,
    and national planning.
4. Definite provision for planning must be made in edu-
    cational organizations in order that planning may
    proceed satisfactorily and attain tangible results.
5. One phase of educational planning should provide the
    basis for organized research. Another phase
    should be built on and utilize fully the results of
    research.
6. Educational planning must be thought of and estab-
    lished as a continuous process requiring constant
    adaptation of plans to emerging needs.
7. Educational planning to be functional must be realis-
    tic and practical but should not be needlessly

limited by existing situations.

8. All educational planning should involve the active and continuing participation of interested groups and organizations.

9. The planning program should result in specific recommendations which are understood and accepted by those who are participating in the program.

10. Provision for continuing evaluation of the planning process is basic to the program (p. 15-16).

About the same time, some 150 educators from 14 southern states stated through Morphet (1945), the editor of a report of their meeting, that education must be geared to change:

It must be an education which is deliberately designed to meet the needs of the people ... which recognizes and accepts the challenges of the past, the demands of the present, and the opportunities of the future [p. 57-60].

The recent problem-solving models for implementing educational change are built around the concepts of the open-system and closed-system approaches. The military and private industries are far ahead of education in the use of these problem-solving models. Although there are many different types, they may be grouped into the systems-analysis approach and the management-control approach. The systems-analysis model considers the input and output from the environment and envisions the method of information and evaluation as a recurrent activity; it also considers the people within the organization and the people influenced by the organization. Considering these characteristics, this approach somewhat resembles some of the major characteristics of the open system. The management-control approach involves the setting of objectives, obtaining measures of progress, comparing these measures against standards to note variations, indentifying the variations, taking action to correct the variations, and stressing reliable and efficient performance throughout the entire planning process. With regard to these characteristics, this approach tends to resemble the closed system and especially the management ideas of Taylor (1923). It should be noted, however, that both problem-solving approaches overlap, and it is difficult to find a pure systems-analysis approach or management-control approach for developing policies and strategies of educational change.

One particular application of the systems-analysis approach was developed by the Rand Corporation and has rapidly spread from the Department of Defense to other governmental agencies in the 1960s; this is called the Planning-Programming-Budgeting-System (PPBS). The system brings together components of planning and programming with components of the system--the system's structure, functions, and capabilities. The basic elements of the system are as follows:

1. <u>Planning</u>: (a) Goals are developed, (b) needs are weighed, (c) priorities are established in relation to the goals and needs, and (d) objectives are established, including ways to measure these objectives usually by considering discrepancies between existing and desired outcomes.
2. <u>Programming</u>: (e) Alternatives are identified, (f) analyzed, and (g) selected. Finally (h) an evaluation procedure is developed in relation to the above, which permits revision if there is another cycle.
3. <u>Budgeting</u>: This includes the fiscal information such as accounting, purchasing, warehousing, delivering, the payroll, etc; it also includes long-range appropriations.
4. <u>System</u>: The system consists of the above three elements being related in a meaningful way while considering the clients, workers and environment, which in the schools represent the students, teaching-administrative personnel, and community, as well as the various subsystems.

An example of the management-control theory is the Program Evaluation and Review Technique (PERT), which has also been introduced by the Defense Department and subsequently spread throughout business and industry in the 1960s, and, like PPBS, it is just beginning to be introduced in the field of education. Progress and interruptions of various facets of a program are computed, analyzed, and made available to administrators. Progress reports are continuously updated, reflecting changes in schedule, possible difficulties, and achievement rates. According to Gross (1964) and Faber and Shearron (1970), the basic elements of PERT can be summarized in six steps.

1. <u>Events</u>: Every event that must occur to achieve the objectives is stated in specific terms.
2. <u>Sequences</u>: The sequences and relationship of events are established on a flow chart, and they are linked by various symbols such as circles, squares, and arrows.
3. <u>Possible Time Values</u>: An estimated time value is placed on each activity, including "optimistic," "most likely," and "pessimistic."

4. Expected Time Values: The three time values
are used to find the "expected" time for each activity; t =
(a+4m+b) ÷ 6. In the formula, a is the "optimistic" time,
m is the "most likely" time, and b is the "pessimistic" time.
Some theorists believe that the "most likely" time should be
weighted 4:1 over the other times.

5. Critical Path: The computer calculates expected
times for all the activities and their related paths on the
flow chart, in turn determining the critical path or longest
distance in time between beginning and end for each path.
The only way of finishing ahead of schedule is to apply more
effort to the activities or rearrange the flow chart to create
parallel paths or reduced paths.

6. Monitoring: Computer printouts indicate where
revisions and corrective action are needed.

The examples above are only two illustrations of the
many problem-solving models being introduced in current organizations. Other examples include the Educational Resources Management System (ERMS), Critical Path Method
(CPM), Planning and Controlling Technique (PACT), and the
Line of Balance (LOB). Each is useful, under certain conditions, and the selection for use should be determined by
circumstances related to specific purposes.

In theory it is possible to combine both the systems-
analysis model and the management-control model into a separate model, one which the author terms the "scientific-
planning" model. The tridimensional systems of knowledge
model prepared by Culbertson et al. and published by the University Council for Educational Administration (1963) may be
considered an example of the scientific-planning approach.
In the diagram below, there is interaction between and among
each of the three separate systems. System I utilizes existing knowledge to create new knowledge. System II is related
to the use of the new knowledge. System III employs school
administrators, and they use the new knowledge to make decisions.

The model is dynamic in as much as it is concerned
with behavior that changes; these changes utilize the principles of the systems-analysis and management-systems approach. The systems-analysis approach is exemplified by
the fact that System I receives input from the environment
transmits it into the entire system. The technological activities within System II transforms the input. Output is for-
warded from System III into the environment. Hence, there

is a continuous regulation process inasmuch as feedback in
the form of output is translated into new input, and the cycle
repeats itself. On the other hand, the management-control
approach is illustrated by the fact that the total system is
directed toward considerations of task performance, in de-
signing new programs, and in improving the learning experiences of the clients. Efficiency and performance are
stressed by virtue of subdividing the total operation into
various subunits and substructures, as well as by virtue of
an evaluation process. The role performance of school administrators is indicated, thus showing an authority structure
and a division of labor. There is unity of command and centralization of decision making, and the total system is coordinated by one or more administrators. In short, Figure
1. 5 may be construed in part as a closed system which takes
into account and recognizes the importance of the external
environment and it may be interpreted in part as an open
system which considers the importance of tasks, efficiency,
specialization, and central authority. Thus, we have a possible scientific-planning model.

It is not our purpose to develop a specific scientific-
planning model for determining decisions or changes in education, modifications which may or may not be concerned
with administrative decentralization or plans involving the
community. Whatever model is used, whether they are one
of the above examples or a special one devised for a school
system or state department, the model should include as
many of the following elements as possible.

1. Problem Identification: The process begins with
a perceived problem or set of problems--dissonance between
"what exists" and "what should exist. " A management-control approach would consider only the administrators' views;
the systems-analysis approach considers the entire educational community which includes students, teachers, administrators, parents, and community representatives. It might
also involve representatives from the various social systems.

2. Goal Identification: Goals are described as broad,
long-range, and value oriented. They can and should be divided into subgoals, and even among the various subsystems
and divisions of labor. Identification of the goals should reflect a pluralistic audience, again people from within and
outside the school. These goals might be weighted in terms
of needs, to determine priorities; however, they will also
reflect political and economic considerations.

Figure 1.5

SYSTEMS OF KNOWLEDGE UTILIZATION IN EDUCATIONAL ADMINISTRATION*

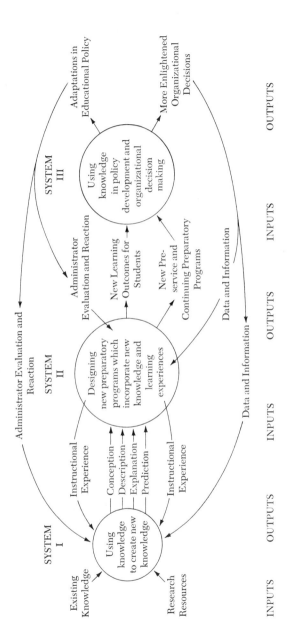

*University Council for Educational Administration (Prepared by Jack Culbertson et al.) Toward the Development of a 1969-74 UCEA Plan for Advancing Educational Administration. Columbus, Ohio: UCEA, 1963; p. 42. Reprinted by permission of University Council for Educational Administration.

3. <u>Objectives</u>: Stemming from the goals, we now need precise, shorter-ranged, quantifiable units. While educators tend to refer to these units as objectives, other organizations tend also to use other terms such as specifications or standards. Whatever terms we wish to use, and assuming the reader in education prefers the usage of "objectives," the point is to find out if we are achieving our objective(s). As an example, one of the goals might be to improve school-community relations, and one of the objectives might be to decentralize the school system into precise unit sizes with given time periods for implementation.

4. <u>Program Structure</u>: Goals and objectives need to be developed into a coordinated program which defines the scope and limits of policies, the kinds of personnel needed to implement policies, and the procedures to follow. In short, tasks and people need to be operative within a functioning framework which considers the entire school operation and the budget (which is discussed below).

5. <u>Data Analysis</u>: Measuring instruments need to be considered. Traditional tests and psychometric procedures may not be applicable to a wide range of change decisions. Observations and interviews may be more appropriate with certain situations. Frequent monitoring may also be required, both at given intervals in the middle of the program (summative evaluation) and at the end (formative evaluation). The evaluating team simply ask questions which in effect say: "Tell me about the program," What problems exist?," How can improvements be made?" In still other cases, actual outcomes may be compared with expected outcomes, and the evaluators attempt to find out the reasons for the discrepancies, what measures are needed to improve the actual outcomes, what preconditions existed that caused some of the problems. Most important, the data analysis must be related to the original problem(s) and the established goals and objectives. If no problems or discrepancies occur with the new program, then it is functioning correctly, or at least according to intended outcomes.

6. <u>Communication of Findings</u>: The evaluation team must be able to communicate the findings to the entire educational community. Several audiences must understand and be able to utilize the data. For this reason, representatives from interested groups should be consulted with and if possible be included in as many stages of the operation that are realistically feasible.

7. Alternatives-Action: Given the findings, and assuming some problems or discrepancies, alternatives need
to be decided.   Again, political and economical considerations will enter the picture.   Alternatives will then lead to
further action which may need to be further analyzed.

8. Budgeting: Budget or cost allocations obviously
need to be considered.   The entire problem-solving elements
and their related costs must be considered and stated;   this
entails the various stages and time tables, the divisions of
labor, the policies, people, and tasks.   Outside funds may
be necessary.

9. Recycling: The control facets of the model involve a continuous reevaluation and reassessment--a continuous attempt to improve the program.   Even if the program
appears to be viable, feedback, modifications, and adjustments are necessary because the internal and external forces
are always changing.

The approach outlined above is general and is not intended to be used as a substitute for one of the more sophisticated problem-solving models;   the model developed by the
author merely helps the reader envision how it is possible to
combine systems-analysis with management-control theory for
purposes of educational change.   The model also helps the
reader ask proper questions and guides him in attempting to
solve problems;   the approach may be considered both theory
and practice oriented.

By the same token, educators can use another scientific-planning approach for evaluating and making decisions
about school programs.   These may include a wide range of
programs, i. e. , analysis of decentralization in school system
A, B, or C for implementation in school system D, or simply an evaluation of compensatory programs for purposes of
financial aid or educational legislation.   The suggested model
includes:

1. Determination of the target population's (i. e. , stu-
     dents, school system, etc.) educational needs.
2. Establishment of a procedure for selecting the pro-
     grams based on objectives, costs, defined inputs
     and outputs (i. e. , student achievement, teacher
     morale and effectiveness, school-community rela-
     tions, etc.) and local conditions.
3. Description of the educational programs being used

which can be implemented for the target population.
4. Determination of the effectiveness and problems of
these programs.
5. Determination of unanticipated outcomes and resistance likely to be encountered.
6. Determination of methods for improving the programs.
7. Provision of methods on how to operationalize the
programs for the target population.
8. Acceptance of the programs intact, or appropriately
modified, or rejection of them--with stated reasons and implications.

The above scientific-planning model can be used to
determine the feasibility of administrative decentralization,
as stated above. Assuming that school system A is already
decentralized, then the responsibilities for the implementation of the model in system A or in another system (D) will
raise related issues of centralization versus decentralization
and the nature of community input. Writes Jacobs (1972):

Any extreme position on these issues does not face
up to reality. The fact is that centralized services
can and should be brought to bear on local school
program development. Such services should be
viewed as another set of resources from which local
schools can draw support. As for delegated authority, no school can operate as an island unto itself.
Certain authority must rest, by law, if for no other
reason, with central administrative heads and the
Board of Education [p. 2].

While there is a trend toward greater community involvement, especially community participation, which in turn results in greater delegation of authority to the local school,
it should be pointed out that the local and central administrators and their respective staffs cannot respond to community needs and expectations without appropriate and measurable authority, nor can they be held accountable to the
community if they have little or no control over the programs.

No matter what planning approach is used, the school
administrators must learn what programs exist to meet specific needs of the school system and what they will cost in
terms of resources, facilities, and personnel; whether the
programs can be realistically operationalized; whether better
system and management policies are required, more training

of personnel or new personnel, new kinds of guidelines; and answers to many other questions. Finally, as Provus (1970) indicates, the school administrators must know what programs to adopt, to modify, to terminate, to continue on an experimental basis, and to try elsewhere in the school system. Given adequate program assessment, administrators and legislators will have compatible data in selecting and funding programs.

CONCLUSION

To some extent, the above systems-analysis and management-control models as well as the combined system-management approaches can be used for planning change and selecting programs in organizing the schools. In terms of administrative decentralization, community participation, and community control, as well as many other educational matters, they can help in:

1. Analyzing, evaluating, and interpreting relevant data in relation to objectives to be achieved.
2. Systematically appraising choices and consequences for achieving objectives.
3. Establishing preferred choices and alternatives.
4. Simulating and portraying tasks and activities, as well as time intervals, for each objective.
5. Determining probability factors involved in implementation.

Morphet, Jesser, and Ludka (1971) point out the need to plan and achieve goals in reorganizing the schools through problem-solving and program-development methods; they write:

> Recommendations involving the reorganization or urban and/or rural school districts [involving] greater community control of schools ... [and] interracial issues ... are representative of areas of controversy that are subject to extensive deliberation in view of present cross currents in public attitude and opinion. ...
>
> Appropriate change techniques can be selected and utilized to increase the probability that goals will be attained in accordance with the circumstances and conditions within a given [school system or] state [p. 86-87].

A comprehensive and coordinated study, with objectives, choices and consequences, time tables, costs, long-range planning, and monitoring for adjustments can bring about rational and peaceful change.   These implications should be obvious in any attempt to organize metropolitan schools.

Morphet et al. (1971) also contend that we must recognize and avoid pitfalls, that unless identified and dealt with promptly, rationally, and realistically, they could result in chaos and conflict.   This is especially true under present social conditions, where various groups are vying for power and have little concern for other groups.   These pitfalls include, according to Morphet et al.:

> (1) the tendency of many people to challenge and attempt to discredit or destroy existing agencies, institutions and values merely or primarily because they have been developed or accepted by 'the establishment'; (2) a strong belief or 'feeling' on the part of some people that changes are so essential that they should be made by 'any necessary means,' without seriously considering the implications or alternatives;   (3) attempts that will undoubtedly be made by some people and groups to control or manipulate the planning and change processes for their own benefit;   and (4) some complacent groups, institutions and agencies that do not see any need for major changes and will tend to resist any bona fide planning efforts [p. 47].

Finally, other pitfalls that should be considered are:

1.   Underestimating the need and pressure for change.
2.   The extreme methods and strategies that some groups will use to foster change.
3.   The ridiculous demands and rhetoric of some change agents.
4.   The complacencies and fears of other groups who in turn surrender democratic principles and problem-solving capacities.
5.   Being swept along by change, with no evidence that the assumptions are viable or really work, and with little or no opportunity to select the best alternatives.
6.   Failing to consider all the social and legal implications, and the economics and politics of the change.

REFERENCES

Argyris, Chris. Integrating the Individual and the Organization. New York: Wiley, 1964.

_____. Understanding Organizational Behavior. Homewood, Ill.: Dorsey Press, 1960.

Baldridge, J. Victor. "Organizational Change: The Human Relations Perspective versus the Political Systems Perspective." Educational Researcher, 1972, 1, 4-10, 15.

Barnard, Chester I. The Functions of the Executive. Cambridge, Mass.: Harvard University Press, 1938.

Blau, Peter and Scott, W. Richard. Formal Organizations. San Francisco: Chandler, 1962.

Burns, Tom and Stalker, G. M. The Management of Innovation. London: Tavistock Publications, 1961.

Carlson, Richard O. et al. Change Processes in the Public Schools. Eugene: Center for the Advanced Study of Educational Administration, Oregon University Press, 1965.

Clark, Burton R. "Interorganizational Patterns in Education." Administrative Science Quarterly, 1965, 10, 224-37.

Etzioni, Amitai. Modern Organizations. Englewood Cliffs, N. J.: Prentice-Hall, 1964.

Faber, Charles and Shearron, Gilbert F. Elementary School Administration. New York: Holt, 1970.

Fantini, Mario D., Gittell, Marilyn, and Magat, Richard. Community Control and the Urban School. New York: Praeger, 1970.

Fayol, Henri. "The Administrative Theory of the State" (trans. by S. Greer). In: L. Gulick and L. Urwick (eds.), Papers on the Science of Administration. New York: Institute of Public Administration, 1937; p. 99-114.

Getzels, Jacob W. and Guba, Egon G. "Social Behavior and the Administrative Process." School Review, 1957, 65, 423-41.

Getzels, Jacob W. and Thelen, Herbert A. "The Classroom as a Unique Social System. " In: N. B. Henry (ed.), The Dynamics of Instructional Groups. Part II. Fifty-ninth Yearbook of the National Society for the Study of Education. Chicago: University of Chicago Press, 1960; p. 53-82.

Getzels, Jacob W. , Lipham, James M. , and Campbell, Roald F. Educational Administration as a Social Process. New York: Harper & Row, 1968.

Gittell, Marilyn. "Urban School Politics: Professionalism vs. Reform. " Journal of Social Issues, 1970, 26, 69-84.

Gouldner, Alvin W. "Organizational Analysis. " In: R. K. Merton, L. Broom, and L. S. Cottrell, Jr. (eds.), Sociology Today. New York: Basic Books, 1959; p. 400-28.

_____. Patterns of Industrial Bureaucracy. New York: Free Press, 1954.

Griffiths, Daniel E. et al. Organizing Schools for Effective Education. Danville, Ill. : Interstate Publishers, 1962.

Gross, Bertram M. The Managing of Organizations. New York: Free Press, 1964.

Guetzkow, Harold. "Relations Among Organizations. " In: R. V. Bowers (ed.), Studies on Behavior in Organizations. Athens: University of Georgia Press, 1966; p. 13-44.

Gulick, Luther. "Notes on the Theory of Organization. " In: L. Gulick and L. Urwick (eds.), Papers on the Science of Administration. New York: Institute of Public Administration, 1937; p. 1-45.

_____, and Urwick L. (eds.). Papers on the Science of Administration. New York: Institute of Public Administration, 1937.

Hague, Jerald. "An Axiomatic Theory of Organizations. " Administrative Science Quarterly, 1965, 10, 289-320.

Hall, Richard H. Organizations: Structure and Processes. Englewood Cliffs, N. J. : Prentice-Hall, 1972.

Hamilton, Charles V. "Race and Education: A Search for Legitimacy." Harvard Educational Review, 1968, 38, 669-84.

Havighurst, Robert J. and Levine, Daniel U. Education in Metropolitan Areas, 2nd ed. Boston: Allyn & Bacon, 1971.

Jacobs, James N. "A Model for Program Development and Evaluation at the Local School Level." Paper Presented at the Annual AERA Conference. Chicago, April 1972.

Katz, Daniel and Kahn, Robert L. The Social Psychology of Organizations. New York: Wiley, 1966.

Levin, Henry M. (ed.). Community Control of Schools. Washington, D. C.: Brookings Institution, 1970.

Levine, Daniel U. and Havighurst, Robert J. "Social Systems of a Metropolitan Area." In: R. J. Havighurst (ed.), Metropolitanism: Its Challenge to Education. Part I. Sixty-seventh Yearbook of the National Society for the Study of Education. Chicago: University of Chicago Press, 1968; p. 37-70.

Levine, Sol and White, Paul E. "Exchange as a Conceptual Framework for the Study of Interorganizational Relationships." Administrative Science Quarterly, 1961, 5, 583-601.

Lewin, Kurt. "Frontiers in Group Dynamics." Human Relations, 1947, 1, 5-41.

Likert, Rensis. New Patterns of Management. New York: McGraw-Hill, 1961.

Linton, Ralph. The Study of Man. New York: Appleton-Century Crofts, 1936.

Litwak, Eugene and Hylton, Lydia F. "Interorganizational Analysis: A Hypothesis on Coordinating Agencies." Administrative Science Quarterly, 1962, 6, 395-420.

March, James G. and Simon, Herbert A. Organizations. New York: Wiley, 1958.

Mayo, Elton. The Human Problems of Industrial Civilization.

New York: Macmillan, 1933.

McGregor, Douglas. The Human Side of Enterprise. New York: McGraw-Hill, 1960.

Merton, Robert K. "Bureaucratic Structure and Personality." Social Forces, 1940, 18, 560-68.

_____. Social Theory and Social Structure (2nd ed.). New York: Free Press, 1957.

Michels, Robert. Political Parties. New York: Free Press, 1949.

Miles, Mathew B. Innovation in Education. New York: Teachers College Press, Columbia University, 1964.

Miller, Harry L. and Woock, Roger R. Social Foundations of Urban Education. Hinsdale, Ill.: Dryden Press, 1970.

Moeller, Gerald H. and Charters, W. W. "Relation of Bureaucratization to Sense of Power Among Teachers." Administrative Science Quarterly, 1965, 10, 444-65.

Morphet, Edgar L. (ed.). Building a Better Southern Region Through Education. Tallahassee, Fla.: Southern States Work Conference on Educational Problems, 1945.

_____, Jesser, David L., and Ludka, Arthur P. Planning and Providing Excellence in Education. Denver, Col.: Improving State Leadership in Education, 1971.

National Council of Chief State School Officers. "Planning and Developing an Adequate State Program of Education." Education for Victory (Official Biweekly of the U.S. Office of Education), December 20, 1944, 15-16.

Ornstein, Allan C. Urban Education: Student Unrest, Teacher Behaviors and Black Power. Columbus, Ohio: Merrill, 1972.

Parsons, Talcott. The Social System. New York: Free Press, 1951.

_____. Structure and Process in Modern Societies. New York: Free Press, 1960.

Provus, Malcolm. "Toward a State System of Evaluation."
    Journal of Research and Development in Education, 1970,
    3, 87-96.

Rogers, David. 110 Livingston Street. New York: Random
    House, 1969. (Vintage ed.)

Schein, Edgar H. Organizational Psychology. Englewood
    Cliffs, N.J.: Prentice-Hall, 1965.

Selznick, Philip. Leadership in Administration. Evanston,
    Ill.: Row, Peterson, 1957.

_____. TVA and the Grass Roots. Berkeley: University
    of California Press, 1949.

Shepard, H. A. and Blake, R. R. "Changing Behavior
    Through Cognitive Change" Human Organizations, 1962,
    21, 88-96.

Taylor, Frederick W. The Principles of Scientific Manage-
    ment. New York: Harper & Row, 1923.

Thompson, James D. Organizations in Action. New York:
    McGraw-Hill, 1967.

Udy, Stanley H., Jr. "The Comparative Analysis of Organ-
    izations." In: J. C. March (ed.), The Handbook of
    Organizations. Chicago: Rand McNally, 1965; p. 678-
    709.

University Council for Educational Administration. Toward
    the Development of a 1969-74 UCEA Plan for Advancing
    Educational Administration. Columbus, Ohio: UCEA,
    1963.

Urwick, L. "Organization as a Technical Problem." In:
    L. Gulick and L. Urwick (eds.), Papers on the Science
    of Administration. New York: Institute of Public Ad-
    ministration, 1937; p. 47-88.

Warren, Roland L. "The Interorganizational Field As a
    Focus for Investigation." Administrative Science Quar-
    terly, 1967, 12, 396-419.

Weber, Max. Essays in Sociology (ed. and trans. by
    H. H. Gerth and C. W. Mills). New York: Oxford

University Press, 1946.

Worthy, James C. "Organizational Structure and Employee
    Morale." American Sociological Review, 1950, 15, 169-
    79.

Chapter 2

RESEARCH PROBLEMS

There is very little current research related to administrative decentralization and community control; most of
the statements about these two concepts are based on dubious
claims, half truths, or unsupported evidence. This chapter
will examine the research related to decentralization and
community involvement; it is divided into four sections.
First we will briefly review the research related to administrative and community organization prior to the controversy
over administrative decentralization and community control.
Next, we will examine the current approaches and limitations
related to this research; then we will explore the current
research concerning community participation and community
control. Finally, we will discuss the present state of research and some suggestions for further research in the
areas of administrative decentralization and community control.

Administrative-Community Organization, 1940s-50s:
The Climate of Opinion

The research on administrative organization during the
20-year period between 1940 and 1959 was largely concerned
with rural consolidation; only limited aspects of the data are
relevant to the present urban setting. The move toward centralization was evident. Dawson (1955) noted that the number
of school districts decreased from 119,000 in 1938 to 48,700
in 1954. Dawson and Ellena (1954) indicated that a total of
1088 centralization proposals were made during the 1952-53
school year and only 93 were defeated.

Gregg (1960) and Stapley (1957) pointed out that the
sparsity of schools and population was considered a factor
which increased costs of educational programs. Centralization provided an equitable program for all students. Morphet,
Johns, and Reller (1959) and Mort and Vincent (1954) pointed

out that centralization reduced the financial handicaps of
poorer districts.   Moehlman (1951), in his influential text
on school administration, argued that centralization raised
professional standards and, up to a point, created efficient
school systems.

In the meantime, two forms of administrative decentralization appeared, one in conjunction with centralization
and the other in opposition to it.   The first type called attention to an intermediate administrative unit which would
provide greater services to local communities.   This administrative unit would permit the existence of small community
school districts at the same time providing services usually
found only in larger systems.   McIntyre (1954) listed 33
states which had developed this type of intermediate administrative unit.   Opinions regarding the ideal size of this reorganized district ranged from 10,000 students with a community population of 50,000 to 60,000, to 50,000 students
with a community population of 250,000 to 300,000, with the
majority of administrators arguing in favor of the smaller
size (McPherran, 1954; Pennsylvania Cooperative Program,
1954).

The second type of decentralization plan corresponded
more closely to present organizational patterns of large
school systems.   Moehlman (1951) described three school
systems: small, medium, and large.   He claimed that "all
the major executive activities present in the most complex
structure [could] be found in embryonic form in the smaller
and simpler structure" (p. 85-86).   However, he maintained
that with overcentralization, flexibility and spontaneity were
reduced, procedures assumed a greater importance, and the
general superintendent and central administration became remote from the school staff.   "The only hope of regaining
dynamism in educational organizations in large urban centers," Moehlman concluded, "appears to be through the process of decentralization" (p. 89).   His concept of decentralization was mainly limited to delegating responsibility to competent staff members within each attendance district.

Mort and Cornell (1941) and Mort, Vincent, and
Newell (1955) developed a method for measuring the effectiveness of a school system based around an adaptability index.   This index was correlated with school characteristics
such as financial policies, curriculum innovation, community
and staff participation, location, size, etc.   These studies
considered the maximally effective school district to comprise

approximately 100,000 students. This estimate was confirmed
by Leggett and Vincent (1947) and Ross (1958).

In still another study on school systems, Mort and
Vincent (1946) stated that large city school systems had become too unwieldly and overcentralized:

> Education ... in the large city ... is as though the
> school of your village were run by somebody way off
> at the state capital. You have no voice, no control,
> your questions go unanswered, your demands on the
> local administration are parried by 'I'm sorry, but
> the matter is completely out of my hands; you will
> have to go to headquarters.' But you can never get
> close enough to the man at headquarters who makes
> the decisions, and you give up [p. 88].

The relation of district size and community participation was also studied. Hicks (1942) hypothesized that New
York City school attendance districts comparable in size but
permitting greater local participation (not control) would rank
highest in adaptability (no significant differences were, however, found). Mort and Vincent (1942) argued that if the
state took steps to overcome the financial handicaps of
smaller districts, education would be better under home rule
than under a centralized system. Westby (1947) contended
that community residents in cities should have greater influence in making decisions regarding the operation of
schools. Morphet et al. (1959), while recognizing the need
for decentralization, pointed out that a large percentage of
the people did not take any interest in school board elections.
This resulted in greater opportunity for incompetent, politi-
cal-minded, and dishonest people to be elected in smaller
school districts. They warned of the possibilities of minority or even majority groups taking over control of the schools
for their own purposes. Similarly Lieberman (1956) and
Norton (1957) argued that administrative decentralization
would foster provincialism and dogmatic views. In short,
many of the arguments for and against decentralization in
this period began to fuse with the related issues of community participation and community control and have reappeared
today with greater intensity.

The period under review was also marked by a concern for identifying the power forces operating within the
community with which the school administrator had to deal,
by concern for the growing criticism of the schools, and by

the desire to find ways for reducing the criticism and height-
ening understanding of the place of schools in the community.

As for identifying the community power sources,
Davis (1954) isolated the power hierarchy of rural communities, and Hunter (1953) isolated the power hierarchy in a
city of half a million. Both studies confirmed that the business and financial elite were policy makers for nearly all
matters. Gleaser (1953) showed that this pattern operated
with regard to school policy in a small New England city.
Wilson (1952) pointed out that the local power system mini-
mized participation of citizens-at-large in influencing local
school policies. Jansen (1940) noted the absence of local
participation of low-income parents in New York City. Data
from Rossi (1954) showed that 61 percent of the citizens in
a large eastern city were indifferent to school matters.
Barnhill (1954) further confirmed that citizens lacked knowledge of and seemed unconcerned about school matters. R.
Campbell (1957) concluded that community control was exer-
cised by a handful of influential people who seemed, for the
most part, to have been willingly accorded their influential
positions by their fellow citizens.

In the midst of this indifference and lack of influence
on the part of most lay citizens, there was growing criticism
of the public schools in relation to national survival. In his
history of progressive education, Cremin (1961) pointed out
that "a spate of books, articles, pamphlets, radio programs,
and television panels burst upon the pedagogical scene, air-
ing every conceivable ailment of the schools, real and imag-
inery" (p. 339).* Scott and Hill (1954) maintained that the
criticism included both soul searching and rhetoric. Anderson (1952) divided the critics into two groups, one composed
of those who were honest, sincere, and generally interested
in education, and the other a motley assortment of "chronic
tax conservationists," "congenital reactionaries," "witch hun-
ters," "super-patriots," "dogma peddlers," "race haters"
and "academic conservatives." The research, however, indicated that the most persistent criticism appeared by organizations and in publications affiliated with patriotic groups
(R. J. Brown, 1955; Knutson, 1958) who savagely charged
the schools with soft pedagogy and subversion (Cremin, 1961).

---

*The harsher attacks were reflected by such authors as Bell
(1949), Bestor (1953, 1955), Hutchins (1953), Lynd (1953),
Rickover (1959), and Smith (1949, 1954).

On the basis of a Phi Delta Kappan survey, including
about 5000 people of various ages and groups, Lovelace
(1955) concluded that the majority of citizens expressed confidence in the schools. Referring to the same data, Rugg
(1955) asserted that criticism was to be expected in an era
of social change. Boss (1955) also reported on a supplementary PDK questionnaire and reported that 85 percent of the
respondents affirmed that the schools were better than they
had been 30-40 years ago.

Spurred by the growing criticism of the schools, there
was a recognized need for greater citizen participation in
school affairs, and for developing cooperative school-community relations. Perhaps the three most influential school administration groups at that period--the National Conference
of Professors of Educational Administration (NCPEA), the
eight regional centers of the Cooperative Program in Educational Administration (CPEA), and the association of the 34
leading universities of the University Council for Educational
Administration (UCEA)--outlined clinical and research programs in administration to identify the role of the school in
community improvement projects, to seek ways for enhancing
school-community relations, and to find types of administrative leadership that would foster desirable school-community
relations.

Counts (1954), Haak (1956), and Sweitzer (1953) all
agreed on the importance of administrators knowing their
community and not forgetting its people when making school
policy. Rothchild (1951) showed that only 15 percent of the
administrators surveyed were satisfied by the amount of
parent participation in school policy. Scott (1957) affirmed
the importance of school-community cooperation through lay
participation as a method for dealing with the criticism.
Rice (1953) polled a sample of superintendents for Nation's
Schools and found support for lay citizens groups, but only
on a temporary basis, to help foster improved school-community relations.

Much information concerning criteria and methods for
improving school-community relations appeared in the literature. Baughman (1957) developed a list of criteria for appraising school-community relations. Pfau (1955) also developed an index for determining effectiveness in interpreting
the school to the community. Polley, Loretan, and Blitzer
(1953) maintained that citizen participation could be augmented
by (1) building a sense of community throughout the school,

(2) developing the machinery for community responsibility in school policy, (3) organizing a professional staff on a community basis, and (4) stimulating interaction between the professional staff and community residents through school conferences.   B. Campbell (1952) identified seven methods by which the school might tell the story to the local community: (1) teach about education as part of the curriculum, (2) teach about education directly to adults, (3) use printed and graphic materials, (4) use motion pictures, television, and radio, (5) have professional staff members participate with community groups, (6) increase the understanding of the staff, and (7) use students as a means of communication.   Oversiew (1953a) also analyzed methods for increasing school-community interaction and ways for keeping the community informed. Butterfield (1953) listed suggestions for improving community public relation through newspapers, parents, PTA groups, and community organizations.   Oversiew (1953b) analyzed data from 80 educators and identified practices for using advisory community groups in policies related to administrative organization, curriculum, and budget.

Perhaps the best way of summarizing this period is to say that centralization was the major trend in reorganizing the schools, and the focus was on the rural areas.   However, there was the growing recognition that the large city schools were bureaucratic and overcentralized.   The criticism of the schools ranged from soul searching and sincere desire for reform to rhetoric and ideology, as is the case today.   Whereas it was once the patriotic, rightest organizations and white conservatives who suffused the school-community atmosphere with politics and race hatred, the present propagandistic movement tends to evolve from anti-establishment, liberal reformers and black militants. Whereas yesterday it was claimed that "vigilante" groups were organized by patriotic, white rightists, today it is asserted that "vigilante" groups are organized by black militants. *   In both cases, however, the targets are the same: teachers, school administrators, and the schools in general.

School administrators sought to encourage community participation (not control) in order to educate the community to the problems of the schools, which is the case today. Most lay people were indifferent and unknowledgeable about school matters, which is also true today.   Because of the vocality of the critics of the schools, and the visibility they

---

*See Chapter 4.

received in the mass media it was (and still is) easy to overlook the fact that most people were indifferent or even had
confidence in the schools; moreover, the majority of the students were succeeding in school--which is the case today as
evidenced by the decreasing drop-out rates, increasing
scholastic achievement test norms, and the percentage of students going on to college.

Administrative Decentralization and Community Control, 1960s-70s: Approaches and Limitations

        In the middle and late 1960s the racial climate in the
large city schools and the pace of change related to decentralization and community control made it difficult for social
scientists to conduct research on these twin trends.   The
problem was aggravated by a growing resentment by school
officials of the wholesale and often overgeneralized criticism
of schools by novice teachers (Herbert Kohl, Jonathan
Kozol, James Herndon and Henry Resnik), liberal educators
(Mario D. Fantini, Marilyn Gittell, William Hazard, and
Henry M. Levin), and black militants (Charles V. Hamilton,
Rhody McCoy, Barbara A. Sizemore, and Preston R. Wilcox).   The problem was further aggravated by the general
lack of communication between the research community and
the practitioner, as well as by the growing militancy of some
blacks who were becoming suspicious of and often rejecting
the social scientist because he was white and subsequently
often viewed him as irrelevant, culturally biased, and antagonistic toward the black community.   Needless to say, very
little empirical data is available on administrative decentralization and community control.   There is, however, a wealth
of expository literature on these two trends which has been
previously explored by other authors but the content is highly
intuitive, subjective, and reflective of the individual authors'
personal biases and political ideologies.

        The research that evolved, then, is "quasi" or "soft"
in nature--mainly, descriptions and reports based on non-
reliable and nonvalid data.   Two types of quasi research resulted, the first of which described the pathologies of the
school bureaucracy and boards of education through personal
recollections, observations, ancedotal data, interviews, and
in some cases descriptions based on nonstandardized measurement instruments.   The second type of quasi research
were the policy reports written for school systems by prestigious educational groups or panels, outside consulting and

management agencies, and inhouse committees usually selected by the general superintendent or board of education.
The methods employed in this type of quasi research include
observations in the schools; interviews with consultants,
school personnel, and community residents; various committees, commissions, task force meetings, public hearings,
community forums, and write-in suggestions. These policy
reports often received wide coverage in the local newspapers
and, in the case of New York City, received national attention.

   Quasi research describing the school system. With
regard to the descriptions of the school bureaucracy and
school boards, Gittell and Hollander (1968) studied six urban
school systems (Baltimore, Chicago, Detroit, New York,
Philadelphia, and St. Louis). Because the tests used in the
various school systems were not comparable, the portrayals
were mainly confined to individual school systems. What
emerged from these individual descriptions was that the
school systems lacked flexibility and innovation; moreover,
they seemed unable to adapt their administrative organizations and programs to the needs of their minority populations.
External agencies such as the federal government and foundations were prime forces in encouraging innovation. Too often, however, the programs were abandoned when funds ex-
pired. With no real empirical data but only reference to
recent trends, these researchers concluded that innovation
could be achieved only as a result of strong community participation.

   Crain (1968), while reporting on the politics of school
desegregation, analyzed eight school systems (Baltimore,
Buffalo, Newark, Pittsburgh, San Francisco, St. Louis, Bay
City, and Lawndale [the last two cities, respectively somewhere in New England and somewhere in the West, were
given pseudonyms because the general superintendents and
several board members objected to the analysis of their respective school systems]). The school boards fell into three
general categories: (1) political appointees (Buffalo and
Newark), (2) professionals and businessmen of high economic
status (Baltimore, Pittsburgh, and St. Louis), and (3) a mix-
ture of political appointees and elected business and civil
leaders (Bay City, Lawndale, and San Francisco), all of
whom attempted to represent various racial and religious
groups but who for the greater part were still not associated
with lower-class groups. The politically appointed school
boards tended to be the most conservative. The high status

elites tended to be the most reform-oriented, suggesting to
this author that white school board members who are economically secure are least threatened by change or demands
from minority groups.   The school boards that comprised
both political and non-political members tended to be the
least cohesive and least able to implement change.

In attempting to "characterize" the typical school
board, Crain asserted that instead of an articulated educational policy there was mainly reaction to satisfy various
complaints.

> The typical school board ... can be thought of as
> making school policy only in a firefighting fashion.
> If an issue comes up, it acts; otherwise, it does
> not.   It may not take a position at all on some of
> the most fundamental issues of school policy, simply
> because those particular policies have not been made
> salient by community discussion.
>
> The typical school board avoids issues that are not
> important for no other reason than to save time for
> issues that are....   The board then appears to be
> defending the status quo.   By the time [a group] be-
> gins to make noise, [it] can rightly claim the school
> board has been ignoring the problem, and the school
> board begins to discuss the issue with one strike
> against it [p. 125].

Lipham, Gregg, and Rossmiller (1967) found that
school board members in school systems of all sizes tended
to avoid the responsibilities of their positions and seldom resolved conflicts in open meetings.   The public, the professional staff, and the school board members in small and
large districts were not in agreement about what they expected the school board to do; moreover, even among
the school board members themselves there was no more
agreement.   The boards of education generally lacked an articulated school policy and had difficulty in coping with
change; they generally engaged in uncritical acceptance.

Individual school systems were also described.
Schrag (1967) pointed out that the Boston school administrators and central office were out of touch with the communities, still operating on the premises of another age when enrollments were largely white and middle class and on the
once glorious reputation derived from an educational history

that went back to Horace Mann and the common school movement. The author emphasized the inbreeding of the school
system (clearly showing their Irish ethnicity), the rigidity
and conservative nature of the system, the administrative
authoritarianism, and the conformity of lower-echelon administrators at the expense of innovation. According to Schrag,
from the very top of the administrative hierarchy to the bottom, the system was characterized by traditional practices,
covert racism, bureaucratization, administrative patronizing
of teachers, and teacher hostility toward their clientele.

Gittell's (1967) description of the New York City
school system emphasized the insulation of the administrative
organization from the public and the monopolizing power of the
school board members, general superintendent, and the middle management staff at the central office. She claimed
there was a tendency for decisions to be made by an inside
core of top personnel who, although divorced from politics,
were also divorced from the local communities. The major
factors which contributed to this condition were the rise of
bureaucracy and professionalism.

Rogers (1969) also analyzed the New York City school
system and concluded it was a "sick" bureaucracy, whose
operations subverted the goals and whose status quo philosophy prevented any flexible accommodation to the rising demands of minority groups. Among the symptoms of the
sickness were overcentralization, headquarters' control over
and suspicion of field administrators, upward conformity of
anxious subordinates, limited communication and coordination
of departments, inbreeding and insulation based on the policies of the board examiners, promotion of supervisors with
a minimum of daring, paternalistic supervision of teachers,
pressure within departments and units to conform to codes
and protect one another, compulsive following and enforcing
of rules, increasing administrative insulation from the communities, and the tendency to make decisions in committees
so as to make it difficult to pinpoint responsibility to individuals.

Joseph Pois (1964), a Chicago school board member,
noted the frustration of school board members in dealing
with an overwhelming number of problems compounded by a
lack of time and resources, unawareness of community needs
and of what was happening in the individual schools, an inert
central administration, and a great many petty administrative
problems. Perhaps the most evident aspect of frustration

was the distorted flow of information upon which decision-making was based.   Pois wrote:

> Manifestly, a board should avail itself of the factual
> material and viewpoints emanating from the general
> superintendent and his subordinates.   Yet, if this is
> the exclusive source of systematic inquiry and analy-
> sis concerning the school system, the board's deci-
> sion-making must inevitably be determined in large
> measure by the attitudes and concepts of the bureau-
> cracy....   The Chicago Board, when it does seek to
> tap the informational, statistical, and research re-
> sources of the school system, is ordinarily expected
> to use its general superintendent as the point of con-
> tact.   Although this may be justified on the basis of
> protocol or recognition of lines of responsibility in
> the administrative hierarchy, the end result is that
> the flow of information is subject to screening, selec-
> tion, or restatement by the general superintendent.
> As organizations expand in size it becomes less ten-
> able to contend that the chief administrative or execu-
> tive officer should be the sole conduit for the trans-
> mittal of data or analysis to the governing body....
> [Even a subordinate duly authorized to deal directly]
> with a board ... will be prone to proceed with con-
> siderable caution lest he incur the displeasure of his
> superior [p. 88-89].

Seven years later Jack Witkowsky (1971) told of his experience as a Chicago school board member for the 1968-70 period.   He too emphasized the feeling of frustration of being caught up in petty details of the daily operation of the schools, and wasted time dealing with irrelevant and trivial issues.   He wrote:

> The format of the Board of Education's bi-monthly
> meetings appeared to be designed to minimize the
> board's effectiveness.   By the time the board strug-
> gled through the superintendent's agenda, which often
> included more than 100 items, members had little
> time or energy left to discuss their own suggestions
> about critical issues facing the school system [p. 91].

Witkowsky spoke about the school board's remoteness from the community:

> Seldom did anything come out of the committee

reports. The general public had an opportunity to
address the board only twice a year, during hearings
on general policy and the budget. The board consistently refused to let the public discuss current problems during its regular meetings [p. 91].

The bigness and bureaucratic structure of the system
was also emphasized. The teachers were reporting to the
school principal, the school principal reported to the district
superintendent, who reported to the area superintendent, who
reported to the deputy superintendent, who reported to the
general superintendent. Each administrator above the principal had his own office and staff of experts. Buck passing
became the norm. When a community group demanded action, low level administrators would "frequently pass the
buck up on the line until it [reached] someone so remote that
he [could not] be subjected to community pressure." Bigness
made it difficult for school board members "to get the simplest information about the school system. No one knew, for
instance, how much money was being spent at each school"
(p. 92).

Similarly Elliot Shapiro, one of the present 32 community superintendents in New York City, was interviewed by
Hentoff (1966) when he was a school principal in one of Harlem's elementary schools. Shapiro spoke about the lack of
communication within the New York school system:

> ... all the way up the chain of command in the school
> system were people with a vested interest in keeping
> the truth away from the person on the next rung up.
> By the time anything came to the top, conditions were
> reported as being fine [p. 39].

Quasi research related to school policy reports. As
previously indicated, the policy reports fall into three categories of authorship: outside educational prestigious groups
or panels, outside consulting management firms, and inhouse
committees. The 15 largest school systems and several of
the medium-sized school systems each have issued recently
at least one such report and in many cases several reports.
The most noted of these are the Passow report (1967) for
Washington, D. C. ; the Mayor's Advisory Panel (1967) in
New York, commonly referred to as the Bundy report; and
the inhouse report District Boundary Lines under the Community School District System (1969), also in New York; the
the Havighurst report (1964), the Booz-Allen and Hamilton

report (1967), and the Commission on Urban Education (1971), commonly referred to as the Peterson Commission report, all in Chicago; the inhouse report in Los Angeles entitled Educational Renewal (1971); the Philadelphia inhouse report entitled A Multiple Option Approach to School-Community Participation (1970); and in Detroit, the inhouse reports, Working Draft of Possible Guidelines ... (1970) and the Public Reaction Draft of Decentralization Guidelines (1970).

With the exception of the Passow report, the above policy reports are the most well known because of the size and relative visibility of the respective cities and school systems. In effect, we are dealing with the five largest cities and school systems of the nation which, because of their size and concurrent influence, receive wide coverage in the national news and educational literature. However, the Passow report is influential because of the author's affiliation with Columbia University and his general influence on the academic community and the field of urban education; likewise, the report is about the school system of the nation's capital, which is also a city with the largest percentage of blacks of any major city.

Viewing the above policy reports in relation to the three categories, the Passow Report (1967) and Havighurst report (1964) were written by outside, prestigious educational groups. While Passow is affiliated with Columbia University, Havighurst is affiliated with the University of Chicago. Both reports relied on some graduate student participation as well as a number of university staff members as consultants. Several task forces were formed and the professors (Passow and Havighurst) were responsible for the respective final reports. Questionnaires were administered to students, teachers, and community leaders. Both reports put total system reform (Passow for the Washington, D. C., public schools and Havighurst for the Chicago public schools) among its many recommendations, some changes directed toward school decentralization and integration. Both reports saw the advantages of strong community participation, but rejected total community control.

The recommendations of the Passow report (1967) were that:

1. The school system be divided into eight areas, each serving approximately 20,000 students.
2. Each area be headed by a community superintendent,

appointed by the central office and responsible to
the deputy superintendent in charge of community
school coordination.

3. Community boards of education be elected by the
    voters from each area, and these boards advise
    the community superintendent and set policy which
    does not conflict with the rules of the central
    board. *

4. Schools be transformed into community schools,
    open 12 to 14 hours a day, six days a week, all
    year.

5. The metropolitan area work toward comprehensive
    educational planning to reduce racial isolation.

The Passow report legitimized the need for decentralization in Washington D. C. and, according to Fantini et al.
(1970), planted the seed for the Adams-Morgan Community
School District, an experimental program based upon the concept of strong community participation.

The Havighurst report (1964) favored:

1. Placing decision-making authority in curriculum and
    instruction as close as possible to the individual
    schools and increasing the authority of the school
    principals.

2. The creation of three regions: (X) with three dis-
    tricts comprising high achievement and college
    preparatory high schools and their feeding schools;
    (Y) with seven districts comprising middle-level
    achievement and comprehensive schools; and
    (Z) with four districts comprising low achievement,
    inner-city schools.

3. The creation of six districts organized to promote
    integration and community development.

In effect, Havighurst was urging homogeneous grouping.
Based on realistic achievement scores, this would have maintained or even reinforced socio-economic and racial segregation, which is in marked contrast to his philosophy. He

---

*The report states, "If the local boards are given complete
responsibility and authority, including power to allocate funds,
the present system would split into six or eight nearly independent school districts. However, tokenism was rejected
and it was recommended that "local boards be given considerable autonomy" (p. 10).

claimed that the grouping of students according to common educational characteristics would lead to the best possible curricula and school program. He realized that he would be criticized for promoting segregation, but urged that the low achieving students usually found in the inner cities would be highlighted so as to increase funding in these schools. (At the time, compensatory education was considered a viable idea and not subject to failure, as it is today.) One might hypothesize that Havighurst recognized that Chicago was (and still is) the most segregated city in the North and perhaps in the entire country,* and that mass integration would not be implemented by the school board, at least not without a court order, and that therefore only the six pilot districts organized to promote integration would be tolerated at that time by the white citizenry.

The two policy reports issued by panels are the Mayor's Advisory Panel (1967) and its Bundy report and the Commission on Urban Education (1971) and its Peterson Commission report. Both panels issued statements in favor of integration but noted that the possibilities were remote and thus proceeded to issue the strongest recommendations in favor of administrative decentralization and community control. The concept of control was advocated as an essential ingredient for promoting participatory democracy at the local level. Both panels seem also strongly influenced by a number of white liberal educators and black militants, thus suggesting the reason for the stand on community control.

Even though the Bundy report is perhaps the most important document in promoting the concept of community control, we will examine it, only briefly now, since it will be discussed in detail in Chapter 4. The Mayor's Advisory Panel (1967) advised that:

1. New York City schools be decentralized into 30 to 60 school districts comprising between 12,000 and 40,000 students.
2. Community school boards have control over curriculum, personnel, and finances.
3. The city board of education retain limited powers, namely over student transfers, contract union negotiations, and school integration policies.

*The 1970 census in Chicago confirms that "Chicago ... is the most segregated city in the nation" (Chicago Tribune, November 5, 1972, Section 1B, p. 1).

The white liberals serving on the panel included McGeorge Bundy, the head of the committee, who was president of Ford Foundation and former dean of faculty at Harvard as well as advisor to Presidents Kennedy and Johnson; Francis Keppel, president of General Learning Corporation and former U. S. Commissioner of Education; Mitchell Svirdoff, the director of the city's Human Resources Administration, the agency which coordinated the anti-poverty services, and close advisor to Mayor Lindsay; and Mario D. Fantini, staff director for the study who has since become noted for his anti-school system viewpoints and favorable views on community control. The other panel members were two minority leaders (Bennetta Washington, director of the Women's Job Corps and wife of the first black mayor of Washington, D. C. , and Antonia Pantoja, social work professor and leader in the Puerto Rican community) and one city school board member (Alfred Giardina)--the only panel member who voiced a dissenting opinion. Consultants included David Rogers and Marilyn Gittell, both liberal educators and noted for their anti-school system views, and a number of black militants such as Roy Innes, head of Harlem Core; David Spencer, one of the prominent educators in Harlem's I. S. 201; and several people connected with the Ocean Hill-Brownsville district as well as anti-poverty agencies. According to La Noue (1972), "ideology and politics seem to have shaped most of its community control-oriented recommendations" (p. 13). Indeed, the black militant community used the report to help advance their ideological and political demands centering around control of the schools, which eventually led to the Ocean Hill-Brownsville controversy between the black community and the predominantly white teacher's union and supervisory association, and the subsequent racial polarization of the city.

The Commission on Urban Education's (1971) basic recommendations were:

1. Legislation to implement decentralization and local control in designated urban areas of the state of Illinois, including the city of Chicago.
2. Elect local boards by members of the respective communities.
3. Insure community control in the following areas: curriculum, personnel, student policy, and financing.
4. Evaluate teachers and administrators, hold them accountable to the community, and establish

criteria for transfers.
5. Establish a position of educational ombudsman to
    serve as a liaison between the central board and
    local boards.

In connection with the above recommendations for community control, the influences of such consultants as the liberal William R. Hazard, associate dean of education at
Northwestern University, and black militants such as Barbara
A. Sizemore, former director of Chicago's Woodlawn Experimental School District; Calvert Smith, director of black
studies at the University of Cincinnati and former member of
the Chicago Center for Inner-City Studies; and Rhody McCoy,
former unit director of the Ocean Hill-Brownsville district
seem apparent. However, the black community failed to respond to the report or force an overt issue over its recommendation in bargaining for greater control of the Chicago
schools. To some degree, this implies a lack of unity among
the Chicago black militants at that time and the fact that many
blacks may be "bought off" in varying degrees by Mayor
Daley's "political machine" with related jobs and favors.
Also, they are already in the power structure of the Chicago
school system, and almost all of the new vacancies as principals and superintendents in ghetto areas have been filled by
blacks. However, the Commission is reconvening at the
time of this writing; a follow-up report is scheduled to be
published in 1974, and one should not underestimate the growing influence of the Chicago black community.

In the meantime, the Illinois General Assembly was
influenced by the 1971 Peterson Commission report and established (Senate Bill 805) in February 1972 a Department of
Urban Education within the State's Office of the Superintendent
of Public Instruction. The bill mandated four functions of
the new department, including the development of a three-
year experimental program in local school governance with
financial grants to participating schools.

In theory, the experiment seeks to determine the best
methods for achieving community involvement. Participation
is limited to school districts with an average daily attendance
of 20,000 or more students. Eight school districts within the
state are eligible; they are Chicago, Decatur, East St. Louis,
Elgin, Mt. Prospect, Peoria, Rockford, and Springfield. In-
centive grants ranging up to $200 per student is to be pro-
vided to participating districts. The experiment is to include such matters as personnel, curriculum, financing,

accountability, and evaluation, with the local governing boards
for each experimental group originally assuming office on
September 1, 1972 and governing their respective districts
for three years [Elsbery (1972) and Local School Governance
Experiment (1972)].   However, all of the school districts except East St. Louis argued that there was not sufficient time
to train the local school board members and that they needed
additional time;   moreover, because of the alleged general
financial crisis in education the funds had not been allocated
by the state to pay the participating districts.   The experiment has been rescheduled to begin sometime in late 1974
or early 1975.   (A side note is that the evaluation was to be
conducted by the Department of Education.   This connotes an
"inside" evaluation;   a more objective procedure would be
to employ an outside evaluation group to monitor the experiment on a continuous basis from the beginning to the end:
such a group would have no stake in the success or failure
of the experiment.)

Only one of the aforementioned reports was written
by an outside consulting and management firm: the Booz-
Allen and Hamilton report (1967).   In 1966 the Chicago school
system commissioned the firm to survey the public schools
and provide a plan for decentralization.   In May of the following year, the company made recommendations that the
board of education:

1.   Retain responsibility for setting policy and deliberat-
      ing major issues.
2.   Establish three standing committees (facilities, fi-
      nance, and community relations) to identify key
      issues and present them to the central board of
      education.
3.   Divide the system into three areas, each headed by
      an area associate superintendent, and retain the
      27 districts (approximately nine districts within
      each area), each headed by a district superin-
      tendent.
4.   Continue to permit the district superintendents to
      have direction over the schools within their
      boundaries and permit the new area associate
      superintendents to have direction over the dis-
      tricts within their boundaries, the latter to be
      accountable to the deputy superintendent at the
      central office.

The Chicago Board of Education adopted the plan;   authority

and accountability continued to be directed upwards to the
central office.

The inhouse reports entailed an initial committee organized by the general superintendent and board of education,
or in the case of New York City the school board itself wrote
the report. The committee members usually interviewed
hundreds of teachers, school administrators, community
leaders, and even students in the case of Detroit and Los
Angeles. The committee members also attended hundreds
of discussions, commissions, public hearings and community
forums. Often, a proposed plan was submitted which was
followed by additional public meetings as well as usually by
thousands of write-in statements. Modifications were made
and the final report was then submitted.

In accordance with the 1969 Decentralization School
Law passed in the state capitol, the New York City five-
member school board issued the report, District Boundary
Lines under the Community School District System (1969),
thus delineating 31 school districts [expanded to 32 in 1973].
The most controversial part of the report was the majority
decision (3-2 in favor) that the three experimental school
districts--Ocean Hill-Brownsville in Brooklyn, I. S. 201 in
Harlem, and Two Bridges in lower Manhatten--be merged
with additional schools to create larger school districts.
(We will return to this report and discuss it in greater detail in Chapter 4.)

The Los Angeles school decentralization commission
members were appointed during the aftermath of the New
York City racial disruptions over community control. The
commission members were influenced by the events in New
York and, in their report, Educational Renewal (1971), they
rejected the concept of community control on the basis that
it could "polarize and intensify all latent racial and potential
conflicts throughout the city" (p. 28). The report listed 26
recommendations which can be categorized into three headings:

1. Increasing the school principal's authority in planning
    curriculum, ordering textbooks, and converting a
    number of unfilled teacher positions to dollar
    equivalents to employ additional personnel.
2. Organizing school-community advisory committees
    for each school--whose members would include
    teachers, parents, and students in secondary

schools--and which would be coordinated by the
school principal.

3. Reorganizing the school system into ten regular and
    three experimental areas, each headed by an area
    superintendent.

In March 1971 the Los Angeles Board of Education
approved the task force's recommendations; however, 12
areas were organized. Although the three experimental districts were approved by the school board, funds were not
forthcoming from the state legislature.

The Philadelphia inhouse committee on school decentralization was also organized at the height of the New York
City issue over community control. The document submitted
to the school board, A Multiple Option Approach to School-
Community Participation (1970), also rejected the concept of
community control and suggested in the introduction that the
"Central Board of Education retain [its] powers ... essential
to the efficient operation of the schools" (p. iii). The report argues for decentralization on an individual school basis
accompanied by greater community participation involving
three options: (1) informal participation without formal
structure, (2) advisory participation through a committee
which advises the school principal in school matters, and
(3) shared authority with a local school board making decisions "consistent with appropriate laws ... and Central
Board of Education policies" (p. 8). In April 1971 the
Philadelphia Board of Education Meeting adopted the commission's recommendations "subject to further consideration,
as soon as funding [could] be undertaken."

Detroit's Office of School Decentralization outlined
two inhouse reports which we will briefly examine now but
further examine in the fourth chapter. The first report was
the Working Draft of Possible Guidelines ... (1970), a two-
part report which assessed the opinions of thousands of students, parents, teachers, and administrators and listed 100
specific issues related to the powers of the central board of
education and regional (decentralized) boards of education.
After several workshops and public meetings, as well as
write-in statements, the Office of School Decentralization
issued the Public Reaction Draft of Decentralization Guidelines (1970). This draft represented the majority or plurality
viewpoint on all issues. The Guidelines recommended that:

1. The school system be divided into eight regions,

each comprising 24 to 56 schools, and each governed by an elected regional board of education.

2. A regional superintendent be in charge of the schools
within his respective boundaries.

3. The regional school boards be granted board powers
over curriculum, instruction, staff organizational
patterns, and inservice training, as well as share
powers with the central school board in such matters as special education, student policy, testing
and evaluation, employment and promotion of personnel, contracting special funds, and school-
community relations.

In October 1970 the Detroit Board of Education made
some minor revisions and adopted the Guidelines for Regional
and Central Boards of Education of the School District of the
City of Detroit, the final plan which led to the decentralization of the system on January 1, 1971; we will return to
these documents in the last chapter.

In summarizing, it should be noted that the above two
research approaches were based on soft data. First, the
research on the school bureaucracies and school boards was
for the greater part action or field-oriented (natural and un-
controlled). The data were based on personal recollections,
observations, ancedotal data, interviews, and nonstandardized
measurement instruments, which may be considered legitimate for some educators but which are of dubious quality for
many members of the research community, especially since
there were few, if any, checks regarding the reliability and
validity of the personal data, observers, and measurement
instruments; little controlling for the value judgments of the
investigators; little or no objective confirmation of the data;
and plentiful conversion of micro-data (or data from a limited sample size or setting) into macro-data (or generalizations concerning larger settings or even the entire school
system). The lack of proper safeguards made the final product susceptible to the personal biases, ideologies, and politics of the investigators. Except for the value of suggesting
hypotheses or perhaps encouraging overgeneralized judgments
about some phenomenon on school bureaucracies and school
boards, the above research on the school systems had little
research value for purposes of drawing valid generalizations
and conclusions.

Second, the policy reports were based on intuition
and logic and were motivated largely by political and racial

pressure.   There was often an attempt to assess the attitudes
of community residents and representatives of social-action,
political, and business groups, which is practical and perhaps
necessary for schools in order to legitimize recommendations
or to find out which recommendations are the most expedient,
but from a strict research viewpoint such procedures are
also highly unreliable and in the main invalid, for these procedures tend to mirror personal biases and political ideologies and are not proof of the educational worth of administrative decentralization or community control.   (For example,
will these two concepts, if implemented, improve the education of the students, and which students, if any?)   All of the
policy reports assumed or implied the merits of decentralization, while the viewpoints on community control varied.   In
every one of these reports, there was no evidence of research to support the policies.   Decisions seemed to be
based on circulated and unchallenged "wisdom," linked to
the urgency for change for the sake of change--a current
fetish in education--and by the demands of liberal educators
and especially the black militant community.   Pressure and
politics seemed to be the key factors, not education per se.

Community Participation and Community Control

        A number of studies can be cited which show that the
traditional form of community participation involving parents
with children attending school, not community residents without children attending school, correlates with increased student development in academic and attitudinal areas.   For
example, Schiff (1963) found that parental participation and
cooperation in school affairs led to increased student achievement and school attendance and fewer discipline problems.
In Hess and Shipman's (1966) study of middle-class and lower-
class mothers' attitudes toward their children in school, the
investigators concluded that involving parents in school activities might help low-income children improve their self-concepts and images of the teachers and school, as well as help
low-income mothers acquire teaching skills which could be
used at home.   Brookover et al. (1965) showed that low-income junior high school students whose parents were involved
in school matters had acquired improved self-concepts and
made significant academic gains in comparison to students
whose parents were uninvolved in school matters.

        Rempson (1972) evaluated an experimental program
for increasing parental participation of blacks and Puerto

Ricans in 27 elementary schools in New York City. He found that participants reported gains in improving their ability to guide their children's growth, a strengthened self-image, and increase of their knowledge of the school functions. It was also found that significantly (the levels of significance were not reported) more Puerto Rican fathers than black fathers participated in the school activities (suggesting in part to some social scientists the theory of the patriarchal Puerto Rican family and the matriarchal black family) and that a greater percentage of black parents than Puerto Rican parents participated in these school activities (suggesting in part to this author that English-speaking ability influences parental participation in American schools).

From personal observations of compensatory programs across the nation, Fusco (1966), Gordon and Wilkerson (1966), and Jablonsky (1968) concluded that the schools which involved parental participation seemed to have greater success in educating lower-income students. However, the recent evaluation reports on compensatory education indicate that increases made by students in the initial years have not been maintained, thus suggesting the influence of the Hawthorne effect which links changes in the subjects' performance with knowledge of the experimental situation itself and not to the variables introduced by the programs. Since there was no follow-up study for the other four successful research studies mentioned above, it is possible that the Hawthorne effect was also operating there.

The effects of low-income parental participation and improved student achievement on preschool children has been reported by Deutsch (1964, 1971). Similarly, Cloward and Jones (1963) reported that parents of all socio-economic classes who were involved with school activities were more likely to stress interest in the academic achievement of their children. Coleman et al. (1966) concluded that the student's sense of control over his environment is a strong factor which affects achievement. It would appear, according to this author, that greater parental involvement could increase the student's sense of control. A similar hypothesis is also stated by Lopate et al. (1970): that "active participation of parents in school affairs ... may enhance cultural identity and self-concept, which in turn [may] raise achievement" (p. 143).

It is important to note that the above data should not be equated with the effects of community control, or even with community participation as defined in the introduction.

It would be wrong to infer that since parental participation in assisting children with school learning seems to enhance student achievement and attitudinal development, as well as strengthen parental self-images and ability to help their children with school work, that the same is true with community control or even the current form of community participation which involves advisory input. This is just as fallacious as assuming that since school administrators favor community participation, they would also favor community control.

Empirical investigations of the effects of community control are limited as of now, since it is a recent development, confined to two major cities on a system-wide basis and a few pilot projects elsewhere, and since adequate research controls have not yet been developed. A few recent studies are discussed below which have some bearing on community control and student or teacher behaviors.

Ravitch (1972) summarized the literature which endorsed the Ocean Hill-Brownsville experiment in New York City and which claimed that students in the district had achieved academic success. These success stories were based on personal observations from liberal educators and literary critics (including I. F. Stone, Alfred Kazin, Dwight Macdonald, and Nat Hentoff), liberal organizations (such as the New York Civil Liberties Union and the New York Urban Coalition), the district's self-evaluation reports, Queens College Institute for Community Studies, which funded more than $1 million in Ford Foundation grants to the demonstration district, and the Ford Foundation which also initiated the Bundy report.

Ravitch points out that the demonstration district lasted from the fall of 1967 to June 1970; throughout 1968 and 1969, Rhody McCoy, the unit administrator of the district, refused to administer reading tests to the students, but "nevertheless continued to release figures attesting to the rapid improvement of reading scores" (p. 72). Ravitch asserts that there was no control group to gauge the district's effectiveness, that there was no systematic or reliable method of record keeping, "and that any other district which handled its internal affairs so inefficiently would have been dissolved by state authorities"(p. 72).

In the Spring of 1971, one year after the district had been dissolved, standardized reading tests (Metropolitan Reading Achievement Tests) were administered to the students

of the eight schools in the district in conjunction with the
city-wide testing program.   According to the results of the
reading scores, the Ocean Hill-Brownsville experiment was
a failure.   Writes Ravitch (1972), "Every school in the [ex-
perimental] district reported poor reading scores--as compared with other schools in the city ... [and] even with other
ghetto schools generally" (p. 72).   The school with the
highest score had 24.5 percent of its students reading at or
above grade level, with the other seven schools reporting
lower scores and as few as 5.5 percent of its students reading at or above grade level.   The results of the 1971 tests
showed that all the schools reported a lower score than they
had in 1967.   For example, seventh graders at J.H.S. 271
had mean scores of 5.4 in 1967 (the normal reading score
should have been 7.7) and 4.7 in 1971;   the same pattern
appeared in the other grades in the other schools of the experimental district.

        One must consider that the district was heavily funded
by supplementary Ford Foundation and state money;   it had
a ratio of one staff member to every eight to ten students,
was supplied with the latest educational "hardware," presumably had the support of the staff since the community
school board allocated jobs (in fact, this latter situation
caused the 1968 New York City teacher strike), and yet it
was a failure in terms of teaching students to read, probably
the most important aspect of the curriculum in terms of
school success.   On the other hand, one must remember
that the district was plagued with a series of conflicts and
controversies, and even though the schools remained open
during the 1968 teacher strike, the school atmosphere was
not conducive to academic learning.   The atmosphere was
politically and racially tense.

        Talmage and Ornstein (1973b) developed a 30-item in-
strument and used a five-point scale ranging from "strongly
agree" to "strongly disagree" to measure perceptions toward
accountability and community control.   (Most of the items
pertained to accountability;   for our purposes, only those
items related to community control are examined.)   As many
as 305 teachers from Chicago were surveyed and divided into
three groups: preservice, student teachers, and inservice;
and then categorized by sex, teaching level, ethnicity, and
school location.   Items administered fell into three major
areas: curriculum and instruction, personnel matters, and
student performance.   Internal consistency reliability and
pre- and post-test reliabilities were satisfactory (Hoyt's

ANOVA reliability--. 700; preservice teachers, Pearson
Product Moment Correlation, r=. 893; inservice teachers,
Pearson Product Moment Correlation, r=. 744).

All differences reported were at the . 001 level, based
on F ratios for the analysis of variance. Minority teachers
had significantly higher scores than white teachers on the
desirability of the "local community members [refering to
adults who did not necessarily have children enrolled in the
schools], having much to add to the school academic program." The mean score was significantly higher for those
who preferred to teach in the outer city and suburban schools
than for those who identified with inner-city schools for the
following items: "Parents [adults who had children enrolled
in the local school] should have a role in hiring the school
personnel"; "the local community should be consulted on
decisions concerning transferring a teacher"; and "parents
should be members of the school's curriculum committees."
This suggested that teachers in the inner city (most of whom
were white) were threatened by current demands of parents
and local community members, or were less likely to look
positively on parent participation and community participation
in matters concerning personnel and curriculum.

Comparing preservice and inservice teachers, the latter were significantly less positive about three items related
to being held accountable to community members for their
instructional performance and to perceiving relations with
the community as a factor that would improve the behavior
of the students. This suggests that preservice teachers are
more idealistic, or at least more likely to favor a greater
amount of community participation. With more exposure to
educational reality, and its political and economic considerations, attitudes of teacher groups tended to become less
positive toward community involvement. The authors concluded that "future studies should probe perceptions of student, parent, and community groups in [the] same areas."
Comparison of perceptions could give leaders a basis for
working out accountability/ school community relations (p. 220).

In summary, the present research on community control is limited, partly because of the ideological and racial
conflicts which have prevented rigorous research and partly
because so few school systems have implemented plans which
approach community control. Detroit and New York are the
only school systems that have effected a system-wide plan;
Louisville is in the process of extending community

participation but there are as of now no specific guidelines for community control; and a few school systems have implemented a model city or experimental school which approaches community control--e.g., in Chicago, Buffalo, Flint, Gary, Indianapolis, New Haven, Oakland, and Washington. For the greater part, student achievement scores of the experimental schools have not been compared with matched control groups, nor have the studies attempted to control for the Hawthorne effect and extra monies allocated to these pilot programs. Much of the data on community control, therefore, has been formulated in terms of a debate or a specific position (for or against). Research is expensive, but lack of research on community control may be more expensive in the long run to the students and society in general. As La Noue (1972) suggests, "Given existing racial hostilities and other problems in our cities, decentralization [also implying community control] will not be easily reversible. If it fails, the human social costs will be great" (p. 25). Until the research clearly shows the effects of decentralization and community control, we should proceed with caution.

The difference between community participation and community control have not been empirically explored either. Talmage and Ornstein (1973a) hypothesize that most professional educators strongly favor community participation, but they have less positive, perhaps even negative views toward community control. At the present, the investigators have obtained data from a sample of 300 teachers, supervisors, and administrators from the Chicago metropolitan area, to learn the views these educators have toward community participation in vs. community control of the schools. The items discriminate within four classifications: curriculum, student policy, financing and personnel. The investigators have not yet calculated the results. Eventually, we hope to use the same instrument for a nation-wide study. A copy of the instrument is found in the Addendum at the very end of this chapter. A class using this book might poll themselves and learn their attitudes toward community participation vs. community control. The reader is cautioned that the outcome of the classroom survey is relevant only to what the specific group thinks. While it would not reflect the attitudes of teachers or administrators in general, the class findings can be used as a source of discussion (and perhaps controversy).

The Present State of Research

    A few years ago Fantini (1970), one of the major pro-
ponents of decentralization and community control, criticized
those who urged caution because there was a lack of empirical evidence. He wrote:

> The first question [of the skeptic] usually is: What
> evidence is there that neighborhood control of urban
> schools improves student achievement? The answer
> is that if there is no evidence it is because there
> really are no community-controlled urban public
> schools.... However, what we do have ample evi-
> dence of is the massive failure that the standard,
> centrally controlled, urban school has produced. It
> is ironic, therefore, that those in control of a failing
> system should ask others offering constructive, demo-
> cratically oriented alternatives to demand results be-
> fore there has been any chance for full implementa-
> tion [p. 52].

    That same year, Clark (1979) reviewed the books
on decentralization and community control and concluded that

> What a considerable portion of the literature on de-
> centralization to date amounts to is special pleading
> for a particular solution.... Very little attempt is
> made to develop ideas coherent enough to warrant the
> term 'theory,' and the casual use of favorable exam-
> ples seldom justify the label of empirical research.
> Where knowledge is incomplete but problems imme-
> diate ... one can still expect generalizing intellectuals
> and amateur politicians to come forth with solutions
> [p. 509].

> ... [D]ecentralization ... may ameliorate some press-
> ing problems. Such efforts can serve as useful ve-
> hicles for social as well as scientific experimentation.
> But unless there is more systematic social scientific
> analysis of these efforts than we have generally had
> to date, we may never understand their many conse-
> quences [p. 514].

    The implications of these two statements clearly re-
flect the liberal educator's position which often seeks change
for the sake of change, often without regard for research or
proven evidence, in contrast to the researcher who often

opposes mass change without evidence. According to Robinson (1972), "this confrontation is by no means new--in fact its very existence may be deemed a necessary requirement for a vital society," but like so many other differences today it appears much sharper and it seems that "there is heightened respect for change per se, quite apart from any presumptions of progress of improvement" (p. 587). Similarly, there appears to be a decline of respect for the value of research and the concurrent claim by those who often do not understand research (including many community activists, teachers, administrators, and professors of education) that the researchers are elitists.

The central fallacy of liberal educators is that their ideas are usually based on bandwagon wisdom, with little research evidence; in fact, they often help create this "wisdom" and expect others to accept their ideas on faith. Many of these liberal educators are anti-scientific and anti-research; they often plunge headfirst, and implement change in one swoop without real knowledge that what they are doing or about to do really works. (For example, compensatory education has cost us billions of dollars before finding out it does not work. By late 1972 there were more than 250 performance contracts, also totaling billions of dollars, with very little proof that these contracts were productive. Across the country educators are advocating the use of behavioral objectives and performance criteria, and most institutions of higher learning can no longer get funds from the federal government unless behavioral objectives and performance criteria are written into the teacher-training programs; yet there is no evidence that these ideas work, improve teacher training, or can be implemented in practice.) Indeed, it is more fun for liberal reformers to think up new programs and ideas than to try to implement them; many of these educators run from their programs and ideas right before the "roof caves in."

It is no longer "fun" but a hint of back-scratching and educational collusion and corruption, when we learn that most federal funded programs, especially the larger ones directed to aiding the poor, the racial minorities, the inner-city, and ghetto schools, are characterized by contract awards on a noncompetitive basis, widespread waste and misappropriation of funds, and little if any systematic evaluation. Edith Green (1972), a Congresswoman who conducted hearings on the appropriation of federal grants and contracts, points out that between 1966 and 1971 82 percent of the grants in the

Department of Health, Education, and Welfare (HEW) and 90
percent of those in the United States Office of Education
(USOE) were awarded on a noncompetitive basis. We are
thus witnessing the rise of a poverty-educational complex in
which the federal government is able to grant hundreds of
millions of dollars, even billions, "in deals that are close
to arrangements between friends" (p. 83). And, the point is,
most of the money is being funded to liberal reformers and
educators who have friends in Washington and black militants
who claim they represent the black community. They seem
to have little regard for empirical evidence; their major
orientation is change for the sake of change and conflict for
the sake of conflict; at best many of them seek reform without real knowledge that what they are doing is educationally
sound, and at worst, many are anti-system and wish to bring
it down.

Ornstein (1968) contends that "little time or energy is
spent on validating the various assumptions, or anticipating
the numerous variables that will affect a program." The
programs are "hurriedly put together to get the money while
it is still available," and the result is the programs generally
fail and end up chiefly "in ambiguous and dismal outcomes"
(p. 253). Green (1972) maintains that officials feel obligated
to spend all the money appropriated to them for the fiscal
year. They are put into a bind of spending the entire federal allotment in order to request additional funds for the
next fiscal year. The result is mass confusion and allocation of millions and even billions of dollars without clear
understanding of the programs. Thus in the fiscal year ending June 30, 1971, the finalizing of federal grants and contacts reached a peak of 1049 in one week in mid-June; a
month earlier the weekly figure was 192 and two weeks after
the mid-June rush the number of transactions had decreased
to 227. This mid-June deluge leads to a great deal of quick
transactions and eventual waste of money.

Abert (1972) points out that funding involves a choice
between competing needs, and these choices "remain based
on value judgments" (p. 65). For example, should the federal government assist the "have littles," or not-so-disad-
vantaged children from working-class backgrounds, though
they are not the most needy, or should we almost entirely
overlook them as we have in the past and assist the less
able students, who may be hopeless. Or, should a library
be built in a moderate economic suburban community, where
the books are likely to be read, or in an inner-city, poor

area, where the books are less likely to be read. Similar
questions arise over the locations of facilities and the funding of programs in all social and economic areas--ranging
from drug rehabilitation centers to manpower training centers. Abert indicates that predetermined factors such as
population density, income, and race are considerations that
guide funding. Therefore, the funds wind up in the hands of
the liberal-minority community. And the past indicates that
the funds are generally wasted--often split among friends or
used to pay off the most vocal and potentially militant groups
in fat consultant fees and salaries--monies are often misappropriated, and programs often fail; then there is the cry
that more money is needed before a dent or change can be
made. To correct this situation, we need to pilot-test our
ideas with matched experimental and control groups. The
trouble is, we often hear the claim that there is no time to
test our ideas. The cycle is repeated: liberal reformers
using catchy slogans and writing professional-looking applica-
tions for grants, and black militants who claim they represent
the black community and warn of impending violence. Many
of the compensatory advocates tend to be opportunists, who
seek personal gain and profit, and regardless of their slogans
and rhetoric they are often not concerned with the target population they claim they serve but instead concerned with self-
interests. As Sidney P. Marland (1972), the former Commissioner of the USOE, put it: "I must say that prudent
program management does not always result in the best immediate circumstances for the children [or target population]
whom the programs are supposed to serve" (p. 88).

Green (1972), Marland (1972), and Ornstein (1968,
1972) assert that there is virtually no monitoring of these
federal programs, nor is there an adequate evaluation.
Green (1972) points out there is no "checking performance
against promise, offering criticism where necessary, and
taking corrective action when called for" (p. 84). Marland
(1972) admits that the programs in the past have not been
evaluated and in other cases the directors themselves carry
out the evaluation. Writes Marland, "I must assume they
[the directors] possessed a natural and healthy bias in favor
of their own enterprises" (p. 88). Ornstein (1968, 1972)
bluntly states that most of the reports, if they are filed at
all, are filled with false data and results. He (1972) wrote,
"Very few directors of a program will jeopardize their
chances for additional funds and admit their present program
is a failure." Even the "outside evaluators are often reluctant to state the truth, because of fear of being blackballed

by the directors" (p. 64-65). Marland (1972) contends that
his USOE is trying to evaluate these programs now, but he
automatically gives the program designers and directors a
way out--by not holding them accountable, by also stating
that "such programs simply cannot be administered totally
free of the risk of falling short of expectations or even failure" (p. 88). This may be partially true, but we should
work toward eliminating these high-risk projects, this waste
of money.

The most obvious waste, and unethical practice, is
the misappropriation of funds. Moynihan (1969) has described
this in detail with regard to many of the community action
programs, and this is true with many educational programs,
too. Green (1972) contends that there are stacks of reports--
the few programs which have been evaluated or audited by
federal officials or outside agencies--which show bizarre and
unfeasible objectives that should never have been funded, and
merely resulted in the waste of millions of dollars per year.
And a random examination of the accounts indicate huge sums
of misappropriated money totaling in the tens of millions;
even worse, these same firms and directors get funded again.
Regardless of this misassignment of money, Green asserts
that "it seems that HEW and USOE officials are determined
to keep certain grant recipients solvent come hell or high
water" (p. 85). In the meantime, Phi Delta Kappan (1973)
reports that the federal auditors indicate that the USOE had
awarded $56 million in grants and contracts illegally. Pres-
ent HEW Secretary Caspar Weinberger has admitted that part
of the illegal practices consisted of back-dating grants so
they would be approved on time. And Richard Fairley (1972),
past director of OE's division of compensatory education, now
claims that of more than 1200 educational projects evaluated
between 1970-72 only ten were found successful on the basis
of measurable data.

Granted the pace of school reform does not lead one
to be optimistic, but it is questionable whether the schools
can solve all the problems of society. Certainly there is no
empirical evidence to expect that administrative decentralization or community control will reform the schools. Without
quality research we are only basing our claims on bandwagon
wisdom--at worst, on politics.

The problem is compounded by the suspicion and distrust on the part of the black community toward the social
scientist (researcher) who is usually white. Billingsley
(1970) writes:

> ... the reason black families have fared so much
> worse than white families in social science is that
> they are black and social science is white. ...   When
> black people have been the object of analysis by white
> social scientists ... the relations between white and
> black people rather than the nature of the life of black
> people ... has been at the center of their interests.
>
> ... these social scientists have been victimized by
> their own Anglo-European history and culture.   They
> have tended to view other cultures primarily as ob-
> jects of assimilation [p. 133-34].

Glazer (1969), on the other hand, reports references
to several prominent studies by sociologists, anthropologists,
and psychologists and contends that:

> History and social research convince me there are
> deep and enduring differences between various ethnic
> groups, in their educational achievement and in the
> broader cultural characteristics in which these differ-
> ences are, I believe, rooted; that these differences
> cannot be simply associated with the immediate condi-
> tions under which these groups live, whether we de-
> fine these conditions as being those of levels of pov-
> erty and exploitation, or prejudice and discrimination;
> and if we are to have a decent society, men must
> learn to live with some measure of group difference
> in educational achievement, to tolerate them...
> [p. 187].

Glazer is concerned about the attitudes we take about these
differences: Do we believe that they are the sole consequence
of the "ill will" and "racist" feelings of teachers, administrators,
social scientists, and society in general?   About these differences, he writes:

> How elaborate are we to make the efforts to wipe
> them out, and how successful can we hope to be no
> matter how elaborate our efforts are?   Are our mea-
> sures to equalize to include the restriction of the op-
> portunities of those groups that seem to find school
> achievement easy [p. 195]?

The conflict of opinion between Billingsley and Glazer
goes beyond the issue of research related to administrative
decentralization and community control, and on to the general

racial conflict that can destroy our society; we are already
heading in that direction. We need to research educational
differences within and between racial and ethnic groups, to
investigate the multiple causes and solutions. We need to
support the right of free inquiry, but will the black community and especially the black militants still permit the social
scientist who is often white to engage in research? And if
there are continued differences how will white society react
to the differences? Will white society use these differences
to rationalize discriminatory practices? And how will black
society react? Will it lead them to explode into a storm of
emotions and rhetoric?

Even though researchers may believe that their efforts
contribute to the cause of poor and minority groups, the
black activists may confront them with hostility. Part of
the problem is related to basic issues which strain the relations between practitioners and researchers. Writes Ornstein (1972):

> While the social scientist is concerned with research
> and knowledge for its own sake, the practitioner is
> concerned with service and the application of research
> and knowledge. The researcher usually is not con-
> cerned with practical problems because what is ap-
> propriate in one situation is often not applicable to
> other situations. On the other hand, most research
> is impractical for the practitioner who is working not
> with mean scores but with individual variability. The
> gap between the social scientist and practitoner is per-
> haps even wider in the black community because the
> problems of the practitioner are more difficult, and
> he feels the research is less applicable to his situa-
> tion. Furthermore, the practitioner in the ghetto is
> often concerned about covering up the inefficiencies
> and problems that he is confronted with; therefore,
> he views the social scientist as a possible threat who
> may uncover the truth or expose the present conditions
> of the school or social agency [p. 132-33].

And Caro (1971) maintains:

> Preoccupied with the immediate, tangible, dramatic,
> and personal, the minority activist is likely to be
> impatient with the evaluator's [researcher's] concern
> with the future, abstract concepts, orderly procedures,
> and impersonal forces. In contrast to the activist

who often seeks to generate open conflict, the evaluative researcher typically emphasizes cooperative approaches to problem solving. The evaluator [re-
searcher] may also find himself in an awkward position in the power struggle between client spokesmen
and professional administrators. If he entered the
program at the invitation of a funding agency or a
professional administrator, the evaluative researcher
is likely to be mistrusted immediately by minority
activists who see him as a potential spy [p. 99].

As the above suggests, part of the problem between
practitioners and researchers is also related to race differences, and this aspect of the problem seems to be worsening.
According to Deutsch (1969) and Ornstein (1972), suspicion
toward the white social scientist has risen to the extent that
in many black communities the white social scientist is no
longer permitted to conduct research. Obradović (1972) contends that the social scientist is already under close scrutiny
and in direct conflict with black activists and black community dwellers. Her research is based on three Southern urban areas, and it is common knowledge that most blacks in
the South tend to be less militant than those in the North.
The findings of the study indicate that among blacks there is
an inherent negative attitude toward the researcher; it brings
to mind the image of a white person and elicits emotional responses "such as 'white man,' 'the man,' ... 'outsider' and
'exploiter' " (p. 6). Blacks contend that their needs and
priorities have been ignored by traditional researchers, that
there is a feeling of exploitation in that the time, efforts,
and money used in the research mainly serve the purposes
of the researcher's publication record and grant opportunities.

Obradović states that the research community must
accommodate itself to the needs of the black community and
that there is need for black researchers to conduct research
in the black community. Few people would dispute this.
She also contends, however, that the black community must
have input on all phases of research--implying agreement
with the respondents of the survey that blacks "monitor all
research done in their communities ... and that research
findings [first] be reported to the people from whom the data
were collected" (p. 4), and recommending that there be
"community members on the student's dissertation committee" if he does research in the black community (p. 9).
Here we need to recognize that monitoring implies censorship
and lay community members, black or white, often lack the

formal education and qualifications to help determine what is
legitimate research. Obradović seems to anticipate this criticism and further maintains that when we study the black
community we must make allowances, to the extent where
the study "may not be readily amenable to a clean research
design or be conductable under controlled conditions." Rather
than suiting the research community, "we must suit the black
community and even find ways of rewarding professors who
do not publish tightly-controlled research" (p. 10). Here,
her implications are anti-intellectual and anti-research; they
imply that many blacks--who will be researching the black
community--are incapable of conducting valid research and
we have to reward them because of their color, not on their
merit or research abilities. Her proposal, in sum, leads to
black censorship and black ideology--not research--and we
should be honest and admit these facts if this is the route
research in the black community is to take, all under the
guise of eliminating so-called middle-class biases and the
bigotry of the white social scientist. Indeed, the reader
needs only to assess these implications in relationship to
Record's (1972) study of what is happening to many white
sociologists across the country who are criticized and harassed by black militant students as being biased, irrelevant,
and racist. Of the 140 of the estimated 750 white sociologists specializing in race relations in the United States, he
found that nearly 25 percent have abandoned their fields of
inquiry.

> All over the U.S., white social scientists who once
> prided themselves on being unprejudiced and basically
> sympathetic to the blacks they studied have found their
> motivation and competence challenged by militants who
> claim that only a black can understand the black ex-
> perience. The antagonism toward these white social
> scientists has also spread through the black ghettoes,
> making it difficult for them to continue their research
> [p. 46-47].

As one sociologist, who specialized in race relations and was
undaunted by taunts of being a "nigger lover" in the 1950s,
stated "It is too much to hassle, to be an impartial behavioral scientist when the sole criterion for knowledge, understanding, or credibility is the color of your skin" (p. 46).

In this connection, Billingsley (1972) calls for the
overthrow of social scientists who are white, over forty,
and studying blacks--to be replaced by so-called more

objective black social scientists who know the black experience. (Question: Will the black social scientist be objective
or will they be promoting a political cause?) And Stone
(1972) contends with the use of popular rhetoric that if blacks
"are going to break the stranglehold of white colonialism"
they must define new criteria and concepts of education and
social science research (p. 5). He contends that the white
social scientists on race relations must be overhauled and
that blacks are "determined to 'do [their] own thing.' " The
author also calls for a black-white "technical assistance
partnership" so long as the ground rules are developed by
blacks (p. 6). (Question: Is this really a partnership?)

     One of the strongest anti-research positions adopted
by the black community is in Boston, and this is purported
by Roscoe C. Brown (1971), director of the Afro-American
Affairs at New York University. The black residents of Boston have established a Community Research Review Committee (CRRC), which also includes black social scientists, and
who insist on screening and approving the researchers of the
black community, being paid ten percent of the total research
project, and screening and approving the findings before they
are submitted to any agency or journal. A sample of some
of the stipulations is presented below [quoted from R. C.
Brown (1971), p. 5-6]:

Requirements for Research to be Conducted
in the Black Community of Boston

All research grant proposals that intend to use members and/or facilities in the Black community must be
reviewed and approved by the CRRC before any such
research may begin, and be subject to continuing approval by this committee....

Projects to be conducted in the community must provide to the CRRC sufficient funds for the committee's
operation. Such funds are calculated as roughly equivalent to 10% of the total project funds.

All research conducted in the Black community must
involve significant Black personnel, including a Black
co-investigator who is approved by the CRRC.... With
respect to the research itself, Black staff and consultants should be involved in all aspects of the study including:
     a. the design and development of the study

    b.   the implementation of the study
    c.   the monitoring of the study
    d.   the analysis and interpretation of the results
    e.   the preparation and publication of reports,
         papers, talks, etc. based on this research.

Copies of all data and subsequent analysis will be deposited with the CRRC as these become available. The confidentiality of such materials will be maintained by the CRRC.

Copies of all project reports, including interim and final reports, as required by the funding institution, must be filed with the CRRC.

... after analyzing the data, summarizing the results, and preparing a preliminary report, but before disseminating this information to the professional or lay public or to the funding source, the principal investigators must:
    a.   circulate a copy of the report to the CRRC for review and comment, criticism and, if necessary, rebuttal. Any consultation services the CRRC requires for competent review of the report are to be paid by the research project. ...
    b.   agree to include (under separate authorship) as part of the final report and as part of any subsequent publication of the findings, a critical presentation of any alternative interpretations of major findings which cannot be reconciled with the investigator's main finding.

There is no question that blacks have a right to be sensitive to the analysis and interpretation of the research data concerning their schools and community, and that a rebuttal report may be in the best interests of both the black community and research community; however, the implications of some of the above stipulations also border on black censorship and black ideology. The stipulations which reflect censorship and implications of not permitting white social scientists to conduct research in the black community, have political and ideological ramifications. Black activists and possible militants could gain control of the information disseminating from ghetto areas and people would have to come to them for information. As Caro (1971) suggests:

> General antagonism toward social research is also
> linked to the activist's political ambitions. The in-
> dependent social scientist who does poverty research
> is a potential competitor for the activist who would
> like to control the flow of information from poverty
> areas [p. 99].

Black activists would also be in the position to demand money
from investigators who wanted to conduct research, as stipu-
lated in one of the above demands by the CRRC; moreover,
they could end up with their own "inside" social scientists
and slant the findings to accommodate their interests.

Under such conditions, the validity of the research on
the black community would become suspect by most social
scientists, just as it is now suspect by most blacks; moreover, the mood of today's racial situation and the inherent
distrust of white social scientists by blacks (with some
justification) suggest that this could happen with community
control of the schools. As Ornstein (1972) writes:

> ... we are reaching the point where there is a lack
> of tolerance toward controversial findings (involving
> racial studies) and where the oppressed minority is
> becoming the oppressive minority.... Hypersensi-
> tivity to racial and ethnic differences (some real,
> some imaginery) can only impede frank discussion
> and legitimate reform--and transform the social
> scientists' tolerance to hostility [p. 135].

This indeed would be a serious problem, since the white
social scientist, by virtue of his expertise and affiliation
with certain prestigious universities, is still influential in
effecting social and political legislation and in effecting overall reform in schools and society.

Before we proceed with some research suggestions on
administrative decentralization and community control, we
need to be aware of the politics of the situation by examining
the results of these twin concepts. Decentralization and especially community control have been advocated as though
they were certain to be successful. Arguments for these
concepts have often been based on dubious hypotheses, half
truths, and intuition, rather than on research evidence.
Knowing the outcomes of these programs has tremendous implications, especially for those who advocate it and who obtain (or lose) jobs from these new policies. Given the usual

discrepancies between rhetoric and reason, as well as between promise and reality, most advocates of community control would wisely prefer to limit outside evaluation. Lack of research, lack of comparable data, and lack of concrete evidence tend to work in favor of those who advocate change, and especially for those who end up controlling the new policies and programs, who in effect obtain political and economic gains from the change. As D. Campbell (1972) suggests:

> There is safety under the cloak of ignorance. ... If the political and administrative system has committed itself in advance to the correctness and efficacy of its reforms, it cannot tolerate learning of failure [p. 188-89].

This especially applies to the new administrative and school board group, as in the case of community control, where the new power group is still quite visible because of the recent change and possibly heated controversy that accompanied the change, and because it has few buffers to ward off criticism or dissipate the energies of the critics since the new political and administrative machinery has not yet matured.

Rossi (1972) points out, "Research might find that the effects are negligible or non-existent" (p. 227). In fact, if we set up controls for the possible Hawthorne effect, this is what would probably happen. New educational programs usually produce non-positive results or minimal changes because there are several other variables associated with school success that the schools themselves have little control over. (For example, reports by Coleman et al. (1966), Jencks et al. (1972), McPartland (1968), the U.S. Commission on Civil Rights (1967), and Walberg (1969) indicate that the most important variable of the child's performance in school has to do with his family characteristics.) The major research studies repeatedly confirm that all the other variables are either secondary or irrelevant. Thus it behooves the critics of teachers and schools and the reformers who advocate compensatory education and other changes to show otherwise. As Guba (1969) suggests:

> Over and over, comparative studies of alternatives in education have ended in a finding of 'no significant difference'.... It is often observed that the educationists are incapable of devising any approaches that are better than those things that they already [are] using. But, if this is so, we ought perhaps to applaud their

remarkable consistency, since they do not devise
alternatives that are any worse either [p. 31]!

One might argue, then, that a new program need only
show no difference in student achievement to be considered
legitimate.   This is debatable.   When advocating change,
Guba (1969) and Rossi (1972) contend that the new program
must demonstrate that it has a positive effect.   But it is
possible that the research will demonstrate a negative effect
on student achievement, as in the case of Ocean Hill-Brownsville and more recently with regard to the entire New York
and Detroit systems (to be discussed in Chapter 4).   Without
research, claims based on unsupported truths, intuition, and
logic can continue to be voiced, and testimonials from the
advocates of change and ideology can always be found.   So
long as there is no adequate research related to administrative decentralization and community control, the bite of the
opponents' criticism is reduced;   moreover, they are put on
the defensive: criticized for resisting change, branded as
pro-establishment and representing the forces of stagnation.

This, indeed, is exactly what happened in Ocean Hill-
Brownsville, according to Ravitch (1972).   The advocates of
community control continuously claimed favorable changes:
"that Ocean Hill had already achieved academic success,"
innovative methods had "succeeded in raising the reading
levels of many children in the districts in a remarkably
short time," and that " 'by February 1, 1970, every young-
ster in that school system [would] be classified as a reader' "
(p. 71).   The opponents could only claim that there was no
available statistical data, since Ocean Hill-Brownsville "was
the only district in the city which had not participated in the
standardized citywide reading tests" (p. 72).   The eventual
comparison of reading scores showed the experiment to be
a failure;   nevertheless, the New York City school system
was pressured into a city-wide policy which approaches community control.

To be scientific and support our claims with evidence,
we must be able to experiment and conduct evaluative research.   We should advocate change that improves education
and conduct research to support the change without political
excess that blinds us to the reality of results or the refusal
to admit that a specific change has no effect or even a negative effect on student achievement.   If, on the other hand,
we are committed to change because of political or economic
reasons and not because of real educational benefits which

can be proven, then there is good reason for maintaining ignorance, preventing research, slanting findings, screening the research, or hiring an "inside" or politically-oriented researcher.

While all this may sound pessimistic, the general practice is well known of administrators attempting to prevent unwanted research or outside evaluation because their jobs may depend on the findings. The ideological and racial factors connected with community control, and the accompanying politics and economics, only increase the possibilities of preventing legitimate evaluation and research--at least what is considered legitimate by most members of the research community. Add to this the conflict between the black militant community and the research community, and it is doubtful whether, at the present, we can conduct honest research related to community-controlled schools. So long as we remain trapped by race and ideology, the advocates of community control, and especially those who gain politically and economically as a result of the change, cannot afford an honest evaluation of the new program; indeed, we can only give lip service to the need for research, knowing full well in advance that it will be politically controlled or censored if the results prove negative.

If a school system initiates change across the board, such as community control, without evidence that the change has positive effects on learning, the change is not only educationally unsound and irresponsible but it also suggests that education is not the real issue. As Aberbach and Walker (1971) (concerning Detroit), Bard (1972) (concerning New York), and La Noue (1972) (concerning both cities) suggest, the real issues of community control were political and economic and the pressure behind the changes were racial and ideological. If the changes in the two cities prove to have a negative impact on the students, return to the former unitary school system is difficult and with the present racial situation, nearly impossible. Indeed, once a group gains power it is usually not willing to surrender it despite the general harm it may perpetuate. Only in a school system where racial tension is minimal or nonexistent, as in the case of the Clark County schools in Las Vegas, could there be change from centralization to decentralization and back to centralization (see Chapter 3).

Research Suggestions for the Future

While the blacks and whites are polarizing in the
cities and vying for political power and diminishing jobs, the
author is appealing for depolarization on social issues such
as education. Although this may sound impractical or uto-
pian, he is appealing for new bridges between blacks and
whites concerning their children--the clientele who are supposed to be educated--concerning students who have been
short-changed in the past but whose interests do not seem
to be of prime importance in the current battle over the
schools. If new understanding can be built, then research
on administrative decentralization and community control can
proceed. But if the issues over decentralization and community control continue on the present course, then little
viable research on these twin concepts will be forthcoming
in the near future.

It is hoped that a climate could exist in the schools
which permitted rigorous research and less rhetoric and
self-deceptive claims. Although this climate probably still
exists in many cities, it does not seem to exist in the school
systems where there is a controversy over community control. Ironically, this is where the research is needed the
most. As educators, we must seek political stances that
permit legitimate research. We must advocate, according
to D. Campbell (1972), "the importance of the problem
rather than the importance of the results" (p. 219). To be
committed to an idea is certainly admirable, but once we
are committed to ideology we cannot risk honest evaluation.
Even when confronted with research evidence, the true be-
liever usually refuses to budge from his original position;
in fact, his resistance is often hardened.

To race pell-mell into any new reform measure, without evidence that it works or that it is beneficial, is to bow
to the demands of unreason and rhetoric, to pressure and
politics. The need is to implement pilot programs, with
randomized and controlled comparisons. Data would be
forthcoming which should tentatively validate or invalidate
our hypotheses. Caution must be applied, for too many of
us expect the results of one experiment in education to settle
issues once and for all. Indeed, scientists and physicians
would never engage in such thinking. Further replication is
called for; moreover, successes or failures in one community or school system may not apply to other communities
and school systems. Different communities and school

systems are likely to formulate different programs; it is
misleading to take the results of one community or school
system or a small number of communities and schools and
conclude that decentralization or community control is successful or unsuccessful for another school system.   There
are no typical cities, no typical communities, no typical administrative decentralization plans, no typical community
control plans.

Unless the analysis includes a large number of communities and school systems where comparative data can be
developed, the findings will be faulty.   Recent research
(Halinsk and Feldt, 1970) indicates that there should be at
least 20 subjects for each variable being controlled.   According to Hickrod (1971), "A single equation ... [involving]
six or seven variables ... requires measurements on about
150 school districts" (p. 145).   This is of course difficult
and therefore the case study approach might be the most
feasible study, especially for the individual school system.
A longitudinal study for about five to ten years would supply
a wealth of data, but because of politics and pressure we
cannot wait that long to obtain data;   this type of study might
be conducted in conjunction with the case study approach with
tentative findings disseminated every few years.   Not only
ought we to conduct rigorous testing in the initial pilot program, but once it has been decided that reform is to be
adopted as standardized practice throughout the system, we
still need to experimentally evaluate it in each of its stages.

Assuming that we still live in a pluralistic society,
and that black and white parents, community residents, educators, and others can still communicate and are still interested in the education of children and youth, we would hope
that legitimate research on the effects of decentralization and
community control would be conducted in the near future.   In
conducting such research, it would be advantageous to extend
the logic and techniques of experimental (laboratory) research
to action-oriented (field) research.

It is not the author's intention to discuss in detail the
strategies of experimental research, but the general aim
would be to conduct "true experiments" by considering threats
to internal and external validity.   When checking for internal
validity, the investigator should ask: Did the independent
variables (treatment or experimental variables, often represented by the symbol X) really produce a change in the dependent variable (criterion or predicted variable, often

represented by the symbol Y) or what did account for the
results? When checking for external validity, the investigator should ask: What relevance do the findings have beyond
the confines of the experiment? To what extend can generalizations of the results be extended to other settings, other
independent variables, other measures of effect?

The aim for the investigator is to eliminate as many
as possible of the problems associated with internal and external validity through well-designed experiments including
where possible random control groups. Where randomized
treatments are not possible, a critical use of experimental
designs is still possible. Because education is a process
involving a number of variables interacting simultaneously to
form an effect, the investigator should also think of conducting experiments which include factorial designs and multi-
variate analysis. Thus we could answer questions such as
what is the main effect of each of the independent variables
that account for the results, and what is the interaction effect, if any, of the independent variables on the results?
Of course, it is essential that the investigator know which
variables to control, for there is always the possibility that
other variables (not controlled) may account for the experimental results.

A suggested experimental design might consist of six
districts. Two districts would have complete control over
curriculum, personnel, and the budget. Two districts would
share authority with the central board, and two would serve
as control groups to function under the traditional organization of the central board. The six districts could be matched
by class and race. Three might be predominantly black (75
percent or more) categorized into three different income
levels and three might be predominantly white (75 percent
or more), also categorized into the three same income levels.
Ideally, the number of districts might be expanded to include
three additional integrated districts (60 to 70 percent white;
40 to 30 percent black), also categorized into the same income levels. Other racial matches could be made in school
systems that had a large Spanish-speaking, Indian or Oriental
population, or any white ethnic group that deemed it necessary to identify itself as a distinct group for cultural purposes.

Besides matching class and race, a number of dimensions of student performance could be measured and controlled
in accordance with objectives. Characteristics of parents,

teachers, administrators, schools, and the community could
also be classified. Specifically which items are included
will vary with the school systems, but each item would have
to be quantified. After making adjustments for initial differences, the next procedure would be to form a multiple regression analysis with the gains in student performance serving as the dependent variable and the other characteristics
related to parents, teachers, administrators, schools and
community serving as independent variables. (Student performance serves as a single criterion or dependent variable
and the other characteristics serve as mutliple predictors
or independent variables. The usual procedure is to derive
a multiple-regression equation with weights that will maximize the correlation between predicted and obtained criterion
measures.)

Future research in the area of administrative decentralization and community control might also focus on the
following survey questions. The questions in Table 2.1 provide school-community background information. Those in
Table 2.2 are specifically related to decentralization and
community control. Within-group differences, which may be
as large as between-group differences, should also be measured.

The questions in Tables 2.1 and 2.2 are related to
conflicting demands at different levels of intensity by various
interest groups. To date, the issues related to decentralization and community control have not been satisfactorily resolved by the various interest groups. Indeed, there is continuing need for research to fill in the unresolved issues and
unknown consequences of the two reorganizational models of
concern, and how to deal with the question of whether the
students and society in general really benefit and to clarify
the roles of the various interest groups in both set of changes
in the school system. As of now we have no research evidence that administrative decentralization and community control improve education; this is especially true with community control. A systematic response to these issues is, of
course, crucial for the proponents of the various decentralization and community control schemes; otherwise, what we
have are unsupported assertions quoted as statements of
fact. Clark (1970) points out that many of the proponents
of decentralization and community control, "including some
of Athenian stature, operate from a number of questionable
assumptions" (p. 513). Similarly, La Noue (1972) contends
that many of the conclusions about decentralization and

Table 2.1

SCHOOL-COMMUNITY QUESTIONS
FOR BACKGROUND INFORMATION

School	Community
1. How does the school provide opportunity for the community to learn about the school?	1. How does the community provide opportunity for the school to learn about the community?
2. How do the school personnel feel about the community? Why?	2. How does the community feel about the school personnel? Why?
3. How does the school support the community?	3. How does the community support the school?
4. How does the school use community resources and leadership?	4. How does the community use the school's resources and leadership?
5. How does the school provide opportunity for the community to participate in the educational program?	5. How does the community provide opportunity for the school to participate in the community program?
6. What can be done to improve the situation?	6. What can be done to improve the situation?

Table 2.2

QUESTIONS RELATED TO ADMINISTRATIVE
DECENTRALIZATION AND COMMUNITY CONTROL

Administrative Decentralization	Community Control
1. Who are the advocates? [question derived from La Noue (1972)]	1. Who are the advocates?
2. What are the motivations of these people? [question derived from La Noue (1972)]	2. What are the motivations of these people?
3. How seriously does the public want to decentralize? (Is it just a small well-organized minority of educators or residents?)	3. How seriously does the public want community control? (Is it just a small well-organized minority of educators or residents?)
4. What are the various roles of the students, parents, community leaders, professional staff, etc.?	4. What are the various roles of the students, parents, community leaders, professional staff, etc.?
5. Do students, parents, community residents, teachers, etc. have a greater voice under decentralization?	5. Do students, parents, community residents, teachers, etc. have a greater voice under community control?

6. What role problems develop among the various interest groups?

6. What role problems develop among the various interest groups?

7. How do various interest groups feel before and after decentralization is implemented? (What are the differences when race and class are controlled?)

7. How do the various interest groups feel before and after community control is implemented? (What are the differences when race and class are controlled?)

8. How do the various interest groups want to be represented? (What are the differences when race and class are controlled?)

8. How do the various interest groups want to be represented? (What are the differences when race and class are controlled?)

9. How do labor unions, political groups, and municipal and community agencies affect decentralization?

9. How do labor unions, political groups, and municipal and community agencies affect community control?

10. How does the current racial and job situation affect decentralization? (What impact has it made on the racial and ethnic distribution of teaching jobs and administrative positions?)

10. How does the current racial and job situation affect community control? (What impact has it made on the racial and ethnic distribution of teaching jobs and administrative positions?)

11. How does decentralization affect the student's learning?

11. How does community control affect the student's learning?

12. What decentralized unit size (in terms of geographical or metropolitan location, area size, number of students and racial composition of schools) is most effective?

12. What type of community control (in terms of geographical or metropolitan location, area size, number of students, and racial composition) is most effective?

13. What administrative levels (central office, district or field office, individual schools) should be decentralized?

13. What administrative functions (curriculum, personnel, student policy, budget) should be controlled by whom?

14. When does bigness lead to inflexibility?

14. When does community control lead to racial discrimination or political chaos?

15. When does smallness lead to reduced range of educational services?

15. When does professional control lead to racial discrimination or status quo education?

16. What is the cost of decentralization?

16. What is the cost of community control?

17. What support (internal and external) does a decentralized unit require to function successfully?

17. What support (internal and external) does a community school board require to function successfully?

18. What changes in educational policy and approaches have decentralized units been able to implement that was not possible under the centralized administration?

18. What changes in educational policy and approaches have community school boards been able to implement that was not possible under the central school board?

19. How does decentralization affect school integration? (Can they be implemented together?)

19. How does community control affect school integration? (Can they be implemented together?)

20. What is the impact of school decentralization on metropolitan development and cooperation? (Can we decentralize and still promote metropolitan cooperation?)

20. What is the impact of community control on metropolitan development and cooperation? (Can we have community control and still promote metropolitan cooperation?)

21. What is the impact of school decentralization and federal reform? (Can they be implemented together?)

21. What is the impact of community control and federal reform? (Can they be implemented together?)

22. How can conflicts be reduced so basic educational issues take priority over power?

22. How can conflicts be reduced so basic education issues take priority over power?

---

community control, either stated or implied, seem unjustified in terms of lack of proven evidence.

As stated earlier, research is expensive but lack of research on administrative decentralization and community control may be more expensive in the long run to students and society in general. Until the evidence is clear, we should proceed with caution. The point is, the so-called "solutions"--administrative decentralization, community control, even community participation--are mainly slogans, rather than closely worked-out concepts with consequences understood and accounted for in the rhetoric. We assume that the "community" voice is the most vocal and articulated, and we have yet to hear from the majority of silent parents who have their own ideas of life's aspirations for their children and how the school should fulfill this. Once these plans are adopted on a system-wide basis, they would be very difficult to reverse in many large school systems, especially where politics is apparent. What we need, then is research that will test the worth of unsupported statements and claims. We have to test our hypotheses and use caution against making unwarranted conclusions. The aim is to develop

experimental designs to obtain reliable and valid data and to
see whether our findings can be replicated in different settings. We need a partnership between practitioners and researchers, among the various interest groups, and especially
between blacks and whites, if a breakthrough is to be made
to a higher level of mutual understanding and quality education for all children and youth.

On a more general level but one still relevant to the
research on administrative decentralization and community
control, it is important to remember that research can produce knowledge which can eventually lead to change. While
research does not guarantee change, it produces knowledge
for helping to determine whether change is necessary or possible. Wynne (1970) writes:

> Research can produce knowledge. This knowledge can
> give the public tools to make new demands on schools.
> The tools can change the power relationship between
> schoolmen and communities. Because researchers
> can make these tools, we are important threats to
> schoolmen. We must be tamed, controlled, restricted,
> and sedated. We are.
>
> While the only important product of research is infor-
> mation, information is the major source of change in
> any society in which people are not killing each other
> on a large scale. ... [N]othing important happens dif-
> ferently in a democracy unless some members of the
> society are told something they didn't realize before.
> Note that I did not say that the communication of
> 'new' information automatically produces change, but
> that such communication is a precondition to change
> [p. 246].

The question of what information will effect what change is
complex and related to political, economic, social, and
scientific factors. Nevertheless, we should not underestimate the long-range value of information generated by research, nor should we underestimate the relationship between the research community and the federal government--
the latter who possess the experts, resources, money, and
legal apparatus to implement reform and effect changes on
a mass scale. In fact, almost all our major reform measures and changes in education (and other social services
such as medicine, health care, employment practices, housing, social and welfare services, etc.) have been derived

from and implemented by the federal government.

The research community has become aware of its
role for improving the educational enterprise; it is increasingly becoming aware that it must be relevant. Popham
(1971) describes one aspect of this new orientation.

> Whereas a decade ago the bulk of investigations being
> reported in educational research journals and at pro-
> fessional meetings could be characterized, kindly, as
> somewhat esoteric, the current drive is for practical
> relevance.

> I am suggesting ... that the mood among American
> educational researchers has clearly changed. They
> now see a crucial national need to improve the schools
> which, though operated by dedicated school personnel,
> are far less effective than they should be [p. 3].

It has become evident that researchers must listen
more closely to the problems and needs of the practitioner
in order to better understand what needs to be studied to
improve education. According to Farmer (1971), educational
research must be restructured "to maximize the relationship
between the basic researcher and practitioner and, consequently, minimize the gap between basic research and practice" (p. 3). A better relationship can exist between both
these groups if the research includes practical goals and
practical concerns of the practitioner. According to Fox
(1969), an improved relationship can exist between the researcher and practitioner if "the practitioner has been present on the research at all stages." If he is "involved with
the research process, he usually feels identified with the
findings" and is more willing to accept them (p. 100). Caro
(1971) points out the need to present clear and concise findings to the practitioner. Sadofsky (1966) warns that delivering results to the public or professional associates without
warning may produce a defensive reaction to the findings.
Weiss (1966) has suggested that instead of judging programs
or reporting research in simple success or failure terms,
the practitioner should be encouraged to seek alternatives.

While we are trying to maximize the researcher-
practitioner interaction in order to yield more relevant and
viable educational research, we must not overlook the black
community. For the greater part, the black community feels
that it has been "surveyed and studied to death" and that

little good has occurred. According to blacks, too often the research has stressed negative findings or things that are not complimentary to their community. Social scientists often look for problems, emphasizing negative traits and behaviors and viewing differences in relation to the norms of the larger society, or white middle-class, as "problems" or "abnormalities." Studies are more likely to focus on the pathologies of blacks than on the people and institutions that have caused them. Not only have the contributions of black social scientists been scanty, but white social scientists have, perhaps wrongly, been considered in the past to be experts on black families and culture. Assuming the problem lies with the social scientist, there is the need to train more black researchers.

It is important to recognize that research concerning the black community is often characterized by public visibility and emotionalism. The findings can be threatening to the black community, the practitioner working in the ghetto, or the power structure (which is often white but is changing). While the social scientist must recognize his role and responsibilities, as well as the potential impact and possible dysfunctional outcomes of his research, the black community must recognize that the social scientist has the right to free inquiry so long as his research does not degenerate into systematic distortion or propaganda. A study may be criticized or rejoinders may be written, but no one has the right to subject the social scientist to harassment or threaten him because the findings do not agree with popular rhetoric or political ideology.

The researcher must go where the current problems are, and he must be allowed to investigate all facets of society; otherwise, his work becomes irrelevant. He, if white, must not be denied access to the black community on the grounds of race, for he can do more good than harm for the black community--especially in helping to effect social change. Writes Deutsch (1969):

> ...[T]he human social scientist can, I think, play a unique role in lowering the barriers to social change by his activities when he arrives at the relevant problems. He can not only study them, but also, by the kind of questioning of tacit assumptions proposed, he can assault the obstacles to their solution. Indeed, many of the implicit assumptions of the social sciences buttress the barriers to change--or constitute major obstacles themselves.

Social scientists are best qualified to remove the ob-
stacles created by their own assumptions, as well as
the realities and pseudo-realities of their cultural context. It would seem necessary that they do so if they
are to participate actively in the evolution of a democratic society. [By following research procedures]
we can get out of ruts we perhaps are not aware of
being in. In the process we can influence, or at
least bring into question, the many aspects of public
policy which may rest on outmoded or invalid assumptions [p. 9].

On the other hand, the black community has the right
to know the overall purpose of a specific study and the right
to cooperate if its people or spokesman feel that the social
scientist is conducting research where the implications are
important. The black community must recognize, however,
that the research controlled and censored by them will be
rejected by most of the research community as invalid. To
reach some kind of compromise with the black community,
Ornstein (1972) suggests that the white researcher do the
following:

(a) include members of the black community as participants in the research wherever possible; (b) control the variable of the investigator's or examiner's
race; (c) select social scientists from the same minority group that is being researched--at least whenever possible; (d) make research more relevant to
the black community and the practitioners working
with the black community; (e) explain the basic ideas
and results of the research to the black community
without contaminating the validity of the study; and
(f) allow for a rebuttal in the form of a minority report or statement which will be attached to the original study--if the black community desires it [p. 137].

R. C. Brown (1971) also points out the need to write two
types of research reports, one for the professionals and research community and the other for the lay public without
the technical jargon. He warns, however: "We must ...
be careful that what we say, in intent and fact, is similar
in both types of research reports, even though the language,
itself, might be different" (p. 9).

There is need for social scientists to give serious
consideration to the complaints of ghetto dwellers, as well

as to be more sensitive to the needs and nature of the black
community.   In fact, the pressure of contemporary events is
forcing social scientists to look at the character of the social order and to reevaluate the theoretical concepts and
models by which they have explained black Americans and
race relations in the past.

CONCLUSION

It must be realized that most of the so-called experts,
whether they are from Harvard University or the black community, are as flummoxed as the rest of us when it comes
to giving precise, specific meaning to solving the problems of
school and society.   To a large extent educational reformers
draw on a shared vocabulary--social justice, racial equality,
equal opportunity, etc.   The difficulties come, and the splits
appear, when the vocabulary has to be translated into action.
One who is familiar with the literature grows weary of the
liberal reformers and black militants who offer few constructive
and realistic solutions.   One begins to feel that their imagination
has outstripped reality.   One begins to grow tired of hearing that
the struggle of the blacks and poor is the central issue, usually
the only issue, in school and society.   What about the overlooked
majority and the ordinary student?

What is even more disturbing is the increasing inability of all sides in the great debate about improving the
schools to find a common language which can bridge their
various concerns.   Write Ornstein and Talmage (1973):

> What we need is a common language ... which per-
> mits self-examination and openness on both sides of
> the philosophical, racial, and ideological dividing
> lines.   We need to put away our political and eco-
> nomic motives, to talk to one another as concerned
> persons for the welfare of our clients (or target pop-
> ulation).   We need to advocate the importance of re-
> search, not rhetoric.   We must provide a forum that
> permits us to fully understand issues ... before ad-
> vocating any idea as one certain cure-all [p. 149].

We certainly have the money and resources to improve our
schools, and to improve the education of all children and
youth;   this includes not only inner-city students, but those
from the outer city and suburbs, even the rural areas.
What we still need is to find this common language;   we

need to put aside our self-interests and ideologies, to reduce
the rhetoric and emotional exchanges, and finally, to depolar-
ize. In short, we still have to learn how to communicate
with one another. As an educator and citizen, the author
cherishes the right to participate in the communication about
improving school and society. He hopes readers recognize
their roles as well. Let us all work for a better tomorrow--
better schools, a better society.

REFERENCES

Aberback, Joel D. and Walker, Jack L. "Citizen Desires,
    Policy Outcomes, and Community Control." Paper Pre-
    sented at the Annual American Political Science Associa-
    tion. Chicago, September 1971.

Abert, James. "Since Grantsmanship Doesn't Work, Why
    not Roulette?" Saturday Review, October 21, 1972, 65-
    66.

Anderson, Archibald W. "The Cloak of Respectability: The
    Attackers and Their Methods." Progressive Education,
    1952, 29, 69-70.

Banfield, Edward C. The Unheavenly City. Boston: Little,
    Brown, 1970.

Bard, Bernard. "The Battle for School Jobs: New York's
    Newest Agony." Phi Delta Kappan, 1972, 53, 553-558.

Barnhill, George D. A Study of Group Opinions Concerning
    the County Superintendent in a North Carolina County.
    Unpublished doctoral dissertation. University of North
    Carolina--Chapel Hill, 1954.

Baughman, M. Dale. "Yardsticks for Measuring School-
    Community Relations." Educational Administration and
    Supervision, 1957, 43, 19-22.

Bell, Bernard I. Crisis in Education. New York: McGraw-
    Hill, 1949.

Bestor, Arthur. Educational Wastelands. Urbana: Univer-
    sity of Illinois Press, 1953.

_____. The Restoration of Learning. New York: Knopf,
    1955.

Billings, Charles E. "Community Control of the School and
    the Quest for Power." Phi Delta Kappan, 1972, 53,
    277-78.

Billingsley, Andrew. "Black Families and White Social
    Science." Journal of Social Issues, 1970, 26, 127-42.

_____. "Forward." In: R. H. Hill, The Strengths of
    the Black Families. New York: Emerson Hall, 1972.

Booz-Allen and Hamilton. Organized Survey: Board of
    Education--City of Chicago. Chicago: The Author,
    May 1967.

Boss, Henry T. "Questionnaire Results Analyzed." Phi
    Delta Kappan, 1955, 37, 68-69.

Brookover, Wilbur et al. Self-Concept of Ability and School
    Achievement, II. East Lansing: Bureau of Educational
    Research Services, Michigan State University, 1965.

Brown, Richard J. Public Criticism of Secondary School
    History Teaching, 1930 Through 1954. Unpublished
    doctoral dissertation, University of Iowa, 1955.

Brown, Roscoe C. , Jr. "How to Make Educational Research
    Relevant to the Urban Community--The Researcher's
    View." Paper Presented at the Annual AERA Confer-
    ence. New York, February 1971.

Butterfield, E. E. "Examining Our Public Relations."
    National Association of Secondary School Principals,
    1953, 37, 357-62.

Campbell, Bernard C. Local Application of Adaptability Re-
    search in the Area of Public Understanding. New York:
    Teachers College Press, Columbia University, 1952.

Campbell, Donald T. "Reforms as Experiments." In: C.
    H. Weiss (ed.), Evaluating Action Programs. Boston:
    Allyn & Bacon, 1972; p. 187-223.

Campbell, Roald F. "Situational Factors in Educational Ad-
    ministration." In: R. F. Campbell and R. T. Gregg
    (eds.), Administrative Behavior in Education. New
    York: Harper & Row, 1957; p. 228-68.

Carmichael, Stokely and Hamilton, Charles V. Black Power.
New York: Random House, 1967. (Vintage ed.)

Caro, Francis G. "Issues in the Evaluation of Social Programs." Review of Educational Research, 1971, 41,
87-114.

Clark, Terry. "On Decentralization. " Polity, 1970, 2,
508-14.

Cloward, Richard A. and Jones, James A. "Social Class:
Educational Attitudes and Participation. " In: A. H.
Passow (ed.), Education in Depressed Areas. New
York: Teachers College Press, Columbia University,
1963; p. 190-216.

Coleman, James S. et al. Equality of Educational Opportunity. Washington, D. C. : Government Printing Office,
1966.

Commission on Urban Education. A Report to the General
Assembly of Illinois. Chicago: State of Illinois,
February 1971.

Counts, George S. Decision-Making and American Values
in School Administration. New York: Teachers College
Press, Columbia University, 1954. (CPEA Series.)

Crain, Robert L. The Politics of School Desegregation.
Chicago: Aldine, 1968.

Cremin, Lawrence A. The Transformation of the School.
New York: Random House, 1961. (Vintage ed.)

Davis, Benjamin F. Community Forces in a Recently Organized School District. Unpublished master's thesis,
Ohio State University, 1954.

Dawson, Howard A. "District Reorganization. " School
Executive, 1955, 74, 86-87.

_____, and Ellena, William J. "School District Reorgani-
zation. " School Executive, 1954, 73, 39-42.

Deutsch, Martin. "Facilitating Development in the Pre-
School Child: Social and Psychological Perspectives. "
Merrill-Palmer Quarterly, 1964, 10, 249-63.

_____. "Organizational and Conceptual Barriers to Social Change." Journal of Social Issues, 1969, 25, 5-18.

_____. "Perspectives on the Education of the Urban Child." In: A. H. Passow (ed.), Urban Education in the 1970's. New York: Teachers College Press, Columbia University, 1971; p. 103-19.

District Boundary Lines Under the Community School District System. Special Committee on Decentralization (Committee on the Whole). New York: Board of Education, December 22, 1969.

Educational Renewal: A Decentralization Proposal for the Los Angeles Unified School District. A Report by the Decentralization Task Force. Los Angeles: Unified School District, February 22, 1971.

Elsbery, James W. (Director of the Department of Urban Education, Office of the Superintendent of Public Instruction for the State of Illinois). Letter to the author, June 2, 1972.

Fairley, Richard L. "Accountability's New Tool." American Education, 1972, 8, 33-35.

Fantini, Mario D. The Reform of Urban Schools. Washington, D. C.: NEA, 1970.

_____, Gittell, Marilyn, and Magat, Richard. Community Control and the Urban School. New York: Praeger, 1970.

Farmer, James A., Jr. "Indigenous Interactional Research." Paper Presented at the Annual AERA Conference, New York, February 1971.

Fox, David J. The Research Process in Education. New York: Holt, 1969.

Fusco, Gene C. "Reaching the Parents." In: R. D. Strom (ed.), The Inner-City Classroom: Teacher Behaviors. Columbus, Ohio: Merrill, 1966; p. 145-61.

Gilbaugh, John W. "S. O. S. from the Small-Town Superintendent." School Executive, 1952, 72, 64-65.

Gittell, Marilyn. Participants and Participation: A Study of School Policy in New York. New York: Praeger, 1967.

_____, and Hollander, T. E. Six Urban School Districts: A Comparative Study of Institutional Response. New York: Praeger, 1968.

Glazer, Nathan. "Ethnic Group and Education: Towards the Tolerance of Difference." Journal of Negro Education, 1969, 38, 187-95.

Gleaser, Edmund J., Jr. The Identification of Certain Alignments of Social Power Impinging Upon Decision-Making of a School Committee and Superintendent in a New England Community. Unpublished doctoral dissertation, Harvard University, 1953.

Gordon, Edmund W. and Wilkerson, Doxey A. Compensatory Education for the Disadvantaged. New York: College Entrance Examination Board, 1966.

Green, Edith. "Education's Federal Grab Bag." Phi Delta Kappan, 1972, 54, 83-86.

Gregg, Russell T. "Administration." In: C. W. Harris (ed.), Encyclopedia of Educational Research, 3rd ed. New York: Macmillan, 1960; p. 19-24.

Guba, Egon G. "The Failure of Educational Evaluation." Educational Technology, 1969, 9, 29-38.

Guidelines for Regional and Central Boards of Education of the School District of the City of Detroit. Adopted in Accordance with Public Act No. 48 of 1970 State of Michigan. Detroit: Board of Education, October 26, 1970.

Haak, Leo A. "The General Public and the Public Schools." Administrator's Notebook, 1956, 4, No. 8.

Halinski, Ronald S. and Feldt, Leonard S. "The Selection of Variables in Multiple Regression Analysis." Journal of Educational Measurement, 1970, 7, 151-57.

Hamilton, Charles V. "Race and Education: A Search for Legitimacy." Harvard Educational Review, 1968, 38, 669-84.

Havighurst, Robert J. The Public Schools of Chicago. A
Survey for the Board of Education of the City of Chicago.
Chicago: Board of Education, 1964.

Hentoff, Nat. Our Children Are Dying. New York: Viking
Press, 1966.

Hess, Robert D. and Shipman, Virginia C. "Material Atti-
tude Toward the School and Role of Pupil: Some Social
Class Comparisons." Paper Presented for the Fifth
Work Conference on Curriculum and Teaching in De-
pressed Urban Areas. New York: Teachers College,
Columbia University, 1966.

Hickrod, G. Alan. "Local Demand for Education: A Critique of School Finance and Economic Research CIRCA
1959-1969." Review of Educational Research, 1971, 41,
35-49.

Hicks, Alvin W. A Plan to Accelerate the Process of
Adaptation in a New York City School Community, the
Report of a Type B Project. Unpublished doctoral dis-
sertation, Teachers College, Columbia University, 1942.

Hunter, Floyd. Community Power Structure. Chapel Hill:
University of North Carolina Press, 1953.

Hutchins, Robert M. The Conflict in Education. New York:
Harper & Row, 1953.

Jablonsky, Adelaide. "Some Trends in Education of the Disadvantaged." IRCD Bulletin, 1968, 4, 1-11.

Jansen, William. The Social Agencies and Public Education
in New York City. New York: Teachers College Press,
Columbia University, 1940.

Jencks, Christopher et al. Inequality: A Reassessment of
the Effect of Family and Schooling in America. New
York: Basic Books, 1972.

Knutson, Howard T. "School-Community Relations." Review
of Educational Research, 1958, 28, 358-69.

La Noue, George R. "The Politics of School Decentralization Methodological Considerations." Paper Presented
at the Annual AERA Conference, Chicago, April 1972.

Leggett, Stanton F. and Vincent, William S. A Program for Meeting the Needs of New York City Schools. New York: Public Education Association, 1947.

Lieberman, Myron. Education As a Profession. Englewood Cliffs, N. J.: Prentice-Hall, 1956.

Lipham, James M., Gregg, Russell T., and Rossmiller, Richard A. The School Board As an Agency for Resolving Conflict. Madison: University of Wisconsin, 1967.

Local School Governance Experiment. Chicago: Department of Urban Education, Office of the Superintendent of Public Instruction for the State of Illinois, 1972.

Lopate, Carol et al. "Decentralization and Community Participation in Public Education." Review of Educational Research, 1970, 40, 135-50.

Lovelace, Walter B. "Surveying the Survey." Phi Delta Kappan, 1955, 37, 61-66.

Lynd, Albert. Quackery in the Public Schools. Boston: Little, Brown, 1953.

McIntyre, Kenneth E. "Significant Trends Indicated in the Progress and Problems of Redistricting." American School Board Journal, 1954, 128, 38-40.

McPartland, James. The Segregated Student in Desegregated Schools. Final Report to the Center for the Study of School Organization of Schools. Baltimore: Johns Hopkins University, June 1968.

McPherran, Archie L. The Nature and Role of the Intermediate District in American Education. Lincoln: University of Nebraska Press, 1954.

Marland, Sidney P., Jr. "A Responsible Stewardship." Phi Delta Kappan, 1972, 54, 87-88.

Mayer, Martin. The Teachers' Strike. New York: Harper & Row, 1969.

Mayor's Advisory Panel on Decentralization of the New York City Schools. Reconnection for Learning: A Community

School System for New York City. New York: Ford
Foundation, 1967.

Moehlman, Arthur B. School Administration. Boston:
Mifflin, 1951.

Morphet, Edgar L. , Johns, Roe L. , and Reller, Theodore.
Educational Organization and Administration. Englewood
Cliffs, N. J. : Prentice-Hall, 1959.

Mort, Paul R. and Cornell, Francis G. American Schools
in Transition: How Our Schools Adapt Their Practices
to Changing Needs. New York: Teachers College
Press, Columbia University, 1941.

_____, and Vincent, William S. Introduction to American
Education. McGraw-Hill, 1954.

_____, and _____. A Look at Our Schools: A Book
for the Thinking Citizen. Lancaster, Pa: Cattell,
1946.

_____, _____, and Newell, Clarence. The Growing
Edge, An Instrument for Measuring the Adaptability of
School Systems, 2 vols. New York: Metropolitan
School Study Council, 1955.

Moynihan, Daniel P. Maximum Feasible Misunderstanding.
New York: Free Press, 1969.

A Multiple Option Approach to School-Community Participation. Report on the Commission of Decentralization and
Community Participation. Philadelphia: Board of Education, July 22, 1970.

Norton, John K. "The Contemporary Scene." In: R. F.
Campbell and R. T. Gregg (eds.), Administrative Behavior in Education. New York: Harper & Row, 1957;
p. 41-81.

Obradović, Sylvia M. "Community Perspectives on Educational Research in Black Communities. " Paper Presented at the Annual AERA Conference, Chicago, April
1972.

Ornstein, Allan C. "Anxieties and Forces Which Mitigate
Against Ghetto School Teachers. " Journal of Secondary

Education, 1968, 43, 143-54.

_____. Education and the Disadvantaged Child. New York: McKay, 1973.

_____. Urban Education: Student Unrest, Teacher Behaviors, and Black Power. Columbus, Ohio: Merrill, 1972.

_____, and Talmage, Harriet. "A Dissenting View on Accountability." Urban Education, 1973, 8, 133-51.

Oversiew, Leon. Emerging Practices in School Administration for Communities, Teachers, Boards, and Administrators. New York: Metropolitan School Study Council and Cooperative Program in Educational Administration, 1953 (a).

_____. "Ten Ways Superintendents Use Human Resources." School Executive, 1953, 73, 74-76 (b).

Passow, A. Harry. Toward Creating a Model Urban School System. A Study of the Washington, D. C. Public Schools. New York: Teachers College, Columbia University, 1967.

Pennsylvania Cooperative Program in Educational Administration. Pennsylvania Surveys its Educational Needs. Harrisburg: Pennsylvania Department of Public Instruction, 1954.

Pfau, Edward. A Study of Selected Aspects of Oral and Written Communication as These Are a Part of School Public Relations Program. Unpublished doctoral dissertation, Michigan State University, 1955.

Phi Delta Kappan. "Washington Report," 1973, 54, 713.

Philadelphia Board of Education Meeting. April 12, 1971. Attached with a letter from Herbert Hazan (Assistant to the Superintendent) to the Author, January 26, 1972.

Pois, Joseph. The School Board Crisis: A Chicago Case Study. Chicago: Educational Methods, 1964.

Polley, John W. , Loretan, Joseph, and Blitzer, Clara F.

Community Action for Education. New York: Teachers
    College Press, Columbia University, 1953. (Institute of
    Administrative Research, Study No. 9.)

Popham, W. James. Statement Presented to the Appropria-
    tions Committee, U.S. House of Representatives. Wash-
    ington, D.C., March 10, 1971. Excerpted in Educational
    Researcher, 1971, 22, 3-4.

Public Reaction Draft of School Decentralization Guidelines.
    Detroit: Office of School Decentralization, Board of
    Education, August 1970.

Ravitch, Diane. "Community Control Revisted." Commen-
    tary, February 1972, 70-74.

Record, Wilson. "Who Is Impartial?" Time, August 7,
    1972, 46-47.

Rempson, Joe L. "The Participation of Minority-Group
    Parents in School Activities: A Study and a Case Study
    with Guidelines." Paper Presented at the Annual AERA
    Conference, Chicago, April 1972.

Rice, Arthur H. "For and Against Lay Communities."
    Nation's Schools, 1953, 52, 50.

Rickover, Hyman G. Education and Freedom. New York:
    Dutton, 1959.

Robinson, Donald W. "Change for its Own Sake." Phi
    Delta Kappan, 1972, 53, 587.

Rogers, David. 110 Livingston Street. New York: Random
    House, 1969. (Vintage ed.)

Ross, Donald H. (ed.). Administration for Adaptability.
    New York: Metropolitan School Study Council, 1958.

Rossi, Peter H. "Boobytraps and Pitfalls in the Evaluation
    of Social Action Programs." In: C. H. Weiss (ed.):
    Evaluating Action Programs. Boston: Allyn & Bacon,
    1972; p. 224-35.

_____. The Publics of Local Schools. Cambridge,
    Mass.: Graduate School of Education, Harvard Univer-
    sity, 1954. (Staff Research Memorandum No. 2.)

Rothschild, Bob K.   High School Teacher-Community Relations in Northeast Missouri.   Unpublished doctoral dissertation, Teachers College, Columbia University, 1951.

Rugg, Earle O.   "Our Greatest Social Achievement."   Phi Delta Kappan, 1955, 37, 69-74.

Sadofsky, Stanley.   "Utilization of Evaluation Results: Feedback into the Action Program." In: J. Shmelzer (ed.), Learning in Action.   Washington, D.C.: Government Printing Office, 1966; p. 22-36.

Schiff, Herbert J.   The Effect of Personal Contractual Relationships on Parents' Attitudes Toward Participation in Local School Affairs.   Unpublished doctoral dissertation, Northwestern University, 1963.

Schrag, Peter.   Village School Downtown.   Boston: Beacon Press, 1967.

Scott, C. Winfield.   "Criticism of Schools Continue."   NEA Journal, 1957, 60, 44-47.

_____, and Hill, Clyde M. (eds.).   Public Education Under Criticism.   Englewood Cliffs, N.J.: Prentice-Hall, 1954.

Shanker, Albert.   "The Real Meaning of the New York City Teachers' Strike."   Phi Delta Kappan, 1969, 50, 434-41.

Smith, Mortimer.   And Madly Teach.   Chicago: Regnery, 1949.

_____.   The Diminished Mind.   Chicago: Regnery, 1954.

Stapley, Maurice E.   School Board Studies.   Chicago: Midwest Administration Center, University of Chicago, 1957. (Studies in Educational Administration, No. 2)

Stone, Chuck.   "The Psychology of Whiteness vs. The Politics of Blackness," Educational Researcher, 1972, 1, 4-6, 16.

Sweitzer, Robert E.   "What They Don't Know Can Hurt You."   Administrator's Notebook, 1953, 2, No. 3.

Talmage, Harriet and Ornstein, Allan C.   "Community

Participation--Community Control Attitudinal Inventory,"
in process, 1973 (a).

_____, and _____. "Teachers' Perceptions of Decision-
Making Roles and Responsibilities in Defining Accountability." Journal of Negro Education, 1973, 42, p. 212-21(b).

United States Commission on Civil Rights. Racial Isolation
in the Public Schools. Washington, D. C. : Government
Printing Office, 1967.

Walberg, Herbert J. An Evaluation of an Urban-Suburban
School Bussing Program: Student Achievement and Per-
ception of Class Learning Environments. Draft of Report to METCO. Roxbury, Mass. : METCO Education
Program, July 1, 1969.

Weiss, Carol H. "Planning an Action Project Evaluation."
In: J. Schmelzer (ed.), Learning in Action. Washington, D. C. : Government Printing Office, 1966; p. 6-21.

Westby, Cleve O. Local Autonomy for School Communities
in Cities. New York: Metropolitan School Study Council, 1947.

Wilson, LeLand C. Community Power Controls Related to
the Administration of Education. Unpublished doctoral
dissertation, George Peabody College for Teachers,
1952.

Witkowsky, Jack. "Education of a School Board Member."
Saturday Review, September 20, 1971, 90-92.

Working Draft of Possible Guidelines for Implementation of
Public Act 244, 2 vols. Detroit: Office of School Decentralization, Board of Education, April, May 1970.

Wynne, Edward. "Education Research: A Profession in
Search of a Constituency. " Phi Delta Kappan, 1970,
52, 245-47.

ADDENDUM

Community Participation   Community Control
Attitudinal Inventory

The questions on the inventory are being used to obtain factual information about the views teachers and administrators have toward community participation in and control of the operations of their schools.   The community is defined as a cluster of adults who reside in the local community and who are concerned about educational issues but who may or may not have children presently enrolled in the local school.

There are three parts to the inventory.   Part I is concerned with your attitudes about community PARTICIPATION in school affairs.   Part II is concerned with your attitudes about community CONTROL of school affairs.   Part III is concerned with data on your background which may correlate with responses in Part I and Part II.

Part I: Community Participation
    Directions: Part I contains 20 statements.   For each of the 20 statements below, indicate your response to the question, TO WHAT EXTENT SHOULD COMMUNITY MEMBERS PARTICIPATE IN THIS AREA?   Indicate your response using the following symbols:

A = in all cases
B = in many cases
C = in some cases
D = in no cases

1. Advise on matters related to evaluating the curriculum.
2. Advise on matters on student discipline.
3. Advise on matters related to spending money for school repairs.
4. Advise on matters on grouping students in classes.
5. Advise on matters related to preparing state and federal proposals.
6. Advise on matters related to recruiting teachers when vacancies exist.
7. Advise on matters related to developing the school's educational objectives.
8. Advise on matters on disagreement between students and school personnel.

9. Advise on matters related to determining local taxes for schools.
10. Advise on matters on formulating new courses.
11. Advise on matters on testing students.
12. Advise on matters on evaluating the fitness of teachers, principals and superintendent(s).
13. Advise on matters on reporting student progress.
14. Advise on matters on selecting books from an approved list.
15. Advise on matters on recruiting teachers, principals and superintendent(s) when vacancies exist.
16. Advise on matters related to implementing the curriculum.
17. Advise on matters on evaluating the fitness of teachers.
18. Advise on matters related to building new schools.
19. Advise on matters related to tenure and promotion of school personnel [teachers, principals, superintendent(s)].
20. Advise on matters related to expenditures per student.

Part II.   Community Control
    Directions: Part II contains the same 20 statements as in Part I.   For each statement indicate your response to the question, TO WHAT EXTENT SHOULD THE COMMUNITY CONTROL POLICY IN THE FOLLOWING AREAS? Indicate your response using the following symbols:

            A = majority vote
            B = equal vote with school personnel
            C = minority vote
            D = no vote

21. Determine matters related to evaluating the curriculum.
22. Determine matters of student discipline.
23. Determine matters related to spending money for school repairs.
24. Determine matters on grouping students in classes.
25. Determine matters related to preparing state and federal proposals.
26. Determine matters related to recruiting teachers when vacancies exist.
27. Determine matters related to developing the school's educational objectives.
28. Determine matters on disagreement between students

and school personnel.
29. Determine matters related to determining local taxes for schools.
30. Determine matters on formulating new courses.
31. Determine matters on testing students.
32. Determine matters on evaluating the fitness of teachers, principals and superintendent(s).
33. Determine matters on reporting student progress.
34. Determine matters on selecting books from an approved list.
35. Determine matters on recruiting teachers, principals and superintendent(s) when vacancies exist.
36. Determine matters related to implementing the curriculum.
37. Determine matters on evaluating the fitness of teachers.
38. Determine matters related to building new schools.
39. Determine matters related to tenure and promotion of school personnel [teachers, principals, superintendent(s)].
40. Determine matters related to expenditures per student.

Part III: Background Data
  Directions: Select the appropriate response.

41. Respondent's sex
    a = female
    b = male
42. Ethnicity of respondent
    a = Anglo
    b = Black
    c = Spanish surname
    d = Other
43. Present professional role
    a = Central Office or Field Superintendent
    b = Principal
    c = Supervisor or department chairman
    d = Teacher
    ·e = Other
44. Type of school community
    a = Rural
    b = Suburban
    c = Urban (low income)
    d = Urban (middle/high income)
45. Ethnic composition of the school community
    a = Predominantly Black
    b = Predominantly Spanish surname

       c = Predominantly White
       d = Predominantly another ethnic group
       e = No predominant ethnic group

46.   Geographic location
       a = East (northeast, central coast)
       b = Middle West (central states)
       c = South West
       d = South (southeast and south central)
       e = West (northwest and west coastal)

47.   Degree of present community participation in the local school system decision making process
       a = Community input through the traditional school organizations (PTA, mothers' club, etc.)
       b = Community input through established community advisory councils
       c = Community input through groups organizing action on specific issues
       d = Little or no community input
       e = Other types of input

Chapter 3

CASE STUDIES: MEDIUM-SIZED CITY
AND SUBURBAN SCHOOLS

For purposes of this chapter, 25 medium-sized city
and suburban school systems were randomly selected and
polled. The technique was first to send out a questionnaire
accompanied by a request for primary source data (task
force reports, general superintendent's recommendations,
board of education's resolutions, etc.) related to administrative decentralization and community participation or community control. [Follow-up questions and requests were made
to each person who responded to the initial communication.
In some cases it was difficult to obtain all the data requested
because the answers and related materials were not readily
available. In still other cases there was an under-staffing
of personnel, as indicated by some of the letters, and the
person responding was reluctant to take time out from his
real work. In no way should this be misconstrued by the
reader as meaning that a particular school system was with-
holding data. If anything, the people who answered my requests were very cooperative; each answered three or four
letters, and filled most of my requests; each read and
checked for accuracy the data about his respective school
system and the conclusion of this chapter. Appropriate modifications have been made.] In response to this questionnaire
16 school systems furnished sufficient data to report to the
reader. [Clark County Public Schools in Nevada, Columbus
Public Schools in Ohio, and Fairfax County Public Schools in
Virginia responded but are omitted in the discussion because
the data furnished was incomplete. Clark County decentralized plans involved community advisory groups, and Fairfax had decentralized its schools and incorporated community input also in form of an advisory nature.]

The technique used for writing this chapter was to report data and refrain as much as possible from subjective
criticism or evaluation while individually discussing the 16
school systems and their various organizational plans. Each

137

school system is introduced by supplying general facts and figures pertaining to the size of the system, the student racial composition, the methods of selecting board of education members, the system's reading levels, and the system's financial situation. The discussion then proceeds to the system's reorganizational plans, wherever such plans have been implemented or are in the process of implementation. For the time being, it should be noted that all but one of the 16 school systems reported some type of administrative decentralization or were considering it, but no system reported any type of community control similar to the pattern established in Detroit or New York (both of which are studied in detail in Chapter 4). Many of the school systems, however, were involved in plans to increase community participation in the form of advisory groups[1] [notes at end of chapter].

Near the end of the chapter there is a summary of the facts and figures and the decentralization and community participation plans; a few subjective interpretations are made in this part of the chapter. There is also a summary table (3.1) of the 16 school systems to help provide the reader with an overview of each system in comparison to the other systems surveyed. For quick reference and a general grasp of the data pertaining to each of the 16 school systems, it might be helpful periodically to refer to this table while reading portions of the chapter. Finally, there is a table (3.2) that combines data from the Anne Arundel survey (1970) of 55 school systems enrolling 50,000 or more students, Ornstein's (1972) discussion of the five largest school systems, and the survey of the 16 school systems for this chapter. We now turn to these 16 school systems; they are discussed in order of student enrollment figures--the largest system first.

Dade County, Florida

Dade County includes the city government of Miami, along with 26 other local municipal governments. According to Johnathan Gillingham (1972d), Director of Administrative Research, the school system covers the entire county which is approximately 50 miles long and 40 miles wide; only 27 percent of the 1.27 million people live in the urban center of Miami while about 33 percent live in towns and small cities (suburban) and over 40 percent live in unincorporated and rural areas. Not only in terms of mileage, but also in terms of geographical diversity, the Dade County school system is different than most other systems in the country.

According to tables[2] compiled by the Administrative Research Division of the Dade County public schools, in 1971 there were 234 schools, 12,209 licensed personnel and 10,057 teachers, and 245,025 students, making it the sixth largest school system in the country. The student racial composition was 22 percent Spanish surnamed (mostly Cuban), 25.8 percent black, and 51.6 percent other. The board of education consists of seven elected members. The Miami Herald (November 24, 1971) shows that students taking the Stanford Achievement Reading Test are one to three months below norm in grades one to five, at the mean at grade six, and two to seven months above the norm in grades seven to twelve.[3] According to Gillingham (1972a), the school tax is $1.03 per $100 of assessed true property value. The chart, "Your School Dollar: 1970-71" indicates that the school budget was $285 million including balances and reserves, of which 39.8 percent was derived from local sources, 45.9 from state sources, and 14.3 percent from federal sources.[4] The table "Comparative Costs Per Pupil ... 1970-71" shows that the county spends $950 per student, which is high for a southern school system.

As a result of former Superintendent Joseph Hall's recommendations in his July 1963 report, Administrative Reorganization in the Dade County Schools, to the members of the board of education, the school system decentralized into four districts. For purposes of moving the instructional and administrative services closer to the schools, each district was provided with a small number of appropriate personnel, including a district superintendent who was responsible for the schools within his unit. The January 1972 school county report, Comparison of Administrative, Supervisory and Technical Positions ... 1962-63 ... 1971-72 and Gillingham (1972b, 1972c) point out that prior to the decentralization move there were three central directors for (1) the senior high schools, (2) the junior high schools, and (3) the elementary schools, and an assistant director for elementary schools. The school principals were directly responsible to the assistant superintendent for instruction at headquarters.

The Organization of the Dade County Schools in Four Districts, a memorandum submitted by the school superintendent to all the principals, in August 1963, indicates that the four districts each comprised from 48 to 60 schools and 42,800 to 49,200 students. One director for secondary

schools and two directors for elementary schools were assigned to each district; these positions were abolished at
the central office.   The principals were directly responsible
to their respective district directors.   Writes Gillingham
(1972c), "At the present, principals have a line responsibility
to the directors in the different district offices organization
wise; in actual practice they may go sometimes directly to
the district superintendent" (p. 1).

In August 1964, the school superintendent recommended
in his report, Reorganization of Dade County School System
into Six Districts, that the boundaries be changed to create
six districts, which became effective in July 1965.   The
main criterion for the new boundaries was to formulate the
districts to provide a minimum of transferring to school
boundaries within the previous four districts, and to delegate
the smallest number of schools in the districts which had the
greatest growth potential at that time, and to effect desegregation at the district level.   The result was that the four
districts with the greatest growth potential contained 30 to
33 schools, and the two central districts with the least
growth potential comprised 36 and 47 schools respectively.
Each district contained from 25,000 to 40,000 students.

At the present, there are 33 to 38 schools in each of
the four districts with the greatest growth potential and between 31,766 and 44,237 students;   the two central districts
comprise 44 and 46 schools respectively and approximately
47,000 students.   Data from the Miami Herald (November 24,
1971) shows that four of the six districts tend to be integrated, but the two central districts remain segregated.   The
schools generally are relatively segregated.   Of the total
234 schools in the system, 22 are 75 percent or more black,
18 schools are 75 percent or more Spanish surnamed, 20
schools are 75 percent or more black and Spanish surnamed
combined, and 74 schools are 75 percent or more white.

The January 1972 report, Comparison of Administrative, Supervisory and Technical Positions ... 1962-63 ...
1971-72, shows that the central office and decentralized district offices have expanded.   The administrative personnel
in the central office has increased from 161 in the 1962-63
school year, to 175 in the 1966-67 school year and to 304
personnel in the 1971-72 school year.   The district administrative officers have increased from 32 in the 1962-63 school
year, to 96 in the 1966-67 school year and to 133 in the
1971-72 school year.   As previously indicated, the directors

for (1) senior high school, (2) junior high school, and (3) elementary school, are now operating from the district offices. The principals are responsible to them; they are responsible to their respective district superintendents; and the district superintendents are directly responsible to the school superintendent. By referring to the Administrative Organization Charts ... (1971), we can describe the present central office: two associate superintendents, one for administration and one for instruction; two central district superintendents, one for vocational, technical, and adult education, and one for desegregation planning and implementation; four assistant superintendents of (1) finance, (2) personnel, (3) physical plant, and (4) supportive services; and four directors of (1) administrative research, (2) central data processing, (3) public information, and (4) employee relations, as well as 29 other directors at the central office--all of whose accountability is directed upwards to the school superintendent. Gillingham (1972b) informs us that the Dade County schools have limited community participatory or advisory groups.

Houston, Texas

The Houston school system is the seventh largest one in the nation. According to William D. Broyles, Jr., (1972), the administrative assistant in charge of community relations, and the Racial Composition ... report (1971) of Houston school employees, the school system consists of 230 schools, 17,000 employees, 10,000 teachers, and 231,500 students. The HEW School Campus Report ... (1971) shows that the student racial composition is 46.5 percent white, 38 percent black, 15 percent Mexican-American, and .5 percent others. The board of education is elected by the people and consists of seven members. Based on A Report of the Results of the Iowa Test of Basic Skills ... (1971), the students' vocabulary and reading comprehension scores for grades three to six rank between the 24th and 32nd percentile on a national basis but between the 33rd and 55th percentile in comparison to large city norms. Thus it is in the average range for city school systems. Tony Aleman (1972a), a consultant for the Community Relations Department, states that the school tax per $100 of assessed property value is $1.70 at 53 percent assessment evaluation. The Public School Finances ... report (1971) for the 1970-71 fiscal year shows that the school budget totals $157 million, of which 53 percent was obtained from local sources, 44 percent from the state and 3 percent from the federal government. The school system spending per student was $680 and its spending on instruction in 1972, according to Aleman (1972a), was $553.

Under the superintendency of George G. Garver, the Houston school system was centralized in February 1971. Based on the November 1970 Houston ... Management Review and Analysis report by the management consulting firm of Peat, Marwick, Mitchell & Co. , as well as on pre- and post-decentralization school organizational models, [5] the central office has been realigned. Separating the responsibilities for administration from that of instruction, the administrative responsibilities of the former superintendent of instruction and administration were eliminated; his instructional responsibilities were enlarged, and his title was changed to that of chief instructional officer. Enjoying the same rank with him are two additional chief administrative officers: the chief of financial and business services, which is a similar position to the former superintendent of business, and the chief of administrative services, a new position which assumes many of the administrative responsibilities of the former superintendent of instruction and administration. The three chief officers are responsible to the school superintendent. The following positions were eliminated: the two deputy superintendents of elementary education and secondary education, the two directors of elementary education and secondary education, and the five assistant superintendents of elementary education and four assistant superintendents of secondary education. These were consolidated under the various department coordinators now responsible to the chief instructional officer. Several other assistant superintendent positions have been eliminated, with the intention of saving money and consolidating the K-12 program. (A few positions of administrative assistant to the school superintendent have been created.) The school superintendent's powers have been increased by virtue of his selecting candidates for all new positions at the central office and decentralized area level, having all reports and communication to the school board by school personnel funneled first to his office, and limiting the participation of administrators in school board meetings to those he invites.

Based on the recommendations of the above consulting firm, further recommended by the school superintendent, and approved by the Houston ... Board Meeting in December 1970, the school system has been divided into six areas, each headed by an area instructional superintendent and an appropriate staff, who is in charge of the schools within his boundaries and responsible to the chief instructional superintendent. The central office is in charge of matters concerning curriculum, personnel, and budget; the area instructional superintendents only make recommendations in these matters. They also prepare the area budget, but this is coordinated with the school-wide budgets and often modified by the chief instructional officer. (Writes Aleman [1972b, p. 3], "The final word rests with the central office.") Each teacher is also formally evaluated by the principal on an annual basis, and an accountability model is now being established.

The Houston Independent School District Bulletin (1971) indicates that the six areas each comprise between 33 to 45 schools, and Aleman (1972b) asserts that they each comprise between 34,219 and 40,148 students. Although the main purposes of decentralization were streamlining the administrative organization and consolidating the K-12 program, court order pressure involving desegregation was also a factor which partially guided the student racial composition of the six areas. Broyles (1972) contends that the students' racial composition for each area tends to correspond to the overall racial composition of the school system; no supporting data was supplied. However, since Ross v. Rogers (1957), the school system has been under litigation to desegregate. Based on Ross v. Eckels (1970a, 1970b), it was found that Houston operated a dual school system; the city was ordered to pair 25 elementary schools to promote desegregation. The plaintiffs have alleged, however, that desegregation was achieved mainly by pairing predominantly Mexican-American schools with predominantly black schools. The Houston school pairing was upheld in the Ross v. Eckles (1971) decision because "the Houston Independent School District ... has always treated Latin-Americans as of the Anglo or white race" for school purposes, even in the day before 1957 and the operation of the dual zones (p. 2). [6]

Judge Clark, in dissent, speaks directly to this question:

Spanish-surnamed Americans ... have been adjudicated to be statistically white. As the majority states, we know they live in the very areas required to be paired with all or predominantly Negro schools. I say it is mock justice when we 'force' the numbers by pairing disadvantaged Negro students and the schools of this equally disadvantaged ethnic group [p. 3].

As for community participation, there are several different school area and system-wide citizen groups advising the school principals and serving on various task forces. Aleman (1972b) points out that most of the community advisory groups work with the principals and are either appointed by each principal or in some cases elected by community residents; this procedure varies according to the six areas and the specific advisory group. He points out, "Their duties include providing input to the school as well as providing output to the community" (p. 2).

According to the National Educational Secretary (1971), a city-wide citizen's group, "The Citizens for Good Schools," was formed in the spring of 1967 to study the problems of the school system. From that time to the present, the citizens' group has continued to analyze the various problems of the schools and to report back to the general superintendent and board of education: it has also developed a political base to help elect school board members who are responsive to the public. In January 1970 a new school board majority was elected, committed to increased community participation; it has appointed nearly one thousand citizens to various committees to help them in developing policies for human relations, special education, vocational education, drug abuse and delinquency, student conduct, desegregation, school building, and general instruction.

Baltimore, Maryland

Howard E. White, Jr. (1972a, 1972b), the Educational Assistant to the Superintendent, points out that the Baltimore City school system consists of 217 schools, 11,665 personnel, 7845 teachers, and 190,735 students, of whom 32 percent are white and the remaining are nonwhite. The board of education is appointed by the mayor of the city and is comprised of nine members, three of whom are replaced or reappointed every two years for a six-year period. On a national basis, the reading scores of Baltimore City students progressively worsen from .8 below the median in the second grade to 1.5 below the median by the ninth grade; the mean scores also worsen from .6 below the national level at the second grade to 1.4 at the ninth grade. To raise their $197 million budget for 1972, the city taxed an equivalent tax rate of $1.19 per $100 of assessed property value. The total tax rate is $5.65 per $100 and as much as 47 percent of the school money is raised locally by taxes, with the state contributing

another 46 percent and the federal government contributing
7 percent. The school system spent $833 per student and
an extra $95 with federal funds for the 1971-72 school year.

Upon assuming the position of school superintendent in
October 1971, Roland N. Patterson listed one of his objectives as developing a plan for decentralizing the Baltimore
public schools. Plans for this endeavor were outlined in
four phases in the report entitled, The Superintendent's Options for Decentralization (1972).

A phase one task force was formed in November 1971
to study the possible methods of decentralizing the school
system and their report was submitted the following month
to the general superintendent. During phase two, which
lasted from January 14 to February 14, 1972, several options for decentralization were disseminated through the mass
media including newspapers and television. Opinion surveys
were made available to community residents and the people
of Baltimore through each of the schools. Phase three began in mid-February when the survey was tabulated and combined with previous studies and used in the development of a
plan for decentralization. At the time of this writing, Phase
four, the last phase, has not yet begun; it goes into effect
when one of the options below is adopted by the board of
school commissioners.

According to The Superintendent's Options for Decentralization (1972), administrative decentralization consisted
of three facets: area organization, administrative reorganization at the central office, and community participation.
The area organization included five options: the first three
recommended nine areas, each evolved from an effort to
coincide in some way with natural geographic boundaries;
the remaining two listed six areas, each evolved from an
effort to retain the existing area distribution of the elementary schools. In option one, there was an unequal distribution of schools and students within the nine areas, partially
as a result of maintaining the boundaries of the inner city
into three of the nine areas. Option two represented the attempt to preserve the natural communities of the entire city
and to equalize the student population in each area. Option
three was an attempt to cluster the inner city with the outer
city, promoting a more racially mixed student body, with
relatively the same number of students, but maintaining only
the natural communities of the outer city. Options four and
five maintained the present six elementary areas of the

school with additions of junior and senior high schools to each of the six areas. In the fourth option, the distribution of schools and students were unequal; in the fifth option it tended to be equal.

There were three options for administrative organization and community participation. The three different choices recommended slightly different areas of responsibility for instruction and management at the central office but in all three choices the principal was responsible to the area superintendent, who in turn was responsible to the deputy superintendent and so on. In all three options, there were two assistants to the school superintendent and three associate superintendents in charge of (1) personnel and services, (2) curriculum and instruction, and (3) administration, finance, and planning--all of whom were also responsible to the deputy superintendent.

As for community participation, White (1972c) points out the three options. The first option provided for community residents to serve at the local school level on an informal basis. The second option permitted residents of the community to serve on a council that would function in an advisory capacity at the local level to each school principal. Option three provided for community residents to serve on a council that would function in an advisory capacity at the area level to the area superintendent and community liaison, if there were one.

In the meantime, although not directly related to the decentralization plans, 10 schools have already been designated as community schools. According to the pamphlet, Baltimore City Community Schools (1971), these schools elect a community council comprising members from community agencies and the professional staff to help advise programs geared to community needs and interests and to advise their respective principals. Each community council is coordinated by an administrative agent assigned to the central office who serves as a liaison with the central office. The Baltimore City Public Schools Organizational Chart (1971) indicates that the coordinators of these councils are responsible to the assistant superintendent of community schools at the central office who in turn is responsible to the associate superintendent of personnel services.

Memphis, Tennessee

The Memphis school system, according to Deputy Superintendent Shelby Counce (1972a, 1972c), consists of 163 schools, 10,000 professional employees, 6300 teachers and 143,280 students. The black student enrollment is 77,484 or 54.1 percent and the white student enrollment is 65,280 or 45.9 percent. Counce (1972b, 1972c) further points out that the board of education is comprised of nine elected members, seven elected by political districts and two at large by popular vote. The system-wide reading level is about average. The 1971-72 school budget was $99 million, of which 57 percent was derived from city and county taxes. The school tax per $100 of assessed property value is $.72; the city tax rate is $1.98 and the school-wide spending per student is $630, not including capital outlay.

In October 1969, Superintendent E. C. Stimbert and the board of education appointed a committee of professional educational and management specialists to study the organization and administration of the Memphis schools. The committee submitted its report, entitled A Staff Reorganization Study of the Memphis, Tennessee School System, in April 1970. Commonly called the Haynes report, after Dr. Ford Haynes, the chairman of the Department of Secondary Education at Memphis State University, and chairman of the committee, it recommended the following: The central administration should be maintained through five departments, namely (1) instruction, (2) pupil services, (3) business affairs, (4) plant management, and (5) personnel services. The department of personnel services should replace the department of administration services and the non-personnel services of the latter should be reassigned to the other departments. Each of these five departments would be headed by a departmental assistant superintendent, with an appropriate staff. The school system would be decentralized into four areas, each comprising an equal number of schools and students within what is geographically feasible. The four areas would each be headed by an area assistant superintendent, along with an appropriate staff, who would be in charge of the schools within his area. The departments of instruction and pupil services would be placed in a service role operating from the four area offices. The position of deputy superintendent should be created and the five departmental assistant superintendents and the four area assistant superintendents would enjoy equal status and be responsible to the deputy superintendent, who in turn would be responsible to the school superintendent. It was suggested that these nine assistant superintendents, the deputy superintendent, and the area superintendent comprise the latter's executive council or the main decision-making committee. The report further suggested an area citizens liaison committee, comprised of 15 residents from each area, appointed by the board of education for a three-year term, to function solely in an advisory capacity to the area assistant superintendents, departmental assistant superintendents, deputy superintendent, and area superintendent.

Following a study of the Haynes report, the general superintendent reported his decisions to the board of education in June 1970 in a statement entitled, Superintendent's Recommendation Staff Reorganization Study. The superintendent's recommendations were basically in accord with the Haynes report with only minor modifications concerning the size of the superintendent's executive council and the method of selecting members for the area advisory councils or citizens' liaison committees. The school board followed the superintendent's recommendations and named a committee to devise the master plan for decentralization. The result was A Plan for Implementation of Decentralization in the Memphis City Schools for the 1971-72 School Year, which was submitted in May 1971 and went into effect in July 1971. The recommendations were basically in accord with the Haynes report. For purposes of our discussion, the recommendations are divided into three parts concerning the central office, decentralized areas, and community involvement.

The central office was divided into the five departments recommended by the Haynes report, but it was considered infeasible for all the services of the departments of instruction and pupil services to be located in the field. The outcome was that some services in these two departments were maintained at the central office, some were shared with the central office and area offices, and some were delegated solely to the area offices. Each of the five departments was headed by an assistant superintendent and staffed by appropriate personnel. The five department assistant superintendents enjoyed equal rank with the four area assistant superintendents discussed below and they were all responsible to the new deputy superintendent. The executive council comprised these ten superintendents along with the school superintendent himself, as suggested by the Haynes report.

The school system was divided into four areas, each

headed by an area assistant superintendent and staffed by the appropriate personnel. Each of these superintendents is in charge of the schools within his area and works closely with the five departments listed above, especially with the departments of instruction and pupil services. Assignments of schools to an area were influenced by geographical location, feeder patterns, proportionate numbers of students and schools, and legal compliance with court orders to desegregate. Each area consists of seven to eight pyramids established around a high school and its tributary junior highs and elementary schools. Based on the general superintendent's recommendations and the school board's approval, and as indicated by the Commercial Appeal (December 6, 1970), a local newspaper, each area comprises between 33 and 41 schools and between 33,300 and 39,400 students. Black students comprise between 11,900 (36 percent) and 24,900 (68 percent) and white students comprise between 11,500 (32 percent) and 23,500 (61 percent). The statistics on the racial composition of individual schools were unobtainable.

The Plan for Implementation of Decentralization ... (1971) also established area advisory councils for each area for the purpose of increasing community participation. "Community" in this context refers to parents or guardians of students in school, residents, teachers, students, and representatives of private and public agencies which function within the four areas. No standard model was suggested; instead, the rules have been drawn up by the advisory council members and area assistant superintendents; the latter coordinate the activities of the council. The councils' members are appointed by the area assistant superintendent who in turn transmits his list to the deputy superintendent for approval. (This is in accord with the June 1970 recommendations of the school superintendent and not with the Haynes report.) The members are supposed to reflect representative segments of the community and the three levels of education. Each school is represented through recommendations from the principal. Students and PTA members are included as advisory council members, the exact number differing with each council. The council's functions are solely advisory, "adhering at all times to the policies, rules, and regulations of the board of education" (p. 37). In their advisory capacity, the councils assist in the development of educational programs of the schools within the respective area, consult with the area assistant superintendent, and establish committees and report to him "as he may specify and as the needs occur" (p. 39). These reports are then transmitted to the deputy superintendent. Representatives of the four councils regularly meet together to discuss and share matters of mutual concern.

A brief summary report dated June 1971 and entitled One Year of Decentralization, concerned with the evaluation of administrative decentralization during the 1971-72 school year, highlighted the reorganizational plan as generally successful. There were some problems that still needed to be worked out with regard to the professional relationships between the area assistant superintendents and principals as well as their respective staffs, and the roles and responsibilities of the area staffs and central office staff. This is minor, of course. An important concept is stressed in the conclusion of the report, that the area assistant superintendents and area advisory councils also recognize the importance of working on system-wide problems and it reaffirms the unitary school system: "We must never forget that this is one system, one Board of Education, and one Superintendent. We all work in the same arena ..." (p. 3).

St. Louis, Missouri

According to Facts for 1971-72 and a St. Louis Information Officer (1972a),[7] the St. Louis school system consists of 179 schools, 7550 personnel including 4175 teachers, and 108,550 students with an approximate 65-35 percent black-white student ratio. The school board consists of 12 elected members. The tax rate for the 1971 fiscal year was $2.86 per $100 of assessed value; the total school budget (which includes Harris Teachers College) was $85 million, of which 62.8 percent was based on local sources, 36.6 percent on state sources, and .6 percent on federal sources. The school system spent $1030 on high school students and $765 on elementary school students.

As indicated in January 1969 by the Office of Superintendent's statement, Recommendations for Greater Local Participation ..., the school system was divided into five districts in 1962 and an additional district was established in 1964, each headed by an assistant superintendent. Each assistant superintendent was responsible for administering the elementary schools within his district and coordinating them with city-wide policies. The assistant superintendent also met on a regular basis with a parent congress, composed of parent representatives from each school in his district, whose functions were advisory.

Moves to extend the assistant superintendent's responsibilities to the high school [there are no junior high schools
and only three middle schools now in the school system (St.
Louis Information Officer, 1972b)] began in 1966 with a pilot
program in one of the districts. The following year a second pilot program was established in another district, and
in the 1968-69 school year this vertical administrative structure was implemented on a school-system basis, thus eliminating the need for an administrator of the high schools at
the central office and establishing the administration of all
the schools (with the exception of the vocational, adult, and
special schools) from the district level. Each of the six
districts served approximately 15 to 30 schools and 17,000
students.

The Office of Superintendent's 1969 recommendations
also reaffirmed the advisory role of the parent congresses;
they were to be elected by the community and the number of
representatives from each school could not exceed four. It
was further recommended that the titles of the six assistant
superintendents be changed to district superintendent, to coordinate with their increased local responsibility. The district superintendent was to attend the parent congress meetings as were two members from the board of education who
would serve as liaison representatives and respond on district matters to the school board.

The Office of Superintendent's report, St. Louis Public Schools Reorganization Plan of June 1970 pointed out further administrative decentralization steps to be taken subsequently by the school system in September 1970. The school
system was divided into ten administrative units, each with
its own parent congress. Two units were paired (mainly on
geographical basis and location of feeding schools) to form a
district--making a total of five districts. (Previously, the
school system had six districts each with its parent congress.) ·Efforts were made to equalize the size of the new
districts. Formerly, the number of schools in each district
ranged from one high school and 14 elementary schools to
two high schools and 28 elementary schools. The official
newspaper of the St. Louis school system, School and Home
(1970), shows that each of the new districts has two high
schools and between 20 and 21 elementary schools. (However, the ten administrative units are not so equal; they
comprised between seven and 15 elementary schools in 1970

and between 10 and 15 elementary schools in 1972, not including the branches some have.) The vocational, adult, and
special schools continue to operate on a city-wide basis.

According to the St. Louis Public Schools Reorganization Plan (1970) and the St. Louis Information Officer (1972b),
each of the five districts has three elementary curriculum
committees, at the primary, middle, and upper grades.
However, the curriculum division which is associated with
the central school system continues to coordinate and determine all curriculum. Whereas teacher committees formerly
were selected from the district offices, representatives to
the district curriculum committees are now selected from
each of the school faculties within the district. These committees make curriculum suggestions for improvement according to local and district needs and work closely with the
curriculum division. The district curriculum committees
have produced some variation in curriculum guidelines,
course electives, and textbook selections.

Each of the five district superintendents has two administrative assistants, each with direct responsibility for
one of the units who are accountable to the district superintendent and who also help him coordinate policies within the
district and with the various central office departments.
Each of the parent congresses of the ten units meets with
its district administrative assistant and district superintendent, and each sends a representative to the board of education meeting to improve communication. They report to the
school board and their own parent congresses.

Each district superintendent is responsible for coordinating the parent congresses and curriculum committees within his district, for evaluating personnel, preparing the budget, coordinating the district's programs with city-wide policies, meeting regularly with the general superintendent to
formulate city-wide policies, and meeting with the board of
education to provide data and interpret the district's needs
and programs.

Indianapolis, Indiana

Indianapolis and Marion County were merged into the
city of Indianapolis in January 1970; while the merger
brought together several city and county social systems under
one government, it did not merge the school systems.

According to Joseph C. Payne (1972a, 1972b, 1972c), assistant to the superintendent and affiliated with the Planning
Division, the Indianapolis school system contains 120 schools,
4500 licensed personnel, and 102,734 students. The white
student population is 62.3 percent and the nonwhite student
population is 37.7 percent; the latter figure includes Spanish-
surnamed, Oriental, and Indian students (who comprise .3
percent.) The board of education consists of seven members
elected at primary time. The school reading level is approximately .5 to .7 grade equivalents below the national
norm. The school tax per $100 of assessed value is $4.88,
plus $1.00 for a cumulative building fund. The 1971-72 bud-
get totaled $84.6 million, of which 56 percent was derived
from local sources; approximately $800 was spent on each
student for instructional costs.

With the exception of the Area Organization Plan ...
(1971) referred to below, Payne (1972b) states that no primary source decentralization or community participation documents were available. He (1972a) points out, however, that
in 1969 the school system "was divided into ten districts,
based upon elementary school areas, [and that] the purposes
of this decentralization ... [was] the improvement of administrative communication between central office and the elementary principal's function" (p. 1). Paul I. Miller (1972),
assistant superintendent for elementary education, adds that
"the 10 elementary areas are put together ... to form 3 regions" (p. 1). Each area is supposed to be headed by an
area coordinator who is responsible to the assistant superintendent in charge of elementary education; however,
as of 1972 both Miller (1972) and Payne (1972a) point
out that only four coordinators have been assigned by
the central office. One of these coordinators is in charge
of the specially funded Model Cities area.

The Area Organization Plan ... (1971) shows that each
of the ten areas contains 8 to 13 schools and between 1552
and 9259 students. While seven of the ten school areas are
relatively integrated (15-85 percent black), the individual
schools for the greater part remain segregated. For example, 15 schools are 98 percent or more black and 34 schools
are 97 percent or more white. Only 23 schools or 25 percent of the school system comprises a black student enrollment of between 15 and 85 percent.

Payne (1972a) points out that community participation

is limited to the usual P. T. A. and parent-teacher groups.
The only exception he mentions is an eight-day charette in
1969 which brought together community representatives and
professional personnel to develop plans for a new school in
the model area.   The charette, according to Payne, was
"moderately successful" (p. 2).

Denver, Colorado

The Denver school system, according to Gerald E.
Elledge (1972a, 1972c, 1972d), supervisor of the Department
of Planning, Research, and Budgeting, consists of 121 schools,
7097 personnel including 4437 teachers, and 94,838 students.
Of this student enrollment, 60 percent are white, 23 percent
are Spanish surnamed, 15.5 percent are black, and the remaining 2.5 percent are Oriental and Indian.   There are
seven persons elected to the board of education.   In 1972,
the school tax was $5.63 per $100 of assessed property
value;   the budget was $123.7 million of which 79 percent
was obtained from local revenues;   the general expenditure
per average daily student attendance entitlement was $918.

The Denver public schools make up a unitary district
and Elledge (1972b) maintains that "it is anticipated that it
will continue as presently organized" (p. 1).   In effect, the
school authorities see little value in decentralizing the school
system, partially because the community and schools work
together well and partially because the size of the school system is not overwhelmingly large.   According to the Denver
School District Administration and Supervision Organization
Chart (n. d.), there are four divisions: (1) faculty planning
and engineering, (2) administrative services, (3) general administration, and (4) education--each headed by an assistant
superintendent who works out of the central office.

Of the four divisions, two are of particular interest
for our purposes.   The division of general administration is
subdivided into eight departments, each headed by an executive director.   Two of these departments include: (1) planning, research, and budgeting and (2) school community relations, both of which supply resource personnel and assistance
to the community school organizations discussed below.   The
division of education is subdivided into five departments:
(1) elementary education, (2) secondary education, (3) adult
and vocational education, (4) instructional services, and

(5) pupil services. Both the above organizational chart and
Elledge (1972b) indicate that the principals of the schools are
directly responsible in a line relationship to the five departmental executive directors of education who in turn are responsible to the four assistant superintendents who are responsible to the school superintendent.

　　　According to the Denver Public Schools Advisory
Committees and Area Councils (1972) pamphlet, community
participation is provided at the school level through local
budget advisory committees under the leadership of the principal. Members of this advisory committee consist of the
principal of each school, at least two teachers selected by
the staff, two parents, three citizen representatives from
local business, labor, and professional agencies, and two
students at the junior and senior levels only. At its own
discretion, the budget advisory committee can expand its
membership. Each budget advisory committee identifies
community and school needs and formulates budgetary priorities and recommendations. Along with the principal, one
member of the committee is elected to serve as a representative to the area council below and liaison between both
community councils.

　　　There are nine area councils, each formed on the
basis of geographical proximity around one of the nine high
schools of the school system. Each of the feeder junior
high and elementary schools sends one elected members
from the budget advisory committee, as well as the principal, to the area council. Each area council decides upon
the number of officers and committees to be elected or appointed. Their main purpose is to analyze the budget priorities and recommendations of the individual budget advisory
committees within the respective areas and relate this data
to the needs of the entire area. An administrative agent
from the department of planning, research, and budgeting at
the central office acts as a resource agent and nonvoting
representative who provides assistance in matters related to
the budget. A consensus of opinion is reached and a majority and minority report is written. An elected representative
from the area council presents the budget priorities and recommendation of the council to the general superintendent and
board of education. Thus in formulating the city school budget, there is advisory input based around the needs of the
local budget advisory committees and the nine separate area
councils. While the powers of the two community groups
are solely advisory, they are "extensive, participatory, and

effective," according to Elledge (1972d), and they are related
to a vital concern--money, which according to Superintendent
Howard L. Johnson reflects the priorities of the community
and helps identify their educational needs.   (In light of the
present financial plight facing the schools of the nation, this
advisory activity is becoming increasingly important.) Thus
while there is no official administrative decentralization policy, these local and area councils result in an indirect but
sanctioned form of decentralization.

Anne Arundel County, Maryland

Anne Arundel County is basically a suburban school
system including the small city of Annapolis, lying between
the cities of Baltimore and Washington, D. C.   According to
H. Lewis Alsobrook (1972a, 1972b), who is the officer for
Program Planning and Evaluation, the population of the
county is 297, 000.   There are 99 schools, staffed by about
3600 professionals with an additional 225 operating from the
central office.   Student enrollment is about 75, 000 of whom
about 9600 or 12 percent, are black.   The remaining student
population is white, with less than 1 percent in "other" categories.   The board of education is appointed by the governor
and consists os seven members.   The school system's reading scores from grades three to eight fall at the 49th percentile in terms of national norms.   The county property is
assessed at approximately $49 per $100 of true value.   The
tax rate is $3. 25 per $100 assessed valuation.   About $38
million was raised in the 1971-72 fiscal year through local
property taxes and an extra $44 million was raised through
other taxes including a local income tax.   About 61 percent
of the total $82 million school budget was raised from local
taxes.   Operating expenditures per student were $833.

Plans for decentralization were submitted to the board
of education in April 1970 in a report entitled, Recommendations Concerning Administrative Decentralization....   The
purpose of the plan is to provide greater continuity of the
K-12 and school program and greater administrative services
to the schools.   As the title of the plan suggests, it is administrative in nature, centering around the central office
and area decentralization.   While it points to the need for
community involvement, it does not suggest a specific plan
for enhancing such contact.

At the central office level, the report recommended

that the advisory units of the general superintendent remain
basically intact.   The department of instruction would be ele-
vated to a higher status by raising the chief instructional administrator to a deputy superintendent.   In line with the K-
12 emphasis, the deputy superintendent of instruction and his
staff would assume the responsibility of two persons currently
involved in administering the educational programs in the elementary and secondary schools.   In addition, the position of
assistant superintendent of administration would be created:
in charge of management, fiscal services, personnel, operations, and information.   Both the deputy superintendent for
instruction and the new assistant superintendent of administration would be equal in rank and responsible to the school
superintendent.   (However, according to Alsobrook (1972b),
the assistant superintendent's position has been shelved for
the foreseeable future.)

It was also recommended that the school system be
divided into four areas, each headed by a director and his
staff who would be in charge of the schools in his area and
responsible to the deputy superintendent of instruction.   The
area directors would also work with parental and community
advisory groups, helping them define their wishes and interpreting the policies of the board of education.   Several positions would be created in each area including a supervisor
of instruction from K-12 (in line with the purpose of coordinating the elementary and secondary program), 12 resource
teachers of various subjects, and a media specialist in charge
of coordinating a media center for the area.   According to
Alsobrook (1972a), each of the four areas is to comprise between four and seven secondary schools, 18 to 19 elementary
schools, and up to two special schools, with a total of approximately 16, 000 to 22, 600 students.

Implementation took place in mid 1973 (Alsobrook,
1972b).   Alsobrook (1972a) also writes, "There are no special plans for additional community involvement in this project as we are interested in implementing a form of administrative decentralization and not community control" (p. 1).

Portland, Oregon

According to the World ... 1971-72 and John Nellor
(1972b), director of the Public Information Department, the
Portland school system consists of 114 schools, 7400 personnel including 3600 teachers, and 72, 306 students.   The

Portland Public Schools Area Organization Plan (1970) indicates the black student enrollment comprises 8.5 percent;
and the white student enrollment, 91.5 percent. [Nellor
(1972a) indicates that there is only a scattering of other minorities.] The World ... 1971-72 shows that seven persons
are elected to the board of education.   The tax rate is $1.34
per $100 true cash value; the instructional spending per
elementary student is $725 and the spending per secondary
student is $900.   The 1971-72 budget is $67 million of which
74 percent is derived from local property tax, 21.9 percent
from state funds, .5 percent from federal funds, and 3.5
percent from other sources.

        In their resolution on the Portland Schools for the
Seventies (1970), the school board adopted six objectives,
among them the need to reorganize the schools to provide
administrative autonomy to the schools, greater communication between the schools and central office, greater participation through citizen advisory committees, and reduction of
the concentration of racial minorities in the schools.   To
achieve these objectives, it was suggested that the central
office be reorganized into three divisions: (1) operations,
administered by the deputy superintendent;   (2) planning, administered by an associate superintendent;   and (3) management services, administered by another associate superintendent.   [Also see Portland Public Schools Central Organization (1971).]   The five elementary areas and two high
school areas would be reorganized into three administrative
areas comprising between 38 and 45 schools and between
22,000 and 29,000 students with 7 to 9 percent black enrollments.   [Also see the Portland Public Schools Directory
(n.d.) and the Portland Public Schools Area Organization
Plan (1970).   There is no indication in these reports whether
the individual schools have a similar black percentage.]   The
principals would be responsible to their respective area superintendent who would "administer the schools within his
area in accordance with the Superintendent's instructions and
policies of the Board of Education" [p. 2].   The three area
superintendents would be responsible to the deputy superintendent of operation who in turn would be responsible to the
school superintendent.   An area advisory committee should
be organized for each administrative area "whose composition, rules of procedures ... and duties [would] be prescribed by the Board of Education" (p. 2).   It was also resolved that radical isolation would be avoided by not permitting the minority student population to exceed 25 percent in
any high school. [8]

In accordance with the recommendations adopted by the board of education, Superintendent Robert W. Blanchard indicated steps for implementation in his June 1970 report, entitled Plan for Administrative Reorganization. His recommendations included the realignment of the services and responsibilities of the various departments at the central office in order to reduce expenses, cut back on the administrative staff, and shift some administrators and supervisors to the field where they would be closer to the schools. Several other administrative positions from the former seven elementary and secondary areas were eliminated and other positions were created to help staff the three new administrative areas, resulting in a net reduction of 15 administrative positions and an estimated yearly savings of $190,646.

Advisory groups have been established for each of the three areas. In the Rules of Procedures for Areas Advisory Commiutees, adopted in June 1971 and further amended in July 1971, the board of education outlined the method of selecting the advisory committee members and conducting procedures of business. As for selection, a five-member city review panel appointed by the school board would select nine members including seven community members (defined as either a resident of the area or parent of a student attending a school in that area), as well as two high school students attending a school from that area. Appointments of community members would be made from a list of candidates reflecting a cross section of each area. A petition signed by 100 registered voters of an area would qualify an individual as a candidate. Student members would be selected from a list of those nominated by the student councils in each high school in the area. Community members would be appointed for two-year terms and could serve no more than two consecutive terms. Student members would be appointed for one-year terms.

The advisory committee procedures reaffirmed that "the area advisory committees [would] at all times be bound by and adhere to the policies of the Board of Education, provided, however, that they may from time to time make recommendations in writing to the Board of Education" (n. p.). It was reaffirmed that their duties were only to advise the area superintendent concerning the educational policy with respect to the area. The area superintendent would be entitled to present any matter to the committee at any of the meetings, even if it had not been placed on the agenda. The area superintendent or his delegate would attend the meetings.

Rules and procedures would be amended or repealed at any time by the board of education.

Pittsburgh, Pennsylvania

According to one Pittsburgh Information Officer (1972a, 1972c, 1972e) the 1971-72 Pittsburgh school system consisted of 116 schools, 3353 teachers, and 70,537 students. The white enrollment is 41,833 or 60 percent and the black enrollment is 28,654 (40 percent). As of June 1972, the board of education consisted of 15 members, 10 white and 5 black people, appointed for a six-year term by the judges of the Court of the Common Pleas of Allegheny County. The Pittsburgh reading levels are slightly below the national averages; 18 percent are above average readers, 54 percent are average readers, and 28 percent are below average readers. The 1972 school budget totaled $92.9 million, of which 55 percent was raised from local taxes, 44 percent from the state, and 1 percent from the federal government. According to the Estimated Receipts of Local Taxes (1972), the tax rate is $2.30 per $100 of assessed value. The table "Pittsburgh Public Schools Comparison of Expenditures" (1971) shows that the total expenditures per student are $938 which is slightly more than $100 higher than the county average.

Prior to 1970, the line administration in the school system flowed through two associate superintendents--one for elementary schools and one for secondary schools. In referring to the "Reallocation of Job Functions ..." the February 1970 Pittsburgh Board of Education Meeting pointed out that the span of control in these two positions was too great and therefore impractical. For example, the associate superintendent for the elementary schools had direct responsibility for 89 schools and the associate superintendent for the secondary schools had responsibility for 23 secondary schools. For purposes of insuring continuity of the K-12 program, reducing the administration span of control, and bringing the administration geographically and personally closer to the schools, the school board approved the creation of three decentralized areas, each headed by an area superintendent and director of education. The duties previously performed by the two associate superintendents were transformed to the three area superintendents. The area superintendents, along with a director of education and an appropriate staff, have responsibility for the schools within their areas, and are accountable to the school superintendent.

The Pittsburgh Information Officer (1972c, 1972d) asserts that the three areas contain 29, 32, and 47 schools respectively; in addition there are eight system-wide schools
serving special students such as the physically handicapped,
educationally retarded, and socially maladjusted as well as
an experimental school mainly designed to implement the
ideas of the open classroom. Two of the three areas appear
to be integrated; 63 percent white, 37 percent black; 74
percent white and 26 percent black, but Area III contains a
majority of black students: 47 percent white, 53 percent
black. (No data was supplied about the racial composition
of the individual schools.)

The Information Officer (1972a, 1972d) also points out
that the school system has numerous city-wide advisory committees. The two most interesting community groups appear
to be the ESEA Title I Advisory Committee and the Reorganization Advisory Committee. Both of these community groups
meet regularly. The first committee advises in Title I programs and, in accord with federal guidelines governing such
committees, consists mainly of parents from the target areas.
Inner-city districts nominate parent candidates who are officially selected by the school superintendent. The other
members are from the school staff, plus one school board
member. The second committee advises on policies pertaining to school reorganization, overcrowding, and school integration. Members are selected by the general superintendent
and comprise a racially representative cross section of the
communities, as well as members from labor management,
religious, and governmental agencies. According to the
News from Pittsburgh Public Schools (1971), this committee
is divided into three subgroups based on the three decentralized areas. Their proposals are presented to the board of
education for consideration. Similarly, the school board's
reorganization plans are then presented to the Pittsburgh community for modifications and suggestions. Only after consulting with the city residents does the school board implement
reorganization plans.

Buffalo, New York

The Ethnic Census of the Buffalo Public Schools (1972)
and Buffalo Public Schools Facts and Figures, 1971-72 show
that the school system consists of 95 schools, plus three
special schools, 4058 licensed personnel including 3549 teachers,
and 68,344 students. The students' racial composition is

57 percent white, 39.8 percent black, 2.4 percent Spanish-surnamed, .7 percent Indian, and .1 percent Oriental. The board of education consists of seven members who are appointed by the mayor with the approval of the Common Council. Reading levels are equivalent to those of other large urban areas. However, Superintendent of Schools Joseph Manch has stated that a concentrated attack upon the reading problems that so many urban children manifest is the number one priority of the board of education (Buffalo Information Officer, 1972a, 1972b).

According to Buffalo Public Schools Facts and Figures, 1971-72, the school system's budget for that school year totaled $86.1 million, of which 52 percent was derived from state aid, 41 percent from local and county taxes, 1 percent from federal aid and miscellaneous, and 6 percent from budget notes. On that basis, total expenditures per student were $1,088 for current operation and maintenance of the schools.[9]

Responsible to the school superintendent is a deputy superintendent of finance and research and three associate superintendents for (1) instructional services, (2) personnel and (3) plant services and school planning. Responsible to these four executive superintendents are various assistant superintendents, directors, and supervisors all working out of the central office. Depending on the school level, the principals are directly responsible to the assistant superintendent for elementary education or assistant superintendent for secondary education in the department of instructional services (... Facts and Figures, 1971-72).

There are several community advisory groups including a Community Advisory Committee for Title 1 ESEA Projects and New York State Urban Education Aid Projects, parents advisory groups for the Follow Through and the Spanish-English Development program (Annual Report of the Superintendent, 1970-71), and the appointment of students and parents to textbook and curriculum committees (Your Schools at Work, 1969; Superintendent's Goals, 1972).

The most extensive type of community participation at the present is the 42 member School-Community Advisory Committee, formed in October 1969 and consisting mainly of PTA members as well as representatives from religious, political, labor and governmental groups; it also includes students. This committee advises school officials on matters related to school-community activities (Buffalo Public Schools

Report, 1969).   The activities of the committee continues to receive wide attention in the local newspapers (Buffalo Courier Express, October 20, November 3, 1969; Buffalo Evening News, August 13, 1969) and official school news bulletins (Your Schools at Work, 1969, 1970; Annual Report of the Superintendent, 1970-71; Superintendent's Goals--1972).

Concerning administrative decentralization, in February 1969 the school board directed Superintendent Joseph Manch to have his staff explore ways to decentralize the Buffalo school system (Buffalo Board of Education Meeting, 1969; Manch, 1969).   An inhouse committee was formed in the following month to review the available literature on decentralization, community participation, and community control.   The report, Decentralization Study, was submitted in January 1970 to the board of education; the report included more than 125 sources, defined the three concepts, and listed their advantages and disadvantages.

Although school board defeated (4-3) the school superintendent's recommendation to use the above report as a tool for study whether or not decentralization should be recommended for the Buffalo schools (Buffalo Board of Education Meeting, 1970a, 1970b).   Dr. Manch continuously recommended his support for a decentralization plan that would increase community participation but would not segregate the communities (Annual Report of the Superintendent, 1970-71; Manch, 1970).   Then in February 1971, the Buffalo school board requested that the general superintendent have a staff committee study the possibilities, problems and implications of: a cross-busing program in Buffalo and the use of existing buildings not used as middle schools for middle school purposes.   Following a preliminary staff study, an advisory Planning Council on Desegregation was established and held its first meeting in November, 1971.   The Council included three members from the central office, five teachers, one elementary school principal, four members from the citywide School-Community Advisory Committee and four additional community representatives (Buffalo Information Officer, 1972b). The council submitted its report, A Study of Desegregation to the Buffalo Board of Education and General Superintendent in February 1972.   The study listed implications not only for desegregation, but also for supportive program and alternatives for community participation, including a mild form of decentralization.

The Council members illustrated the feasibility of

creating "five somewhat pie-shaped districts or expanded
neighborhoods with the narrowest point of each located in the
central city and the broadest at the city's periphery" (p. 26).
Approximately 19 schools were designated to make up each
expanded district.   A number of these schools were either
predominately white or predominately black.   Utilization of
a plus or minus 10 percent variance from black-white student
percentages would, according to the study, insure racial balance in each school and district.   [The Council pointed out
that 22 percent of the schools comprised a 16 to 85 percent
black student enrollment and 43 percent comprised a 0 to 15
percent black student enrollment.   As many as 35 percent of
the schools were considered integrated, with a 16 to 85 percent black student enrollment.   The elementary schools were
slightly more segregated;   only 30 percent of these schools
were comprised of 16 to 85 percent black students.]

The maximum distance required for transportation
within any of the expanded neighborhoods was calculated at
5.2 miles.   It was estimated that 50 percent of the system's
elementary pupils would have been transported under the five
district organization, at an estimated cost of $2.9 million
per year of which 90 percent, or approximately $2.6 million,
would be reimbursable through state funds.

The study contended that desegregation including a
form of decentralization for community participation could
be implemented together.   It listed several implications for
a combined effort in school reorganization, program development and desegregation and outlined two alternative approaches
to achieve decentralization and community participation.

Both approaches visualized five districts, each headed
by a district superintendent, a supportive staff transferred
from the central offices into the districts, district councils
and local councils for each school.   In each alternative, the
general superintendent and board of education would make
final decisions regarding policy.   District superintendents
would be responsible to the school superintendent, and the
district and school councils would have advisory responsibilities.

Alternative I reaffirmed that the district superintendent
would implement the decisions of the board of education and
the general superintendent, as required by law.   He would
have limited powers over curriculum and personnel within his
district and would share with the district council the right

to make final selections of teachers referred by the central office.   District councils would screen applicants for district superintendent and submit three names qualified according to Buffalo school standards, one of whom would be chosen by the school board.   The district councils would deal with problems of and make recommendations for dealing with curriculum, personnel, plant facilities, and community relations.   The district superintendent would be responsible for presenting the concerns of the council members to the school superintendent and in turn advise the council members of the policies and decisions of the general superintendent and board of education.   The district council would consist of six parents, four principals, six teachers, four high school students, and a representative from each local school council.

The local school council--comprised of the school principal, two teachers, four community residents (at least two with children enrolled in school), as well as two students from the middle, junior, and senior high councils--would be organized to serve the individual schools.   The council members would discuss the problems and progress of matters related to each school and help develop closer cooperation and understanding between the school staff and community residents.

Alternative II also implied that the school superintendent and school board be responsible for implementing policy. Each of the five districts would be headed by a district administrator appointed by the board of education from recommendations of the district advisory council.   The district administrator would implement all policies established by the school superintendent and board of education.   He would hear the recommendations of the district advisory councils and make their views known to the board of education.

The district advisory councils would be made up of representatives from each school within the district, with equal representation from administrators, teachers, parents, and students.   Their function would be to advise the district administrator, and they could recommend to the board of education the removal of the district administrator for nonperformance of his duties.

Each principal would provide a method for creating the initial school advisory council, which would consist of two elected staff teachers, two parents elected by the community, and two elected student representatives for the

secondary school councils. Their functions would include advising the principal, and evaluation of teachers and administrators. They would confer with the community and the district and central board advisory councils on educational matters.

A school-wide advisory council would be established
to recommend and advise the board of education on all matters. The council would also serve as a liaison with the
district advisory councils. Members would be limited to the
five district administrators, two parents, one teacher and
one student from each district advisory council, and two
representatives from the teacher's bargaining unit.

On March 29, 1972, in a 4-3 vote, the school board
approved a letter to inform State Education Commissioner
Ewald B. Nyquist that it was unable to plan for further desegregation of the city public schools. In a further action,
with the same 4-3 vote, the school board received and filed
A Study of Desegregation (1972). In another motion the members of the board of education stated that the "Board, as it
is presently constituted, is vigorously opposed to any form
of cross busing" (Buffalo Information Officer, 1972b). In
this connection, Knapp (1972) contends that the views of white
segregationists and black militants prevailed.

Minneapolis, Minnesota

According to the Annual Report: 1970-71, the Minneapolis school system consists of 94 schools and 3260 teachers
that serve over 67,160 students. As of 1971 the minority
student population was 13 percent: comprising 9 percent
blacks, 3 percent Indians, and .5 percent each of Orientals
and Spanish-speaking children. The board of education consists of seven members, elected for six-year terms on a
2-2-3 staggered basis. Ralph H. Johnson (1972), director
of the Department of Guidance Services for the Minneapolis
schools, states that the median reading level "compares
favorable with national norms," but the schools comprising
the two pyramids below "are inner-city schools" with a large
number of disadvantaged students and "the test results ...
are somewhat below those for the city" (p. 1). The Annual
Report: 1970-71 shows a 72.8 million operating budget of
which 59 percent is derived from local sources, 36 percent
from state sources, .8 percent from federal sources, and the
remaining from other sources. According to August Rivera

(1972), director of Information Services, the school tax is
$1.39 per $100 of assessed property value; and the expenditure per student in 1970 was $876.

Upon assuming the superintendency in January 1967,
John B. Davis, Jr. stated in his first policy address before
the Citizens Committee for Public Education the need for decentralizing and thus improving the administrative facility of
the school system by establishing a "pyramid" consisting of
one high school and its feeding junior and elementary schools
with local authority and discretionary power. The purpose
would be to break down what is referred to as the bureaucracy, enhance communications among the schools and with
the community, develop cooperative programs among the
schools, and permit decision-making at the local level.

According to the school superintendent's report, Decentralization of Schools in Minneapolis (n. d.), the first
pyramid was established in August of 1967. It is based
around one high school and its 11 feeding schools and serves
approximately 10,000 students. The pyramid is headed by
an area assistant superintendent who is in charge of the
schools and who has a small staff including a director of
educational services and a community involvement planner
who work actively with the community. The Organization
Chart ... (1970) shows that the area assistant superintendent
is responsible to the two central office associate superintendents for (1) elementary education and (2) secondary education, who in turn are responsible to the school superintendent. (There are two other associate superintendents in
charge of personnel and business affairs also responsible to
the school superintendent.)

Based on the Decentralization of Schools ... (n. d.)
report and the North Pyramid News (1968), the official newsletter of the pyramid, each of the three junior high schools
and its feeding elementary schools in the pyramid, form what
is called a "complex." Each complex has a steering com-
mittee--a representative group of three teachers from each
school--that meets monthly to provide communication among
the schools. Representatives from the three complexes meet
together twice annually with the area assistant superintendent.
Each complex also has an elected community advisory council whose members represent each school, to express school
needs felt by the community. A pyramid advisory council
has also been formed which includes one parent representative from each of the schools in the pyramid.

The Minneapolis Board of Education Meeting of January 1969 indicated the desire to extend to the community some decision-making powers and a voice in determining educational policy at the local level. Thus the school board voted unanimously to develop a second pyramid, based around two high schools serving 13 feeder schools including 12 whose community fabric had been developed previously by the Model Neighborhood program, and serving approximately 10,000 students. These schools are also headed by an area assistant superintendent who is responsible to the two aforementioned associate superintendents at the central office and who is assisted by personnel who coordinate plans with community agencies, especially the Model Neighborhood program. In addition, the Decentralization of Schools ... (n.d.) report indicates that there is an elected 60-member advisory group called the community council, composed of parents, community resident, faculty, and students who meet regularly to evaluate programs within the area and reports of various standing committees. There is also a teacher advisory committee which meets regularly with the area assistant superintendent to recommend priorities for expenditure of funds, to evaluate current programs, and to suggest new programs. The power of these committees, in both areas, is advisory in nature.

Supervisory personnel and supportive services continue to come from the central office; thus the two units are not completely decentralized. Based on the Annual Report: 1970-71, both pyramids have consolidated their services in reading instruction, and a single coordinator along with resource reading teachers provide supportive services and inservice instruction to teachers. One component of the program includes an instructional materials center which produces and distributes reading materials to teachers. The team work and cooperative efforts between both pyramids in reading instruction have implications for establishing and coordinating other types of teaching-learning centers for the two decentralized units in Minneapolis and among decentralized units in other school systems.

El Paso, Texas

The city of El Paso has two independent school districts, El Paso and Ysleta. Keith H. Ferrell (1972a, 1972b, 1972c), technical writer of the Division of Administration, informs us that this is the result of two smaller cities

expanding until they merged. El Paso several years ago an-
nexed Ysleta, and since that time the residents have had one
city government and two public school districts. The El
Paso school system consists of 63 schools, 3123 certified
personnel including 2800 teachers, and 62,363 students; the
Ysleta school system is nearly two-thirds this size. The
official student enrollment at the El Paso schools is approximately 53 percent Mexican-American, 43 percent Anglo, 3
percent black, and 1 percent other. The board of education
consist of seven members elected by the registered voters.
According to Ferrell (1972b, 1972d), the reading levels are
slightly below national norms.[10] The school tax rate is
$1.84 per $100, and the tax rate is applied to 65 percent
of the assessed valuation. The 1971-72 budget totaled $41.3
million, of which 36.4 percent was from local sources, 57.2
percent from state sources, and 6.4 percent from federal
sources. The estimated average expenditure per student was
$653. In the 1972-73 school year, the budget was increased
to $43 million and the cost per student had risen to $673.

The Organization Chart ... (1971) showed that there
were three assistant superintendents of (1) instruction, (2)
Mexican-American education, and (3) supportive services,
as well as a business manager, and a deputy superintendent
of administration sharing equal rank. The first four administrators were directly responsible to the school superintendent, and the school principals were responsible to
the deputy superintendent, who in turn was also responsible to the school superintendent.

After studying various administrative decentralization
plans for two years, a plan for decentralization was announced in the summer of 1972 and the school system proceeded to decentralize in September 1972, the basic purpose
being to bring the schools closer to the community. According to Ferrell (1972d) and the El Paso Times (July 21, 1972),
the school system was divided into three areas, each with
about 21 schools and 21,000 students, and each headed by an
area superintendent who in effect replaced the above three
assistant superintendents. Each area superintendent is in
charge of the schools in his area and reports directly to
Superintendent H. E. Charles. Under the new organization,
the position of deputy superintendent remained in charge
of the supportive services while the various departments
of student personnel, finances, school construction,
research and evaluation, vocational education, personnel,

and the newly created department of curriculum and staff development continue to be operated from the central office by
their respective directors who report to the deputy superintendent. The Administrative Communication of El Paso Public Schools (1972) indicates that the 21 curriculum specialists
from the central office, however, have been reassigned to
the area offices, as well as an administrative assistant for
each area superintendent. According to the El Paso Herald-
Post (July 20, 1972) the president of the board of education
has reaffirmed the fact that no new jobs were created, but
that the duties were changed of those people already employed.

Ferrell (1972c) and the school board's summary of
"Community Involvement" (n. d.) indicate that within the last
three years several different community participatory groups
have been formed to enhance communication among the students, parents, and staff, and among the community, school,
and central office. They include (1) a student advisory com-
mittee--consisting of three high school students (two selected
by the students and one by the principal) from each of the
nine high schools for a total of 27 high school students--
which meets twice each month with the school superintendent
and periodically with the school board to discuss pertinent
school problems and affairs; (2) an advisory committee on
Mexican-American educational needs--a group of 12 Mexican-
American school employees appointed by the school superin-
tendent--which meets weekly to enhance communication between the Mexican-American community and school administration; (3) an ad hoc committee on technical and vocational
education, consisting of 14 El Paso businessmen who meet
with and inform the administration and board of education on
types of vocational training most suitable for the students and
metropolitan area of El Paso; (4) an ad hoc committee on
student dress and grooming--a group of 16 students, eight
parents, and eight teachers selected by the groups they represent and formed to study the system's dress codes and suggest changes; (5) a committee planning task force--a group
of 35 (selected by the groups they represent) of community
action representatives, parents, students, teachers, administrators, and school board members who study all aspects of
education for the school system and recommend changes;
and (6) a Title I parent advisory committee--a volunteer
group of parents who are recommended by the principals and
who are receiving services under Title I provisions of the
1965 Elementary and Secondary Act. This committee advises
school officials in planning, implementing, evaluating, and

revising the program services. Ferrell (1972b) also points
out that recently a new group has been formed, called the
home-school community agents, consisting of paid community
residents from the inner-city area who communicate with the
parents and others much more successfully than do teachers
and administrators. These community agents have direct
access at any time to the deputy superintendent. As a result of their work, lines of communication have been improved in areas which were formerly considered difficult.
Finally, the El Paso Times (July 21, 1972) points out that
as a result of administrative decentralization each area superintendent is in the process of establishing a parents' advisory council to meet regularly with him to discuss school
curriculum and services.

Oakland, California

        According to the school superintendent's December
1970 report, Plan for Creation of Administrative Regions and
the pamphlet, Statistical and Financial Data, 1970-71, the
Oakland system consists of 91 schools and 61,600 students.
The student population is 58.8 percent black, 26.2 percent
white, 8.4 percent Spanish-surnamed, 5.1 percent Oriental,
.6 percent Indian, and .9 percent other. The board of education consists of seven elected members. As many as 64
percent of the students are reading below the national norm.
The tax rate is $4.74 per $100. The 1971-72 total budget
was $56.2 million, 62 percent of which was income derived
from local sources, 26 percent from state sources, 9 percent from federal sources, and the remaining 3 percent from
other income. The school system's spending per student
was $895.

        Upon assuming responsibility as superintendent in
July 1970, Marcus A. Foster received permission from the
board of education to hire a management consultant firm to
study the school system. Price-Waterhouse submitted its
report, Recommendation for Improving the Management Effectiveness of the Oakland Unified Schools, in September
1970. Among the major recommendations were (1) to re-
align several offices and departments at the central office
and to replace the existing four divisions into three, namely
(a) educational development (related to curriculum and instruction), (b) pupil personnel, and (c) planning, research,
and evaluation; (2) to create three administrative regions,
each headed by a regional associate superintendent who

would be in charge of the schools within his boundaries;
(3) to clarify the authority and technical responsibilities of
the central office and at regional levels; (4) to adopt and
implement basic management principles to plan, operate,
and evaluate the system's goals and priorities (which include
budget items) and related objectives; and (5) to increase the
level of citizen participation in policy and planning. Methods
to implement these recommendations were also listed.

The first steps taken toward administrative decentralization came in December 1970, when Dr. Foster listed his
recommendations to the board of education in a report entitled Plan for Creation of Administrative Regions. These
recommendations were subsequently approved by the school
board in January 1971. The central office was divided into
three divisions and reorganized according to most of the
basic recommendations of the Price-Waterhouse report. The
minor differences were mainly due to financial limitations
and the desire to reduce costs. Three administrative regions were established, each headed by a regional associate
superintendent appointed by and responsible to the school superintendent, without changing school attendance boundaries
and feeder patterns in the existing regions. Administrative
practicality was the major reason for maintaining the boundaries and feeder patterns. Each region comprised between
20,000 and 23,000 students and the racial composition of the
students tended to coincide with the racial mix of the entire
school system; data on the racial composition of each school
was not provided.

In his March 1971 report entitled Administrative Regions, the school superintendent implemented the remainder
of the system's decentralization plans. The position of regional coordinator was established to assist the regional associate superintendent. Transfers of several administrative
personnel from the central office to the regions, as well as
adjustments in title, work, and salaries, were also implemented.

In the spirit of the Price-Waterhouse report, the
Master Plan Citizens Committee was formed in April 1971
to study six major aspects of the system's policies, operations, and future programs: (1) curriculum and instruction,
(2) school buildings, (3) community resources, (4) decentralization, (5) school finances, and (6) desegregation. This
Citizens Committee was developed by the Oakland citizens,
school administrators, and board of education. By February

1972, it consisted of 370 members from public and private agencies, as well as community and student representatives from each of the system's 91 schools. (Also see Oakland Unified School District Master Plan Citizens Committee, 1972.)

Each of the 91 schools also has its own School Site Planning Committee for purposes of focusing on local issues and problems. According to the Master Plan Citizens Committee Guidelines, adopted by the board of education in January 1971, every interested citizen, including students, may participate in these local school meetings. The local school committees send representatives to the Master Plan Citizens Committee, thus enhancing communication between the local and city-wide committees. Each elementary and junior high school sends one representative per 500 students to the Citizens Committee, as well as at least one community representative. Each high school sends one representative per 250 students, and dropouts may serve as representatives from the schools they last attended. Students who serve as representatives may receive elective credit by making proper arrangements. Students are selected by the school's student governing council. Representatives selected by the school serve on various city-wide task forces. Representatives are to report to the local School Site Planning Committee and the city-wide Master Plan Citizens Committee. (Schools may send observers to the task forces to ensure proper communication between both groups.) It should also be noted that one of the subgroups of the Site Planning Committee, with the participation of the staff, selects three candidates who they feel are desirable for filling the vacancy as principal. There are no written guidelines per se, but the final selection is made by the school superintendent.

The Master Plan Citizens Committee is divided into six task forces which in turn are subdivided into smaller resource groups to enhance communication and permit intensive study of the problems being examined. Each resource group contains about 15 members, including a cross section of the larger task force. Each task force is assisted by an administrator from the Oakland schools and has $12,500 annually to contract for consultant services. The task forces send two representatives to a Master Plan Coordinating Committee which regularly discusses activities and shares ideas among the other task forces and in addition periodically meets with the board of education to exchange ideas and discuss problems. The Master Plan Citizens Committee Guidelines

(1971) state that "The Master Plan Citizens Committee is
directly responsible to the board of education" (p. 5), which
connotes that the school board has final authority over their
decisions.   However, according to Edwin P. Larsen (1972),
the director of research, "the administering Board have committed themselves to be responsible to the recommendations
which the master plan Citizens Committee makes" (p. 2).

In sum, the local school committee and the city-wide
citizens committee enhance communication and understanding
among the community, local schools, central office, and city.
The committees and their various subcommittees serve as
vehicles for interested students, parents, and community and
city residents to educate themselves, voice their opinions,
and participate in school policy and planning.   They serve
as illustrations of extensive forms of community participation, advising on policy and planning, not controlling or deciding on ultimate decisions, but nevertheless advising in a
forceful manner.

Gary, Indiana

According to the Gary Public Schools Staff and Pupil
Enrollment Census ... (1971), in the 1971-72 school year
there were 49 schools, 2331 personnel including 1821
teachers, and 45,332 students.   The student racial composition was 67.5 percent black, 23.6 percent white, 8.6 percent
Spanish surnamed, and .3 percent Oriental and Indian.   According to William Malloy (1972), special education officer,
the board of education consists of five members or trustees
who are appointed by the mayor with the approval of the city
council.   The 1971-72 budget totaled $38.5 million, of which
61 percent was derived from local sources, 30 percent from
state sources, and 9 percent from federal funds.   Haron J.
Battle (1972a), the assistant superintendent of educational
services, points out that in the primary grades, the Gary
reading levels tend to be above national norms, but "by the
third grade and thereafter, the average falls below such
norms" (p. 1).   The school tax rate is $4.95 per $100 of
the adjusted valuation with an additional $1.25 for a building
fund.   The school system spent $919 per student in the 1971-
72 school year (Battle, 1972b).

The school system operates as a unitary district for
the secondary schools and a decentralized district for the
elementary schools.   To understand this organization, the

reader needs to be familiar with the administrative line-staff organization at the central office. The "School City of Gary Professional Staff Organizational Table" (1971) and A Report to the Community ... (1972) indicate that at the central administrative level there are two assistant superintendents, one for educational services and one for business services, who report to the general superintendent, and five directors-- (1) developmental programs, (2) research, (3) career education, (4) instruction, and (5) special services--who are directly responsible to the assistant superintendent of educational services. According to the above organizational table and the School City of Gary District Organization of Secondary Schools (1971) there are eight junior high and middle schools, whose principals are directly responsible to the director of instruction. There are seven high schools, whose principals are directly responsible to the assistant superintendent of educational services.

At the elementary school level, however, there are three decentralized districts. In 1972, under the superintendent Gordon McAndrew, the school system adopted this plan for more effective administrative and supervisory purposes. According to the School City of Gary District Organization of Elementary Schools (1971) and report of the Kindergarten-Elementary Council (1972), each of the three units is headed by a district administrator and a small staff, including a district instructional supervisor, psychologist, and a number of resource teachers, which had been reduced from seven to four to save money then restored to seven as a result of a teacher strike. The principals of the elementary schools are responsible to their respective district administrators and these three administrators are responsible to the assistant superintendent of educational services. In 1972 District I contained nine schools and 7282 students; District II contained 11 schools and 7660 students, and District III had 10 schools and 7984 students.

Based on the Gary Public Schools Staff and Pupil Enrollment Census ... (1971) and the School City of Gary District Organization of Elementary Schools (1971), the racial composition of the elementary schools within the city-wide system is 14,887 (68 percent) black; 5128 (24 percent) white; 1889 (8 percent) Spanish surnamed (with 18 Orientals and four Indians). When we look at the three elementary school districts in relation to school wide figures, Districts I and III are relatively integrated. The racial composition of District I is 54 percent black, 33 percent white, and 13 percent

Spanish surnamed.   District II is 49 percent black, 35 percent white, and 16 percent Spanish surnamed.   District III
is segregated: 89 percent black, 2 percent white, and 9 percent Spanish surnamed.   Looking at the individual schools,
however, we see a different picture.   One of the 30 schools
is relatively integrated in relation to the school-wide figures
(717 black, 106 white, and 275 Spanish surnamed).   Nine of
the remaining schools are predominantly white and the other
20 schools are overwhelmingly black.   Here it should be
pointed out that the power structure of the city government
and board of education are predominantly black and the administrative central office is more than 50 percent composed
of black individuals;   the actions of blacks in Gary might
thus lead one to conclude they do not seek school integration.
Battle (1972b) disagrees with this conclusion, contending that
the three school districts and individual schools are organized to achieve maximum integration within housing pattern
restrictions.

Community participation is mainly limited to advisory
roles in a number of different programs and committees.
This includes: (1) the Pulaski Area Council, organized in
1969 in conjunction with the Pulaski Learning Center which
is federally funded, helping parents plan and utilize teaching
resources and techniques to motivate their children at home
(Pulaski Area Council, 1972;   Pulaski Early Learning Center,
1972);   (2) the Parent-Child Mobile Classroom, also funded
by ESEA money, which takes a mobile classroom on a bus
to the various communities, to provide educational lessons
to pre-kindergarten children and supplementary teaching techniques to parents which they can share with and supplement
their children's learning at home (Title III, ESEA Parent-
Child Mobile Classroom, n. d.);   (3) the Kindergarten-Elementary Council, whose purpose is to extend communication
between the parents and professionals and the home and
school, and where parents meet with representative school
teachers, principals, and district administrators to discuss
teaching-learning services within each of the three newly
formed elementary school districts (Kindergarten-Elementary
Council, 1972);   (4) the Secondary School Parents Council,
which is organized for the same purpose as the above council, but geared for the secondary schools and on a city-wide
level (Secondary School Parents Council, 1972);   (5) the Reciprocal Education Program, organized in 1969 and supported
by foundation money and divided into nine school areas,
to train people in leadership roles in the community and to
develop a pool of leaders who could train other community

residents as leaders (Reciprocal Education Program, n. d.);
and (6) the Coalition to Save Our Schools, organized in 1971
to deal with the financial crisis of the school system and
consisting of interested parents and citizens of the city,
whose members also communicate to other community groups
and state legislators the problems of the school system and
arouse citizens of the city to send letters to state legislators and the governor to pressure the state to advance
money to the school system and keep the schools open
(Coalition to Save Our Schools, 1972).

Torrance, California

Torrance is a suburban community outside Los
Angeles; according to one Torrance administrative superintendent (1972b, 1972c) and the school system's 1972 Statistical Report, the community consists of approximately
139, 000 people whose mean income is at about the $10, 000
level. The school system has grown from four schools and
2000 students in 1947 to 42 schools and 32, 625 students in
1972. In 1971-72, Torrance schools employed 1409 teachers,
and the student racial-ethnic composition was 89. 3 percent white
and 10. 7 percent minorities, most of whom were Mexican-American. A five-member board of education is elected by the
community. On reading tests required by the state, the
first- and second-grade reading scores ranked at the 50th
percentile and the third grade scores ranked at the 52nd
percentile. Whereas in 1947 Torrance had more than
$16, 000 in taxable wealth per student's education, in 1972
it had approximately $14, 800. At the present time, the as-
sessed property value per child is approximately $24, 000
and the tax rate is $4. 95 per $100 of assessed valuation.
The 1971-72 school budget is approximately $32 million, of
which 66 percent is raised from local sources, 32 percent
from state sources, and 2 percent from federal sources.
The instructional spending per child is $790.

Under the leadership of Superintendent Lloyd G. Jones,
the Torrance schools were decentralized for administrative
purposes in September 1971. According to the Torrance
Unified School District Organizational Chart (1971), the administrative structure is now divided into four geographical
areas, each headed by an area administrator responsible for
the schools in their respective areas. Each of the four area
administrators, along with three central office assistant superintendents of (1) business, (2) personnel, and

(3) instruction, is responsible to the deputy superintendent
who in turn is responsible to the general superintendent and
five-member elected board of education. The central office
still maintains control over curriculum, personnel, and the
budget. Parent advisory groups are basically limited to the
traditional PTA. Whatever responsibility and power the
community has in deciding educational policy it is mainly
voiced at the polls when they vote on school bonds, taxes,
and construction.

Summary of the 16 School Systems

Some of the data pertaining to the 16 school systems
are here summarized through a narrative. Table 3.1 below
also summarizes most of the same data in a quick overview.
The reader may find it profitable to refer to this table before and while reading the narrative.

Briefly summarizing the introductory facts and figures,
we find that the city school systems, with the exception of
Portland and Minneapolis, have large minority student populations, which in most cases are growing, as evidenced by
increasing minority elementary school enrollments. In Portland and Minneapolis, where the black student population is
still a small minority, redrawing boundaries and even busing
are considered viable devices for integrating the schools
while still maintaining a white majority in every school.
The nation's suburban schools of course have fewer minority
students and in some cases an exclusively white population,
and this corresponds with the 1970 census which reports that
50 percent of the black population is concentrated in the 50
largest cities and about 33 percent in the 15 largest cities,
while about 5 percent live in the suburbs. Two exceptions
are noted with the suburban schools in this survey: Torrance, California, which has an 11 percent minority student
population, mostly Mexican-American, due to its proximity
to Mexico; and Anne Arundel County, Maryland, which has
a 12 percent black student population, due to its proximity
to Baltimore and Washington.

Approximately 85 percent of the school boards in the
nation are elected by popular vote (Vaughn, 1970). In 1968,
11 of the 50 largest school systems had appointed school
boards (National School Boards Association, 1968), illustrating that larger school systems tend to use appointive methods more frequently than smaller school systems. With

regard to the 16 selected school systems, the members of
the central board of education were usually elected. A few
exceptions were (in New York, as indicated in the next chapter and) Baltimore, Anne Arundel, Pittsburgh, Buffalo, and
Gary. But regardless of how the school board members are
selected, their orientation is usually system-wide, not community or local oriented. One difference between many large
or medium-sized city and suburban school systems is often
the size; the suburban school district is usually small
enough so that the school board's orientation, while it may
be system wide, often coincides with the community or local
residents.

The reported reading levels cannot be compared because the reported methods varied; moreover, many of the
school systems used general terms such as "low," "slightly
below the norm," "below the norm," and "average." In general, the city students read below the national norm, and
this is correlated to some extent with minority enrollments.
A gross generalization can be made between Spanish-surnamed students and black students, that the former group
does not have as intense a reading problem as the latter
group. For example, the city school system of El Paso
comprised a 53 percent Mexican-American enrollment and a
3 percent black student enrollment, yet the reading scores
were reported as slightly below the national norm. (Of
course, "slightly below" is a vague phrase.) The Dade
County school system reported more precise data, showing
that black students started off two months behind in reading
at the first grade and ended up more than 2.5 years behind
the norm at the twelfth grade (not counting dropouts whose
scores are often lower than those who remain to finish high
school), while white students started off two months ahead of
the reading norm in the first grade and ended up more than
one year ahead of the national norm at the twelfth grade.
Thus the reading discrepancy between the black and white
students was more than 3.5 years by the twelfth grade; this
corresponds with the Coleman et al. (1966) data. It should
be noted that the Dade County Spanish-surnamed students,
mostly Cuban, started out one month behind the norms at the
first grade and ended up five months behind the norm at the
twelfth grade.

The financial plight of the schools has recently become a major problem; in fact, the President's Commission
on School Finance, in its report School, People and Money
(1972), believes it is the most urgent problem facing the

schools. In general, the city schools spend less money per student than the suburbs, partly because of a limited tax base and municipal overburden. The HEW Urban Education Task Force's report (1970), submitted to President Nixon, sums up the current situation: "Far more money is being spent on the suburban child who generally enjoys the advantages of educational motivation, educated parents, resources to provide additional tutoring, etc. , than on the inner-city child whose educational needs are greater and whose extra school resources to meet them are fewer" (p. 47). Moreover, the states' "equalization aid" among districts within their boundaries perpetuate these differences. [11]

It is impossible to make valid tax comparisons among the selected 16 school systems, because tax rates were not always based on a 100 percent assessment ratio and the assessment levels varied considerably. For example, the tax rate for Anne Arundel County schools was $3. 35 and the assessment rate was at 49 percent. The school system could drop its rate to $1. 67, simply by raising the assessment to 100 percent of true value. On the other hand, the Dade County tax rate was $1. 03 but the assessment rate was already 100 percent of true value.

While the expenditures per student are listed in Table 3. 1, it is still difficult to make very useful comparisons. Three school systems reported instructional costs, while the remaining reported total spending. The trouble with total costs is that school systems have various methods for determining such costs; some do while others do not include reserves and balances, capital improvement, and contracted funds. Comparisons are difficult and confusing.

According to the Digest of Educational Statistics (1972), the nation's collective elementary and secondary school budget totaled $48. 8 billion during the 1971-72 school year. Of this total, 54. 3 percent was derived from local sources, 36. 7 percent from state sources, 8. 8 percent from federal sources, and . 2 percent from other sources. The average school system in this survey derived between 50 and 65 percent of its budget from local sources, about 35 to 54 percent from state sources, and less than 10 percent from federal sources. This corresponds with the national averages. Exceptions to the rule were Dade County, Baltimore, Buffalo, and El Paso which derived less than 50 percent from local sources and Denver, Portland, and Torrance which were granted more than 65 percent from local sources. It is also abstruse to determine a pattern to this spending, only that perhaps the latter school systems are able to tax their local residents more heavily to supplement state and federal monies.

After introducing facts and figures about each school system, data related to administrative decentralization and community participation were outlined. What tends to emerge is that 15 out of 16 medium-sized school systems have decentralized or are considering decentralization. The one exception is Denver, but even Denver has an indirect type of decentralization based on nine official community advisory groups for each of its nine high schools and feeding schools. Twelve of the 14 school systems started the administrative decentralization process in or since 1969. The three exceptions were St. Louis (in 1962), Dade County (in 1963) and Minneapolis (in 1967). There were two types of decentralization: that in which the entire school system decentralized, which was most frequent, or in which part of the system decentralized--this was the case in Minneapolis (inner-city schools) and Gary and Indianapolis (elementary schools). In still another case, but not dealing with any of the 16 selected school systems, the Clark County school system decentralized and later returned to centralization. [12]

The reasons for decentralization were mainly administrative: to break down the bureaucracy, to reduce the span of administrative control, to bring the administration closer to the schools, and to enhance communication between the schools and central office. (To achieve these objectives, there was usually a realignment of administrative personnel from the central office to the field. Often there was a concurrent problem of financing and an attempt was made to reduce the number of administrative personnel to save money.) In a fewer number of cases, the reasons were to bring continuity to the K-12 program and to make the schools more responsive to the needs of the community. (To achieve these objectives, the departments and superintendent offices of elementary and secondary education were often dismantled or merged together at the central office and subdistrict level and a number of community advisory groups were formed to enhance school-community relations.) The most extensive list of reasons for decentralization were purported by Baltimore:

1.   Improve the quality of education for all students;
2.   Preserve the uniqueness of communities;

3. Maintain racial heterogeneity and a multi-ethnic society;
4. Increase community participation;
5. Shift decision-making responsibilities from the central administration to the administrative areas;
6. Provide accountability at the area level;
7. Provide responsible autonomy at the school level;
8. Increase supervisory and supportive staff at the area and school levels;
9. Coordinate the curriculum from pre-kindergarten to adult education; and
10. Increase flexible enrollment policies. [The reader should note that school desegregation is not mentioned as one of the ten objectives.]

The decentralized unit names varied and included such terms as "areas," "districts," "regions," "units," and "pyramids," with the first term being used in more than half the school systems. In two cases, St. Louis and Indianapolis, the decentralized unit was further divided into smaller units; this is a similar organizational pattern once used by Los Angeles (second largest school system) which had four zones subdivided into 12 areas and still used by Chicago (third largest school system), which has three areas subdivided into 27 districts.

The number of decentralized units varied: from as little as two pyramids in Minneapolis to as many as ten units in St. Louis and ten areas in Indianapolis. At the present, the greatest number of decentralized units organized has been in New York City (largest school system), with 32 community school districts (see Chapter 4). The approximate number of students per decentralized unit varied from as little as 5000-9500 students in Indianapolis and 7000 to 8000 in Gary to as much as 34,000 to 40,000 in Houston and 31,000 to 48,000 in Dade County. As a point of comparison, the most common size was between 20,000 and 25,000 students: this corresponds with the Anne Arundel survey (1970) of 55 school systems, where the most common decentralized unit comprised between 18,000 and 25,000 students. In this connection, Havighurst and Levine (1971) contend that the ideal size for an administrative decentralized unit is from 25,000 to 30,000 students--contending that this should be large enough to carry on necessary local functions and instructional and innovative services with a good deal of efficiency yet still have some room to grow without becoming too large for effective administration. Similarly, the Mayor's

Advisory Panel (1967), which wrote the now famous Bundy report, maintained that the figure should be 12,000 to 40,000 students--each unit large enough to implement a full range of educational services, yet small enough to maintain proximity to community needs and to promote diversity and administrative flexibility. Although there is no validity to these recommended sizes, the general idea is to provide a broad base of educational services and professional expertise with increased administrative efficiency but without extreme dilution.

Most of the school systems appeared to have racially integrated student bodies at the decentralized level; it appeared to stop, however, at this level. Whenever statistics or legal data on the racial compositions at the individual school level were supplied, such as in the case of Dade County, Houston, Denver, Buffalo, and Gary, most of the individual schools remained de facto segregated. Even if the schools are desegregated the classes most likely will remain segregated to a large extent, since such homogeneous grouping still exists in most schools across the country. The Buffalo school system seems to be the only school system surveyed which was trying to combine decentralization with desegregation on the individual school level, but this part of the plan has already been vetoed by the school board after pressure from a vocal number of black and white opponents.

As previously mentioned, none of the 16 school systems reported any type of community control--that is, legal provisions for an elected community school board as in the case of Detroit or New York City (to be discussed in the next chapter). A far more frequent arrangement beyond the usual PTA and school voluntary groups was the appointment of advisory committees on the school, subdistrict, and/or central-wide basis. These committees were usually appointed by the administration from one or more of these three organizational levels; only in a few cases (and not in toto in any school system except apparently Houston) were these advisory groups elected by the community. Nevertheless, in all cases these committees were advisory in nature, as their names suggest, and whenever guidelines had been established the school boards reaffirmed their own power and expectations that the advisory committees abide by the rules and regulations.

The advisory groups often included parents, community

residents, representatives from various agencies, students, teachers, and administrators. Parents were usually defined as adults with children enrolled in school, and community residents were usually defined as adults who did not necessarily have children attending the public schools. The community agencies most often represented were business, labor, church, political, and social governmental groups. Students readily appeared on advisory groups, probably as a result of the recent interest in students' rights and the increased willingness to permit them to express themselves about policies that affect their education. There also tended to be a desire by the school system to have a representative racial mix from the community.

The extent of community participation ranged from limited to extensive. The one school system (Denver) that had no formal plans for administrative decentralization permitted average to extensive community participation, illustrating to a limited extent that a medium-sized city school system need not necessarily decentralize to implement community participation. On the other hand, there were decentralized school systems--such as Dade County, Indianapolis, Anne Arundel County and Torrance--which appeared to limit community participation; moreover, three of these four school systems are either partially suburban or exclusively suburban, thus indicating (at least in this survey) that the suburban schools which commonly are considered to have extensive community participation, and sometimes even community control, do not necessarily have such extensive local input. [13]

In sum, most of the selected school systems were willing to adopt or consider plans for administrative decentralization and community participation. As mentioned in Chapter two, the reasons tended to be based on intuition, logic, and polemics from educational literature, possibly an unwritten reason was the pressure to change the system under some notion of reform, and these two organizational plans were the most acceptable for school authorities. In the same vein, only one of the reporting school systems (Oakland) indicated that an evaluative procedure for administrative decentralization or community participation had been implemented and only one school system (Anne Arundel County) pointed out the need for pilot-testing some of the assumptions, goals, and recommendations made in their respective reports.

As for community control, this apparently was not a major issue with the aforementioned school systems; there were no data indicating that the school authorities were even seriously considering it.   Similarly, accountability was always directed towards the central office, and not toward the community.   In the 15 school decentralized plans, the principal was accountable to a decentralized unit or field superintendent, who in turn was accountable to another superintendent at the central office, who in turn was usually accountable to the school superintendent.

Educators who advocate community control, such as Mario D. Fantini and Marilyn Gittell (who comprise part of the liberal movement in education) and Charles V. Hamilton and Preston R. Wilcox (who comprise part of the black power movement in education), are apparently not convincing many school administrators, school board members, and state legislators.   They do not appear to have persuaded the educational and political authorities of the selected school systems in this survey, and these school systems represent various geographical areas across the country.   If anything, it seems that these educators are writing from an eastern, and more precisely a New York City, viewpoint which may not represent most educators of the country.   In arguing for community control, these educators and groups may represent a provincial viewpoint that is probably atypical in the field of education.   They have managed to mislead educators, in part because of the political and economic support of the Ford Foundation, the Center for Urban Education, the respective writing abilities and publishers of some liberal and black educators, and more probably because of the size and influence of the New York City school system and the nationwide headlines connected with the Ocean Hill-Brownsville experiment and the concurrent 1968 teachers' strike.   It is time that we recognize that what a small number of educators from the East, and especially New York City, vocalize is not necessarily wholly valid at this time to the rest of the country.   Granted the Detroit school system has also responded to the advocates of community control, but this is the only other one.   Granted a number of educators may become seduced by slogans and myths, but the number is small, and most educators running the schools have managed, for the greater part, to maintain control.

Table 3.1 summarizes most of the above data.   The school systems are listed in order which they first appeared in the discussion, the system with the largest enrollment

Table 3.1

MEDIUM-SIZED CITY AND SUBURBAN SCHOOLS
A SUMMARY OF SELECTED DATA

School System	Schools	Teachers	Students	Board of Education	Budget in Millions	Source of Income in Percent Terms			
						Local	State	Federal	Other
1. Dade County	234	10,057	245,025	elected	285	39.8	45.9	14.3	--
2. Houston	230	10,000	231,500	elected	157	53	44	3	--
3. Baltimore	217	7,845	190,735	appointed	197	47	46	7	--
4. Memphis	163	6,300	143,280	elected	99	57	--	--	--
5. St. Louis	179	4,175	108,550	elected	85^d	62.8	36.6	.6	--
6. Indianapolis	120	4,500^a	102,734	elected	84.6	56	--	--	--
7. Denver	121	4,437	94,838	elected	123.7	79	--	--	--
8. Anne Arundel County	99	3,600^a	75,000	appointed	82	61	--	--	--
9. Portland	114	3,600	72,306	elected	67	74	21.9	.5	3.5
10. Pittsburgh	116	3,353	70,537	appointed	92.9	55	44	1	--
11. Buffalo	98	3,549	68,344	appointed	86.1	41	52	1	6
12. Minneapolis	94	3,260	67,160	elected	72.8	59	36	.8	4.2
13. El Paso	63	2,800	62,363	elected	43	36.4	57.2	6.4	--
14. Oakland	91	--	61,600	elected	56.2	62	26	9	3
15. Gary	49	1,821	45,332	appointed	33.5	61	30	9	--
16. Torrance	42	1,409	32,625	elected	32	66	32	2	--

a. Total number of professionals
b. Instructional costs
c. Still considering options
d. Including Harris Teachers College

Table 3.1 (continued)

	School System	Expenditures per Student	Status of Decentralization	Decent. Unit Name	Number of Units	Approx. No. of Students/Unit	Extent of Community Participation[i]
1.	Dade County	$950	decent., 1963, 1965, 1971	district	6	31,000-48,000	limited
2.	Houston	680	decent., 1971	area	6	34,000-40,000	avg-extens.
3.	Baltimore	833	consid. it since 1971	area	6-9[c]	20,000-30,000[c,h]	average
4.	Memphis	630	decent., 1971	area	4	33,500-39,500	average
5.	St. Louis	1,030[e] 765[f]	decent., 1962, 1964, 1970	district unit	5 10	20,000[h] 10,000[h]	average
6.	Indianapolis	800[b]	decent., 1969[f]	region area	3 10	20,000[h] 5,000-9,500	limited
7.	Denver	918	no plans [informal decent. based on community particip.]	--	--	--	avg-extens.
8.	Anne Arundel County	833	consid. it since 1970; implem. in 1973	area	4	16,000-22,500	ltd-avg
9.	Portland	900[b,g] 725[b,f]	decent., 1970	area	3	22,000-29,000	avg-extens.
10.	Pittsburgh	938	decent., 1970	area	3	20,000-25,000[h]	average
11.	Buffalo	1,088	consid. it since 1969	district	5	12,000-15,000[c,h]	average
12.	Minneapolis	876	decent. [inner-city] 1967, 1969	pyramid	2	10,000	ltd-avg
13.	El Paso	673	decent., 1972	area	3	21,000	avg-extens.
14.	Oakland	895	decent., 1971	region	3	20,000-23,000	extensive
15.	Gary	919	decent., 1971[f]	district	3	7,000-8,000	average
16.	Torrance	790[b]	decent., 1971	area	4	7,000-9,000[h]	limited

e. High schools only
f. Elementary schools only

g. Secondary schools
h. Estimated number

i. Based on information supplied to author; no validity or model involved

Table 3.2

DECENTRALIZATION PLANS OF LARGE AND MEDIUM-SIZED
METROPOLITAN SCHOOL SYSTEMS

	School System[a]	Student Enrollment		Status of Decentralization[b]
**1	New York City	(1,100,000)	1,096,894	D
**2	Los Angeles	(750,000)	654,421	D
**3	Chicago	(576,000)	574,230	D
**4	Detroit	(300,000)		D
**5	Philadelphia	(290,000)		D; consid. D at indiv. school level
*6	Dade Co., Fla.	(245,025)	242,486	D
*7	Houston	(231,500)	234,449	D
*8	Baltimore (City)	(190,735)	193,150	consid. D
*9	Prince George's Co., Md.		155,000	D
*10	Memphis	(145,850)	134,500	D
11	Hawaii State		141,802	no plans
12	San Diego		130,398	no plans
13	Fairfax Co., Va.		130,157	D
14	Baltimore Co., Md.		129,661	D
15	Montgomery Co., Md.		124,500	D
16	Broward Co., Fla.		112,452	D
17	New Orleans		111,939	D
18	Atlanta		111,656	D
19	Columbus		110,000	no plans
*20	St. Louis	(108,550)	109,550	D
21	Hillsborough Co., Fla.		103,457	no plans
*22	Indianapolis	(102,734)	107,747	D (elem.)
23	Metropol. Nashville		96,000	D
24	Boston		95,312	D
*25	Denver	(94,838)		no plans (informal D based on community particip.)

---

*data based on current survey
**data based on Ornstein (1972)
[no asterisk] data based on Anne Arundel survey (1970)
a. As many as 55 out of 70 school systems (79 percent) responded to the Anne Arundel survey. For the chapter, 19 out of 25 school systems (76 percent) responded, but three school systems were omitted (Clark County, Nevada; Columbus, Ohio; and Fairfax County, Virginia) because the data furnished were incomplete.
b. D stands for decentralized, or decentralization.

Table 3.2 (continued)

	School System		Student Enrollment		Status of Decentralization[b]
26	Jefferson Co., Ky.			89,835	no plans
27	Fort Worth			86,415	consid. D
28	Seattle			85,502	D
29	Cincinnati			84,843	consid. D
30	Pinellas Co., Fla.			82,000	no plans
31	Orange Co., Fla.			81,577	no plans
32	Tulsa			79,566	no plans
33	San Antonio			78,352	D
34	Clark Co., Nev.	(	76,000)		D; then centralized
35	Newark			75,876	no plans
*36	Anne Arundel Co., Md.	(	75,000)	70,660	D
37	Mobile			73,076	no plans
*38	Portland, Ore.	(	72,306)	77,684	D
39	Kansas City, Mo.			72,702	no plans
*40	Pittsburgh	(	70,737	73,062	D
*41	Buffalo	(	68,344)	70,803	consid. D
*42	Minneapolis	(	67,160)	69,000	D (inner-city)
43	Wichita			66,651	no plans
44	Jefferson Co., Ala.			65,792	no plans
*45	El Paso	(	62,363)	62,000	D
46	Toledo			62,145	D
47	Omaho			62,000	consid. D
*48	Oakland, Cal.	(	61,600)		D
49	Fresno, Cal.			57,387	no plans
50	Dayton			57,015	no plans
51	Akron			56,838	no plans
52	Norfolk, Va.			56,500	no plans
53	San Juan, Cal.			--	no plans
54	Decatur, Ala.			--	no plans
55	Garden Grove, Cal.			--	D
56	Greenville Co., S. C.			--	no plans
57	Jacksonville, Fla.			--	no plans
58	Jefferson Co., Col.			--	no plans
59	Sacramento			--	no plans
60	Salt Lake City			--	no plans
*61	Gary, Ind.	(	45,332)		D (elem.)
*62	Torrance, Cal.	(	32,625)		D

first and so on in descending order. Some of the data is incomplete, as indicated by small dashes in certain columns,
because it was unavailable.

In order to widen the reader's knowledge of school decentralization, Table 3.2 is presented; it combines data
from the Anne Arundel survey (1970), Ornstein's (1972)
discussion of the five largest school systems, and the current
data on the 16 medium-sized city and suburban school systems. There is some overlap among the three sources of
data. Of the five school systems discussed by Ornstein (1972),
three were also polled in the Anne Arundel survey (1970).
Of the 16 school systems polled for this chapter, 11 were
also polled by the Anne Arundel survey (1970). This means
there is overlap with 14 schools, as illustrated by the two
sets of student enrollment figures for these school systems;
in total there are 62 different school systems.

The school systems are listed in descending order according to student enrollment. The student enrollment figures
on the right side correspond with data from the Anne Arundel
survey (1970), and it is derived mainly from the 1969-70
school year. The student figures on the left side in paren-
theses correspond with the data collected from Ornstein's
(1972) discussion which is based on the 1970-71 school year,
as well as from the current survey for this chapter which is
based in 1971 and 1972 data.

Of the 55 school systems polled in the Anne Arundel
survey (1970), 20 had decentralized and seven were considering it. In the Ornstein (1972) document, all five school systems had some form of administrative decentralization. In
the aforementioned survey, 15 of the 16 school systems had
decentralized or were considering it. Four school systems
(Houston, Memphis, Buffalo, and El Paso) that reported no
plan for administrative decentralization during the Anne
Arundel survey (1970), had decentralized or were considering
it by the time of this survey.

Conclusion

Fifty-five out of 70 school systems (79 percent) responded to the Anne Arundel survey (1970). Although 19 out
of 25 school systems (76 percent) responded to the current
survey, only sixteen were included. The Anne Arundel

survey also included three school systems mentioned by Ornstein (1972) and 11 school systems mentioned in the current
survey. Combining the three sources of data, 62 school systems were listed; 35 of these systems comprised 75,000 or
more students; 27 of these decentralized or were considering
it; and in addition, one school system moved from decentralization to centralization. Twenty-five school systems
comprised between 50,000 and less than 75,000 students.
Eight of these had decentralized or were considering it. The
two school systems with student enrollments below 50,000
students had surprisingly decentralized. Of the 62 school
systems, only two had implemented legal provisions for community control--Detroit and New York City which are discussed in the last chapter.

NOTES

1. These findings tend to correspond with the 1970 Anne
   Arundel survey, Decentralization Plans Followed by
   Public School Systems With Student Enrollments of
   50,000 or More. In formulating their own plans for
   decentralization, the Anne Arundel school system
   polled seventy other school systems enrolling 50,000
   or more students. At that time twenty-seven of the
   fifty-five responding systems had either completed the
   process of decentralization or were considering it.
   Detroit had not yet decentralized or implemented control; thus "only one of the respondents [New York
   City] ... made legal provisions for elected, local-
   community school boards. A far more popular arrangement [in lieu of] ... community control [was]
   the appointment of advisory committees at the subdistrict level" (p. 2).

2. From the tables: (1) "Ethnic Composition of Pupil Population ... 1965-71," September 1971; (2) "Employed
   Personnel ... December 1971," January 1972; and
   (3) "Dade County Public Schools by District: 1971-
   72," September 1971.

3. The increase in reading scores at the secondary level is
   correlated with the larger percentages of whites in the
   secondary schools. Whites constantly showed improvements, starting two months ahead of the norms at the
   first grade and 14 months ahead in the twelfth grade.
   However, black students, mostly from low-income

families constantly showed lower scores, starting
about two months behind in the first grade and ending up 32 months behind by the twelfth grade.
Spanish-surnamed student scores started one month
behind at the first grade, reached a maximum low
of eight months behind in the ninth grade, then
showed improvement by ending up five months behind the norm at the twelfth grade.

4. One might ask why it is that Dade County schools are
    able to obtain such a large percentage of their bud-
    get from state and federal sources. Gillingham
    (1972c, 1972d) points out that money from the state
    ranges from 35 to 55 percent annually. Most of the
    state's outlay (73 percent) is determined by average
    daily attendance of students but "the legislature some-
    times allows several years to elapse before increas-
    ing the dollar value of an instructional unit or pro-
    viding other funds" (p. 1). Much of the federal
    money is geared toward defraying the cost of edu-
    cating the Cuban refugee children.

5. Pre-decentralization model: Houston Independent School
    District Tentative Chart of Organization (1961), Cur-
    rent Upper-Level of Organization Structure (n. d.);
    post-decentralization: Houston Independent School
    District (n. d.), Instructional Division (n. d.).

6. For a summary of the court cases regarding desegre-
    gation of the Houston schools, see Kelly Frels, at-
    torney at law, office of Bracewell & Patterson, let-
    ter to William D. Broyles, Jr. , Administrative As-
    sistant in Charge of Community Relations, Houston
    Independent School District, December 3, 1971.

7. School officials who communicated to the author from
    St. Louis, Pittsburgh, Buffalo, and Torrance did
    not want to be quoted by name. Their requests
    have been respected.

8. In answer to my questions, James M. Voigt (1972),
    public schools specialist, points out the Portland
    school system has no specific transfer plan for the
    elementary schools. However, the school system
    is "continuing to study methods to achieve integra-
    tion. " Neller (1972b) asserts that only one high
    school exceeds the 25 percent concentration level,

and steps are being taken to reduce this racial proportion.

9. The 1972-73 proposed school budget for operation and
maintenance totaled $84.8 million, and considering
slight changes in student enrollment figures this
would have brought Buffalo's average per-student
cost to approximately $1,120 (Proposed Expendi-
tures, 1972-73). However, the approved operating
budget totals only 78.1 million, a per-pupil cost of
approximately $1,116.

10. One might ask why the reading levels are well only
slightly below national norms. Remember, there is
a large percentage of Mexican-American students,
most from low-income levels and many who probably
have difficulty (at least in the early grades) com-
municating in English. Schools with a large Spanish-
surnamed student population might explore the reasons for relatively high norms with the El Paso
school personnel. One should also note that most
of the school budget is derived from state money.
This is unusual, indicating in part the financial
plight of the city or the political influence the city
has at the state level.

11. Lekachman (1972) points out that equal dollars spent for
each student do not lead to genuine equal education,
much less equality of results. Reaffirming the findings of the Coleman report, that family characteristics are more important than the best schools or the
amount of school expenditures, he contends that the
school system need not add to the present handicaps
of poor and inner-city children. He argues the need
for more money for poor schools than rich schools,
and to tax the rich to educate the poor.
    Strong opposition to this view can be found by
Finn and Lenkowsky (1972), who argue that school
monies are not correlated with school achievement,
as evidenced by the Coleman data and the failure of
compensatory education. Increased educational expenditures will not produce educational achievement;
rather, it will lead to the poor and "have-little" taxpayers paying more money so that teachers can earn
more. (A side note: about 70 percent of school expenditures is devoted to salaries for teachers and
administrators.) Moynihan (1972) takes a similar

position, also contending that until we find out effective ways to achieve the goals of education, increasing costs will in effect mean a waste of money.

12.   Charles A. Fleming (1972a, 1972b), information services coordinator, points out that the Clark County
school system, consisting of 280,000 people who are
mainly concentrated in Las Vegas, Nevada, comprises 91 schools, 5200 personnel including 3000
teachers, and 76,000 students.   He (1972b) states
that the school system moved from centralization to
decentralization then back to centralization.   "We
are completing our third year after doing away with
the zones, each headed by a zone superintendent,
and we are quite happy with the present arrangement" (p. 1).

13.   This tends to confirm the research by Minar (1966):
that the affluent communities have lower levels of
school electoral participation and conflict than working class communities.   Wood (1958) has shown that
suburban dwellers are indifferent toward most school
matters and take on a non-political ideology.   Banfield and Wilson (1936) point out that the middle-
class ethos of suburbia rejects the idea of the political machine and politics in education.   Working-
class and lower-class people tend to seek personal
benefits from the political machine and recognize
the legitimacy of conflicts between groups with nar-
row and special interests, in turn giving rise to
local politics and politics in education.   Boyd (1971,
1972), and O'Shea (1971) have pointed out that middle-class suburban communities tend to define public
interest in terms of the whole community and are
more impartial and disinterested in school matters
than working-class and lower-class communities.

REFERENCES*

DADE COUNTY, Fla.

Administrative Organization Charts: Dade County Public
    Schools Miami, Florida. Miami: Administrative Re-
    search Division, Dade County Public Schools, Decem-
    ber 1, 1971.

Administrative Reorganization in the Dade County Schools.
    Submitted by Joseph Hall, Superintendent of Schools to
    Members of the Board of Public Instruction. Miami:
    Dade County Public Schools, June 12, 1963.

"Comparative Costs per Pupil for Operation of Schools,
    1965-66, 1970-71." Miami: Administrative Research
    Division, Dade County Public Schools, (n. d.).

Comparison of Administrative, Supervisory and Technical
    Positions in the Dade County Public Schools, 1962-63,
    1966-67, 1970-71, 1971-72. Miami: Administrative
    Research Division, Dade County Public Schools, Jan-
    uary 1972.

"Dade County Public Schools by District, 1971-72." Miami:
    Administrative Research Division, Dade County Public
    Schools, September 1971.

"Employed Personnel, Number and Average Salary, Decem-
    ber 1971." Miami: Administrative Research Division,
    Dade County Public Schools, January 1972.

"Ethnic Composition of Pupil Population by District and
    Countywide, 1965-71." Miami: Administrative Research
    Division, Dade County Public Schools, September 1971.

Gillingham, Johnathan. Director of Administrative Research,
    Dade County Public Schools. Letter to the Author,
    January 28, 1972 (a).

_____. Letter to the Author, March 14, 1972 (b).

---

*To facilitate matters, the references have been arranged in
this chapter according to the order in which the school systems were discussed, then alphabetized. Finally, supplementary references appear at the back of these groupings.

_____. Letter to the Author, April 21, 1972 (c).

_____. Letter to the Author, June 28, 1972 (d).

Miami Herald, November 24, 1971.

Organization of the Dade County Schools into Four Districts.
    Submitted by Joseph Hall, Superintendent, to all Princi-
    pals and Members of the Board of Public Instruction.
    Miami: Dade County Public Schools, August 14, 1963.

Reorganization of Dade County School System into Six Dis-
    tricts. Submitted by Joseph Hall, Superintendent, to
    Members of the Board of Public Instruction. Miami:
    Dade County Public Schools, August 24, 1964.

"Your School Dollar: 1970-71." Miami: Administrative Re-
    search Division, Dade County Public Schools, n. d.

HOUSTON

Aleman, Tony. Consultant for Community Relations, Houston
    Public Schools. Letter to the Author, March 10, 1972
    (a).

_____. Letter to the Author, March 29, 1972 (b).

Broyles, William D. , Jr. Administrative Assistant in Charge
    of Community Relations, Houston Public Schools. Letter
    to the Author, February 1, 1972.

Current Upper-Level of Organization Structure. Houston:
    Independent School District, (n. d.).

Frels, Kelly. Attorney at Law, Office of Bracewell & Pat-
    terson, Houston. Letter to William D. Broyles, Jr. ,
    December 3, 1971.

HEW School Campus Report: 1969-71. Houston: Public Ac-
    counting Department, Houston Independent School District,
    October 18, 1971.

Houston Independent School District. Houston: Houston In-
    dependent School District, n. d.

Houston Independent School District Bulletin. Houston:

Independent School District, February 25, 1971.

Houston Independent School District Board Meeting. December 14, 1970.

Houston Independent School District Management Review and Analysis, Vol. I. Submitted by Peat, Marvick, Mitchell & Co. to the Superintendent of Schools. Houston: The Author, November 1970.

Houston Independent School District Tentative Chart of Organization. Houston: Independent School District, October 3, 1961.

Instructional Division. Houston: Independent School District, (n. d.)

National Educational Secretary, November 1971.

Public School Finances in Harris County, Texas 1970-71. Houston: Tax Research Association, February 1972.

Racial Composition of H. I. S. D. Certified Employees, 1969-71. Houston: Personnel Service Office and the Research Analysis Office, Houston Independent School District, August 25, 1971.

A Report of the Results of the Iowa Tests of Basic Skills Elementary Schools--Grades 3-6. Houston: Group Testing Support Services, Houston Independent School District, November 11, 1971.

Ross v Rogers. (S. D. Tex. , No. 10444), October 15, 1957.

_____. (317 F. Supp. , 512, S. Ct. Tex.), May 30, 1970 (a).

_____. (434 F. 2nd, No. 1140, 5th Cir.) August 5, 1970. Summary reprinted by the HISD. (b).

_____. (S. D. Tex. , No. 10444), May 24, 1971.

BALTIMORE

Baltimore City Community Schools. Baltimore: Community Schools Division, Baltimore City Public Schools, 1971.

The Baltimore City Public Schools Organizational Chart.
    Baltimore: City Public Schools, October 9, 1971.

The Superintendent's Options for Decentralization. A Mes-
    sage from Roland N. Patterson, Superintendent of
    Schools, to the People and School Staff of Baltimore.
    Baltimore: City Public Schools, January 1972.

White, Howard E., Jr. Educational Assistant to the Super-
    intendent, Baltimore City Public Schools. Letter to the
    Author, February 14, 1972 (a).

_____. Letter to the Author, March 24, 1972 (b).

_____. Letter to the Author, June 28, 1972 (c).

MEMPHIS

Commercial Appeal, December 6, 1970.

Counce, Shelby. Deputy Superintendent of Schools, Memphis
    Public Schools. Letter to the Author, February 2, 1972
    (a).

_____. Letter to the Author, March 10, 1972 (b).

_____. Letter to the Author, June 27, 1971 (c).

One Year of Decentralization. Report by Shelby Counce,
    Deputy Superintendent. Memphis: Board of Education,
    June 12, 1972.

A Plan for Implementation of Decentralization in the Memphis
    City Public Schools for the 1971-72 School Year. Sub-
    mitted by the Superintendent's Executive Council to the
    Board of Education. Memphis: Board of Education,
    May 1, 1971.

A Staff Reorganization Study of the Memphis, Tennessee,
    School System. Submitted by the Committee to Study
    the Organizational Structure of the Memphis, Tennessee,
    Public Schools to the Board of Education. Memphis:
    Board of Education, April 15, 1970.

Superintendent's Recommendation Staff Reorganization Study.
    Submitted by E. C. Stimbert, Superintendent of Schools,

to the Members of the Board of Education.   Memphis: Board of Education, June 19, 1970.

ST. LOUIS

Facts for 1971-72.   St. Louis: Public Schools, (n. d.).

Recommendations for Greater Local Participation in the To-
    tal Operation of the St. Louis Public Schools.   From the
    Office of the Superintendent of Schools.   St. Louis:
    Public Schools, January 14, 1969.

St. Louis Information Officer.   Letter to the Author, n. d. ,
    1972 (a).

_____.   Letter to the Author, June 28, 1972 (b).

St. Louis Public Schools Reorganization Plan.   From the
    Office of the Superintendent of Schools.   St. Louis:
    Public Schools, June 9, 1970.

School and Home, September 1970.

INDIANAPOLIS

Area Organization Plan for Elementary Schools, Ten Areas--
    1971.   Indianapolis: Planning Division, Indianapolis Pub-
    lic Schools, December 23, 1971.

Miller, Paul I.   Assistant Superintendent for Elementary
    Education, Indianapolis Public Schools.   Letter to the
    Author, May 2, 1972.

Payne, Joseph C.   Assistant to the Superintendent, Planning
    Division, Indianapolis Public Schools.   Letter to the
    Author, March 15, 1972 (a).

_____.   Letter to the Author, April 11, 1972 (b).

_____.   Letter to the Author, June 26, 1972 (c).

DENVER

Denver Public Schools Budget Advisory Committees and Area

Councils. Denver: Department of Planning, Research, and Budgeting, Denver Public Schools, 1972.

Denver School District Administration and Supervision Organization Chart. Denver: Public Schools, (n. d.).

Elledge, Gerald E. Supervisor of the Department of Planning, Research and Budgeting, Denver Public Schools. Letter to the Author, February 2, 1972 (a).

_____. Letter to the Author, March 13, 1972 (b).

_____. Letter to the Author, April 10, 1972 (c).

_____. Letter to the Author, June 27, 1972 (d).

ANNE ARUNDEL COUNTY, Md.

Alsobrook, H. Lewis. Officer for Program Planning and Evaluation, Anne Arundel County Public Schools. Letter to the Author, March 10, 1972 (a).

_____. Letter to the Author, June 17, 1972 (b).

Recommendations Concerning Administrative Decentralization of the Anne Arundel County School System. Submitted by the Superintendent's Committee on Decentralization. Annapolis, Md: Anne Arundel County Public Schools, April 1970.

PORTLAND, Ore.

Nellor, John H. Director of the Public Information Department, Portland Public Schools. Letter to the Author, February 28, 1972 (a).

_____. Letter to the Author, June 29, 1972 (b).

Plan for Administrative Reorganization. Submitted by Robert W. Blanchard, Superintendent of the Schools, to Members of the Board of Education. Portland: Public Schools, June 1, 1970.

Portland Public Schools Area Organization Plan. Portland: Public Schools, March 23, 1970.

Portland Public Schools Central Organization.   Portland:
    Public Schools, July 1971.

Portland Public Schools Directory.   Portland: Public Infor-
    mation Department, Portland Public Schools, (n. d.).

Portland Schools for the Seventies.   From the Board of Edu-
    cation, Resolution No. 3553, Adopted by the Board of
    Education on March 23, 1970.   Portland: Public Schools,
    1970.

Rules of Procedures for Area Advisory Committees.   From
    the Board of Education, Resolution No. 5292, Adopted
    by the Board of Education on June 28, 1971, and Resolu-
    tion No. 5332, Adopted by the Board of Education on
    July 12, 1971.   Portland: Public Schools, 1971.

Voigt, James M.   Public Information Specialist, Portland
    Public Schools.   Letter to the Author, April 10, 1972.

The World: A Tabulation of Facts and Figures, 1971-72.
    Portland: Public Information Department, Portland
    Public Schools, 1971.

PITTSBURGH

Estimated Receipts of Local Taxes.   Pittsburgh: Public
    Schools, 1972.

News from Pittsburgh Public Schools.   Pittsburgh: Office of
    Information Services and Community Relations, Pittsburgh
    Public Schools, November 9, 1971.

Pittsburgh Board of Education Meeting, February 24, 1970.

Pittsburgh Information Officer.   Letter to the Author,
    March 13, 1972 (a).

_____.   Letter to the Author, March 22, 1972 (b).

_____.   Letter to the Author, April 13, 1972 (c).

_____.   Letter to the Author, April 24, 1972 (d).

_____.   Letter to the Author, June 28, 1972 (e).

"Pittsburgh Public Schools Comparison of Expenditures."
    Pittsburgh: Public Schools, March 25, 1971.

BUFFALO, N.Y.

Annual Report of the Superintendent, 1970-71.   Buffalo:
    Board of Education, (n.d.).

Buffalo Board of Education Meeting, February 26, 1969.

_____.   January 14, 1970 (a).

_____.   February 11, 1970 (b).

_____.   March 29, 1972.

Buffalo Courier Express, October 30, 1969.

_____.   November 3, 1972.

Buffalo Evening News, August 13, 1969.

Buffalo Information Officer.   Letter to the Author, May 15,
    1972 (a).

_____.   Letter to the Author, September 8, 1972 (b).

Buffalo Public Schools Facts and Figures, 1971-72.   Buffalo:
    Division of Finance and Research, Board of Educ., 1972.

Buffalo Public Schools Report. Board of Education, 1959.

Decentralization Study.   Submitted by the Decentralization
    Study Committee to the Board of Education.   Buffalo:
    Board of Education, January 1970.

Ethnic Census of the Buffalo Public Schools, 1971-72.   Buf-
    falo: Division of Finance and Research, Buffalo Board
    of Education, February 1972.

Knapp, Roger. Assistant Professor of Education, Canisius Col-
    lege in Buffalo. Conversation with the Author, May 5, 1972.

Manch, Joseph. "Statement on Decentralization." Submitted
    by the Superintendent to the Board of Education. Buffalo:
    Board of Education, March 11, 1969.

_____. Superintendent of Schools.   Letter to the Mem-
    bers of the Board of Education, January 14, 1970.

Proposed Expenditures, 1972-73.   Buffalo: Department of
    School-Community Relations, Buffalo Board of Education,
    April 21, 1972.

A Study of Desegregation.   Submitted by the Advisory Plan-
    ning Council on Desegregation to the Superintendent.
    Buffalo: Board of Education, February 21, 1972.

Superintendent's Goals--1972.   Buffalo: Board of Education,
    (n. d.).

Your Schools at Work.   Buffalo: Department of School-
    Community Relations, Buffalo Board of Education,
    September 1969.

Your Schools at Work.   Buffalo: Department of School-
    Community Relations, Buffalo Board of Education,
    September 1970.

MINNEAPOLIS

Annual Report, 1970-71.   Minneapolis: Public Schools, 1971.

Decentralization of Schools in Minneapolis.   Submitted by
    John B. Davis, Jr. , Superintendent of Schools, to the
    Members of the Board of Education.   Minneapolis:
    Public Schools, (n. d.).

Johnson, Ralph H.   Director of the Department of Guidance
    Services, Minneapolis Public Schools.   Letter to August
    Rivera in Response to the Author's Inquiry of March 17,
    1972.

Minneapolis Board of Education Meeting, January 14, 1969.

North Pyramid News, September 1968.

Organization Chart of Minneapolis Public Schools.   Minneap-
    olis: Public Schools, 1970.

Rivera, August.   Director of Information Services, Minneap-
    olis Public Schools.   Letter to the Author, March 21,
    1972.

EL PASO, Texas

Administrative Communication of El Paso Public Schools.
    El Paso: El Paso Independent School District, August 1,
    1972.

"Community Involvement. " El Paso: El Paso Independent
    School District, (n. d.).

El Paso Herald-Post, July 20, 1972.

El Paso Times, July 21, 1972.

Ferrell, Keith H.   Technical Writer, Division of Adminis-
    tration, El Paso Public Schools.   Letter to the Author,
    January 31, 1972 (a).

_____.   Letter to the Author, March 17, 1972 (b).

_____.   Letter to the Author, April 18, 1972 (c).

_____.   Letter to the Author, November 9, 1972 (d).

Organization Chart, El Paso Independent School District.   El
    Paso: El Paso Independent School District, 1971.

OAKLAND, Cal.

Administrative Regions.   Submitted by Marcus A. Foster,
    Superintendent of Schools, to Principals and Central Of-
    fice Administrative-Supervisory Staff.   Oakland: Public
    Schools, March 4, 1971.

Larsen, Edwin P.   Director of Research, Oakland Public
    Schools.   Letter to the Author, February 21, 1972.

Master Plan Citizens Committee Guidelines.   Adopted by the
    Oakland Board of Education on January 19, 1971.   Oak-
    land: Public Schools, 1971.

Oakland Unified School District Master Plan Citizens Commit-
    tee.   Request for Proposals: Technical Assistance for
    the OPS Master Plan Citizens Committee.   Oakland:
    The Author, February 1, 1972.

Plan for Creation of Administrative Regions.   Submitted by

Marcus A. Foster, Superintendent of Schools, to Members of the Board of Education. Oakland: Public Schools, December 15, 1970.

Recommendations for Improving the Management Effectiveness of the Oakland Unified Schools. Submitted by Price-Waterhouse Co. to the Superintendent of Schools. Oakland: The Company, September 1970.

Statistical and Financial Data, 1970-71. Oakland: Public Schools, 1971.

GARY, Ind.

Battle, Haron J. Assistant Superintendent of Educational Services, Gary Public Schools. Letter to the Author, March 28, 1972 (a).

_____. Letter to the Author, June 29, 1972 (b).

Coalition to Save Our Schools. Mimeographed, 1972.

Gary Public Schools Staff and Pupil Enrollment Census by Ethnic Groups for the 1969-70, 1970-71, and 1971-72 School Years. Gary: Office of Research and Developmental Services, Gary Public Schools, October 28, 1971.

Kindergarten-Elementary Council. Mimeographed, 1972.

Malloy, William. Special Education Officer, Gary Public Schools. Letter to the Author, June 15, 1972.

Pulaski Area Council. Mimeographed, 1972.

Pulaski Early Learning Center School City of Gary. Gary: Public Schools, 1972.

Reciprocal Education Program. Mimeographed, n. d.

A Report to the Community from the School City of Gary. Gary: Public Schools, 1972.

School City of Gary District Organization of Elementary Schools. Gary: Office of the Assistant Superintendent of Educational Services, Gary Public Schools, September 17, 1971.

School City of Gary District Organization of Secondary
    Schools. Gary: Office of the Assistant Superintendent
    of Educational Services, Gary Public Schools, Septem-
    ber 17, 1971.

"School City of Gary Professional Staff Organizational Table."
    Gary: Office of the Assistant Superintendent of Educa-
    tional Services, Gary Public Schools, September 23,
    1971.

Secondary Schools Parents Council. Mimeographed, 1972.

Title III ESEA Parent-Child Mobile Classroom. Mimeo-
    graphed (n. d.).

TORRANCE, Cal.

Torrance Administrative Superintendent. Letter to the Au-
    thor, February 25, 1972 (a).

_____. Letter to the Author, March 2, 1972 (b).

_____. Letter to the Author, July 6, 1972 (c).

Torrance Unified School District Organizational Chart. Tor-
    rance: Unified School District, October 1971.

1972 Statistical Report. Torrance: Unified School District,
    1972.

SUPPLEMENTARY REFERENCES

Anne Arundel County Public Schools. Decentralization Plans
    Followed by Public School Systems with Student Enroll-
    ment of 50,000 or More. Annapolis, Md: The Author,
    March 5, 1970.

Banfield, Edward C. and Wilson, James Q. City Politics.
    New York: Random House, 1963. (Vintage ed.)

Boyd, William L. "Community Status and Conflict in Subur-
    ban School Politics. " Paper Presented at the Annual
    AERA Conference. Chicago, April 1972.

_____. Community Status, Citizen Participation, and

Conflict in Educational Decision Making. Unpublished doctoral dissertation, University of Chicago, 1971.

Coleman, James S. et al. Equality of Educational Opportunity. Washington, D. C. : Government Printing Office, 1966.

Digest of Educational Statistics. Prepared by K. A. Simon and W. V. Grant. National Center for Educational Statistics. Washington, D. C. : Government Printing Office, 1972.

Finn, Chester E. , Jr. and Lenkowsky, Leslie. "Serrano vs. the People." Commentary, September 1972, 68-72.

Fleming, Charles A. Information Services Coordinator, Clark County Public Schools, Las Vegas, Nevada. Letter to the Author, April 4, 1972 (a).

_____. Letter to the Author, May 8, 1972 (b).

Havighurst, Robert J. and Levine, Daniel U. Education in Metropolitan Areas (2nd ed.). Boston: Allyn & Bacon, 1971.

HEW Urban Education Task Force. Urban School Crisis. Washington, D. C. : National School Public Relations Assoc. , 1970. (Praeger ed.)

Lekachman, Robert. "School, Money and Politics: Financing Public Education." New Leader, September 18, 1972, 7-14.

Mayor's Advisory Panel on Decentralization of the New York City Schools. Reconnection for Learning: A Community School System for New York City. New York: Ford Foundation, 1967.

Minar, David W. "The Community Bases of Conflict in School System Politics." American Sociological Review, 1966, 31, 822-34.

Moynihan, Daniel P. "Equalizing Education--in Whose Benefit?" Public Interest, No. 29, 1972, 69-89.

National School Boards Association. Comparison of Board of Education in School Districts with a Core City Population of 300,000 or More. Evanston, Ill.: The Association, 1968.

Ornstein, Allan C. Urban Education: Student Unrest, Teacher Behaviors, and Black Power. Columbus, Ohio: Merrill, 1972.

O'Shea, David. School Board-Community Relations and Local Resource Utilization. Unpublished doctoral dissertation, University of Chicago, 1971.

Schools, People and Money: The Need for Educational Reform. The President's Commission on School Finances. Washington, D.C.: Government Printing Office, 1972.

Vaughn, Freeman H. "School Board Selection of Members." In: L. C. Deighton (ed.), Encyclopedia of Education, Vol. VIII. New York: Macmillan, 1970; p. 73-77.

Wood, Robert C. Suburbia. Boston: Mifflin, 1958.

Chapter 4

CASE STUDIES: DETROIT AND NEW YORK

This chapter will examine the recent experiences of
Detroit and New York City, the fifth largest and the largest
school systems in the nation. These are the only two school
systems, at the time of this writing, that have implemented
administrative decentralization with community control. As
indicated in the Introduction, "community participation" connotes only listening to the opinions of parents and community
residents but not giving them any real power and authority.
On the other hand, "community control" permits the parents
and community residents to determine to a large degree what
goes on in the schools.

Many people still recall the nationwide headlines and
bitter conflict over community control in New York City, especially the events which pitted the black community of Ocean
Hill-Brownsville against the predominantly white teachers' and
administrators' organizations, one of the key factors which
polarized the city. Because the events of the New York City
schools and Ocean Hill-Brownsville have been analyzed by
many authors elsewhere [see Fantini, Gittell, and Magat
(1970), Gittell and Hevesi (1969), Mayer (1969), and Shanker
(1969)], the discussion below on New York City will not
stress the events connected with community control; rather,
it will emphasize the various decentralization and community
control plans. The discussion will also bring readers up to
date with the recent aftermath of events that have not been
mentioned by other authors.

The experiences of Detroit are less widely known to
most educators even though the issues surrounding community
control also led there to some conflict between the black and
white communities. The present discussion, therefore, will
emphasize these events and only touch on the various decentralization and community control plans. We now turn to the
Detroit schools.

DETROIT

Based on Facts with Figures, Detroit ... (1971) and
Lucille Quamby (1972), coordinator of Information Services,
the school system consists of 325 schools, 12,388 teachers,
746 administrators and 1874 specialized personnel, and
289,484 students. The 1972 racial composition of the schools
was 63.8 percent black, 34.8 percent white, and 1.4 percent
other. The seven-member central board of education was
increased to 13 as a result of decentralization on January 1,
1971. Five members are elected by city-wide elections, and
one member from each of the eight decentralized regions
serves on the school board. According to the Detroit Public
Schools Directory 1971-72, the central administration comprises a general superintendent, executive deputy superintendent, business manager, and six deputy superintendents with
equal rank and in charge of the following divisions: (1) administration, (2) curriculum and educational research,
(3) governmental relations and fiscal planning, (4) staff relations and chief of labor negotiations, (5) school housing,
and (6) school-community relations. The eight decentralized
regions are each headed by a five-member regional board of
education and a regional superintendent. The number of
schools and students, in each region range from 29 and
26,000 in Region 7 to 54 and 40,000 in Region 2.

The reading scores for Detroit students are more
than one year below the national average. Facts with Figures,
Detroit ... (1971) points out that the schools spend approximately $755 per student. The state provides a tax ceiling
of $15 on each $1000 assessed valuation to cover the operation and maintenance costs of the Wayne County government,
the Detroit public schools, and the Detroit libraries. The
Detroit school system for several years has received $8.26
from the $15, which represents about 17 percent of the
school income. The remaining school funds are derived
from local (50 percent), state (40 percent), and federal and
miscellaneous (10 percent) sources. According to Birger
Bakke (1971), assistant to the general superintendent, Detroit
residents pay a school tax of $22.86 per $1000 of assessed
valuation, including an additional $24.15 city tax and $7
county tax--totaling about $54 per $1000. Even with this
unusually high tax, the New York Times (June 4, 1972) points
out that the school system has experienced a deficit since
1967, like many of its large-city school counterparts. The
latest school budget figures show that in 1972 the budget was
$270 million but revenues were about $40 million short.

According to the New York Times (June 4, November 12,
1972), the system has already reached the brink of bank-
ruptcy; in fact, the central school board voted in late 1972
to close down the schools for seven weeks to save money;
this measure was rescinded only after the state legislative
promised to give Detroit "top priority" in 1973 when the
legislature convened (Detroit Information Officer, 1973[1]).

Ironically, the Detroit taxpayers pay higher taxes
than most of the surrounding suburban residents, and the
city dwellers can least afford it in comparison to the suburban people. In the suburbs, most of the taxes go for the
schools while in Detroit most of the taxes go to cover the
entire city costs.[2] In a vicious cycle, the slow collapse of
the Detroit schools is one of the factors that has led to the
general out-migration of whites from the city; this, in turn,
has reduced the tax base and has increased the school deficit; moreover, it was a factor in Judge Roth's ruling that
the Detroit schools were segregated and had to be integrated
with the suburban schools. With school cutbacks implemented
and with insufficient state monies forthcoming, this integration will probably increase the exodus of whites from the
city. This is a classic problem facing most large cities:
as whites flee to the suburbs, the proportion of low income
and racial minorities in city schools and the cities in general increase and it reduces the abilities of the cities to
provide sufficient revenues for the cost of education and
other social services.

From the goal of integration to community control.
Coinciding with the administration of the liberal mayor
Jerome P. Cavanagh in the mid 1960s, the board of education managed to swing to a majority coalition of white liberals and blacks in 1964. The school board outlined an integration policy in 1965; hired a new school superintendent in
July 1966, Norman Drachler, who was committed to school
integration; changed school boundaries and junior high school
feeder patterns, and permitted open school transfers to promote integration; more than tripled the proportion of black
administrators from 11 percent in 1966 to 37 percent in 1970;
and hired two blacks outside the system to be the school system's first black deputy superintendents.

Despite these efforts to integrate the schools, almost
75 percent of the Detroit black students were enrolled in
schools that were 90 percent or more black. In addition,
according to Facts with Figures, Detroit ... (1971), the

number of racially unmixed or totally segregated schools in
1970 was similar to the number in 1965, except that the racial composition was the opposite.   Thus in 1965 as many
as 30 schools were all white;   in 1970 11 were all white.
In 1965 as many as 10 schools were all black;   five years
later, there were 30 all black schools.   The problem was,
the movement of the whites to the suburbs was continuous
and correlated to some extent with efforts to integrate the
schools, and the black student population increased from 53. 8
percent in 1965 to 63. 8 percent in 1970, making it still more
difficult to integrate the schools.   In addition, as Grant (1971)
points out, there was little sentiment among whites to provide money to finance busing, which was the only way to integrate the city schools.

By the late 1960s, as more blacks became disillu-
sioned about school integration and the concept of black power
gained political momentum, the concepts of administrative decentralization and community control acquired growing support and importance.   This shift of opinion was reflected,
for example, by the growing militancy since 1963 of the Rev.
Albert Cleage, Jr. , and his Inner-City Parents Council.
Cleage gained attention in June 1967 when he presented to
the school board the first formal demand for black control
of black schools.

Grant (1971) explains that the concept of community
control soon acquired two political advocates in the Michigan
State Legislature.   One of these people was James Del Rio,
a black Democrat from Detroit.   Early in 1968, Del Rio introduced a bill to divide the Detroit schools into 16 autonomous school systems, each of which would be totally independent like the other 650 Michigan school systems.   The
bill was supported by the Rev. Cleage but denounced by almost everyone connected with Detroit education, including all
of the school board (four whites, three blacks), city-wide
PTA, teachers' union, Board of Commerce, the city's Urban
Coalition, and the influential black weekly Michigan Chronicle.
The bill was overwhelmingly defeated in the legislature.   Virtually unnoticed during the heated debate over the Del Rio bill
was another bill introduced by the liberal white Democrat
Jack Faxon, also from Detroit, which called for the division
of the Detroit school system into regions, each with its own
elected school board and superintendent, but which also re-
tained and enlarged the existing central school board.   Faxon's
bill was defeated in committee and never reached the floor
for a vote.

The same year a city-wide black group was organized, the Citizens for Community Control. The group organized several conferences on community control which also included participants from the Ocean Hill-Brownsville demonstration district; and subsequently, the chairman of the citizens group declared in the Michigan Chronicle that "equality of education through integration [was] politically and geographically unworkable." He declared that blacks would accept nothing less than the control of their own schools, and the "principal should have the power to hire and fire teachers, and the community the power to hire and fire the principal."[3] Neither the Inner-City Council nor the Citizens for Community Control had a large following, according to Grant (1971). But the school board was willing to discuss the issues of decentralization and community control; furthermore, the school superintendent favored some form of administrative decentralization.

In the beginning of 1969, the Del Rio and Faxon bills were reintroduced, only to be tabled again. However, in April 1969, Detroit's NAACP delivered a formal request for decentralization and "community centered schools" with elected local school boards. The same month, Senator Coleman Young, a black Democrat from Detroit, introduced a new version of the Faxon proposal which after little debate was passed in the summer and subsequently signed into law by Republican Governor William G. Milliken on August 11, 1969.

Public Act 244, the new bill, required that the Detroit Board of Education divide its school system into no fewer than seven nor more than 11 regional districts. Each regional district was to elect its own school board as well as one member to sit on the central school board; each regional school board was to operate in accordance with the guidelines established by the central school board. In compliance with the new legislation, the Detroit Board of Education held nine public hearings on how to divide the school system. Writes Bakke (1971):

> It would be fair to summarize these by stating that the majority of white citizens who participated were opposed to decentralization while the blacks were for it--but with stronger demands for community control [p. 134].

And writes Grant (1971):

> It quickly became clear that the black community was
> less than enthusiastic about creating racially integrated
> regions. 'Consideration should be given to those areas
> where a sense of community prevails,' an NAACP rep-
> resentative stated. 'This decentralization bill is not
> a vehicle for integration.' New Detroit, the city's
> Urban Coalition group, declared: 'Elimination of de
> facto segregation should be the result of and not the
> object of education.' The representative of another
> black group reported that 'Throughout all our discus-
> sions, integration has been the least sought-after
> variable.'
>
> Such sentiments were aptly summed up by a spokes-
> man for the largely black first Congressional District
> Democratic organization, who said, 'Redistricting must
> guarantee black control of black schools.'
>
> The willingness of blacks to forsake integrated regions
> stemmed from the simple demographic fact that, al-
> though 65 percent of Detroit's public school students
> were black, only 44 percent of the city's electorate
> was black. If the regions were fully integrated--with
> each region's racial mix duplicating the mix of the
> city as a whole--they all would have black student
> majorities and black voter minorities [p. 3].

In the meantime, A. L. Zwerdling, the president of
the city's board of education, as well as the board majority
still viewed integration as the primary goal. Speaking in
late 1969 before a group of school administrators in Washington, D. C. , Zwerdling (1969a) stated that "no one who has
come to our public meetings on decentralization is interested
in integration. Everyone wants segregation so they will be
assured a little piece of control." He contended that "you
cannot have both integration and community control." And
if it came to a choice between the two, Zwerdling's (1969b)
decision was clear. "I did not become the president of the
Detroit Board of Education to preside over the liquidation of
an integrated school system," he stated to the League of
Women Voters after returning from the nation's capital.
Zwerdling and the majority of Board of Education members
(four whites, three blacks) were trying to couple decentralization with integration. Zwerdling (1970) said in the early
part of the following year, "If we drew boundaries that put

blacks into one region and whites into another region there could never be any integration" (p. 3A).

Under Zwerdling's leadership, the Detroit Board of Education obtained a $360,000 planning grant from the Ford Foundation; the final plan mapped out seven decentralized, racially integrated regional districts, and on April 7, 1970, the board of education voted 4-2 in favor of it. The proposed attendance areas meant genuine integration not only at the district level, but also at the school level. As many as 11 of the city's 22 neighborhood high schools would have been substantially affected, and the three remaining predominantly white high schools would have been integrated from approximately 2, 2, 3 percent black to 29, 31, 53 percent black. The plan included integration both ways, requiring for the first time in Detroit that whites travel to black schools and vice versa. It called for a three-year phasing period.

The reaction was swift; it included floods of protest letters, angry black and white parents demonstrating in front of the board of education, and large-scale boycotts of schools by black and white students. On April 9, only two days after the school board's action, the Michigan State House of Representatives amended Public Act 244 by voting that there should be no fewer than 11 regional districts, that high school attendance boundaries be drawn so that each student attend the school nearest to his home, and that the final plan be placed before the voters as a referendum. On the following day, the State Senate repealed 244, and the two houses then quickly agreed and passed a new bill, Public Act 48 of 1970, superseding 244 as amended by the House. The new bill stated that the Detroit school system would be divided into eight regional districts, each having a five-member board with the candidate receiving the most votes becoming chairman of the regional board and sitting on the central school board; that the central board have five members elected at large by the people of Detroit, who, added to the eight regional representatives, would form a 13-member central board of education. The precise guidelines were to be worked out by the Detroit Board of Education, and they are discussed below. The bill quickly passed the House 93-1 and the Senate 30-1; the governor signed it into law on July 7, 1970.

The state legislature was unable to agree on the exact boundary lines of the regional districts; the governor, in accordance with one of the clauses of the law, named a three-man commission to establish them. According to Bakke

(1971), this group was guided by the statement of the law which said that "regions shall be as compact, contiguous, and nearly equal in population as practicable." Making only minor adjustments, the commission developed the boundaries of the eight regions, resulting "in four regions predominantly black and four white" (p. 137).

At this point, the NAACP instituted a suit in the federal court, claiming that the boundary lines of Public Act 48 willfully promoted segregation. The suit also asked that the school system return to the April 7 plan, but with immediate and full implementation of changed attendance boundaries, rather than the three-year planning program. The suit was denied and this action was upheld by the District Court of Appeals, which, however, declared unconstitutional that part of the Act requiring a student body composition similar (in racial makeup) to the neighborhood population. The Court of Appeals then set a new trial in November on the issue of segregation. This paved the way for the famous Roth decision, which we will return to later in this chapter.

In the meantime, a recall movement had been initiated in April against the four school board members who had voted for the integration plan. Within two months the required 125,000 signatures had been obtained and filed on June 15, and the four were recalled by almost a 2-1 margin on the August 4 primary election ballot. Grant (1971) points out that the election turnout was light--only 23 percent of the eligible voters bothered to go to the polls. A high turnout was evidenced in the white communities, especially in the areas where the integration plans would have required that white students be bussed into black communities. The white vote on the recall was about 90 percent; the black turnout was low, reflecting in part, according to this author, the mixed feelings of blacks about integration versus community control; nevertheless, the blacks that did vote generally opposed the recall. As one school official was quoted in the Detroit Free Press (August 5, 1970), "The song is 'community control' and the tune is 'Dixie'" (p. 3a). Wrote the black Michigan Chronicle (August 15, 1970), white segregationists supported the plan, while blacks supported it as a means for "achieving black power over black schools" (p. 8).

Assessing what happened, Alberbach and Walker (1971) pointed out that many whites objected to integration and went into action and organized groups and informed their sympathizers to go to the polls. There was no comparable

organization and intensity of interest within the black community, for there was a general waning of interest in the pur-
suit of integration and a rising interest in community control.
The disparity of turnout between whites and blacks was reflected in the authors' survey, taken several months after
the recall election.   When respondents were asked if they
remembered the recall election, the whites were more likely to
say they did at every level of education;   the total percentage
of whites so remembering was approximately 75 percent (N=
249), and for blacks it was approximately 45 percent (N=161).
The authors went on to state:

> Whites were not simply reacting against the idea of
> decentralizing the schools in the recall, but rather
> against the threat of increased racial integration.
> Among whites, there was a correlation of (Gamma)
> .43 between preferences for racially segregated school
> districts and support for the recall motion.   It seems
> clear that many whites saw a vote for the recall as a
> vote for the maintenance of segregation.

> The apparent apathy over the recall motion in the
> black community is more difficult to explain.... No
> citizens' committee or ad hoc coalitions supporting
> integrated decentralization plans had sprung up prior
> to the recall, however, an indication that the idea had
> not developed deep roots in the black community....
> One must speculate about the reasons for the black
> leadership's relative inactivity, but the principal causes
> probably lie in their developing ambivalence about the
> idea of racial integration. [and] support ... for in-
> creased neighborhood control over the schools ...
> [p. 14].

General support for integrated schools still existed in
the black community, but the commitment was waning.   For
example, in the same research paper, the two authors (1971)
report data on another survey of 394 whites and 461 blacks
in 1967 and 391 whites and 174 blacks in 1971 in Detroit on
many social issues pertaining to choices of integration, separation, or something "in between."   Among white respondents in 1967, 30 percent maintained that blacks and whites
should attend separate schools, while 70 percent favored
school integration.   The same year blacks expressed overwhelming support for the goal of integration.   Of the 98 percent of the blacks who favored school integration, as many
as 66 percent were willing to risk violence to achieve it.

When the same question was asked in 1971, the whites were less enthusiastic about school integration, but 59 percent still favored it.   The black community, however, had undergone a major change which had political implications related to black power.   Although 88 percent still favored integration (a drop of 10 percent), only 29 percent were now willing to risk violence to achieve this goal (a drop of 37 percent from four years past).   Thus while the idea of school integration existed for blacks, the intensity and commitment to the idea were fading.

While the preference of blacks for integration was duplicated in most other social areas, Alberbach and Walker (1972) point out that it had clearly lost its favored position with issues involving local business ownership and police matters.   In the area of housing (which in turn reflects the neighborhood schools and the extent of integration with bussing), 59 percent of the surveyed blacks prefered to build more and better housing in and around black areas and only 37 percent of the blacks preferred integrated housing in other parts of the city or suburbs.   ("In between" statements totaled 4 percent.)   The white segregationist point of view was keenly illustrated with the housing question: 80 percent were for segregated housing, 17 percent were for integrated housing, and 3 percent were "in between. "

The authors (1971) also pointed out that respondents' commitment (in an interview) to an interracial society in 1967 and 1971 showed that the attitudes of whites had changed very little but that the black commitment to the concept of integration was waning.   In 1967 blacks overwhelmingly favored integration, while most whites were "in between. "   The attitudes of whites toward integration increased 3 percent in 1971, but black attitudes, while still favoring it, had declined 20 percent.

It is only conjecture, but this author hypothesizes that had the survey stimulus-word "separation" been changed to "community control, " a concept connected with today's black power movement and connoting a more favorable position to blacks, more blacks would have responded.   This hypothesis is supported to some degree by the poor voting record of blacks in the August 1970 referendum.   In any event, it is important to note that integration as a viable goal was waning, while the goal of community control was gaining in popularity among blacks.   White conservatives also recognized the latter concept as a means for preventing integration.   It would seem that the majority of whites suddenly embraced decentralization and community control as they realized that it would protect them from integration that the Zwerdling plan had outlined.

On the day of the recall election, the eight regional boundaries were announced. As previously stated, these were four black-dominated and four white-dominated regions. The boundaries tended to coincide with the existing school boundaries while still taking into consideration the Supreme Court's "one-man, one vote" ruling.

The November elections soon followed, which Grant (1971) contends was a clear victory for the white segregationists. The new 13-member central school board consisted of ten whites, six of whom were anti-integrationists, and only three blacks, of whom only one was elected on a city-wide basis--giving blacks the smallest representation on the central school board in 15 years. [4] Contrary to expectations, blacks won a voting majority in only two out of the eight regional school boards, although black students were in a majority in six of the eight regions. In three regions, where the opposition to integration was intense, not one black was elected to the regional school board. Of the total 43 central and regional board positions, 30 were filled by whites, including ten by Polish-Americans, and only 13 were filled by blacks. The Detroit Free Press (November 7, 1970) summed up the election as "the city's most conservative school board in at least six years" (p. 12a). In short, blacks, with more than 40 percent of the city's population and almost 65 percent of the student population (as of the 1970 census), received only 30 percent of the combined school board positions and only 23 percent of the central school board positions: The latter is where the major decision-making authority is vested. And as Grant (1971) says:

> ... [A]t no point during the debate on decentralization was education the prime consideration. The arguments were all political....
>
> The blacks who pressed for decentralization were the losers; they ended up with less power and less influence than they had before decentralization.... Meanwhile, the devastating political conflict that accompanied the process of decentralization has not yet quieted down....

[The whites] who worked to recall the school board
did so in order to fight integration....

... [T]he Detroit experience does offer convincing
evidence that integration and community control are
not easily compatible [p. 4].

Thus it would appear that education or the students'
welfare was not the issue, as it is often claimed to be by
the advocates of community control in the educational literature.   As pointed out in Chapter 2, and as in the case of
New York City, discussed below, the issue boiled down to
politics and race--which group would control the schools,
and in turn economics, and which group would make decisions regarding who would be hired and fired.

> Administrative decentralization and community control
plans.   In accordance with the law, the decentralized school
regions went into effect on January 1, 1971.   Following is a
discussion of some of the important documents that were designed to help the Detroit school system through this transition period.   Public Act 244 did not describe specific ways
in which the law was to be carried out or the exact authority
and responsibility of the central and regional school boards.
The first list of conceivable guidelines, entitled Working
Draft of Possible Guidelines for Implementation of Public
Act 244 (1970), involved approximately 3000 persons--stu-
dents, parents, teachers, and administrators--and was released in two parts, in April and May 1970, by the Detroit
Board of Education and its Office of School Decentralization.

About 100 issues were identified that involved decisions which could be made by the central school board, the
regional school boards separately, or by both school boards.
For each issue, the range of choices for making decisions
were defined within the limits of the law.   In a few cases,
there was only one choice which the law permitted.   In most
cases, however, the law permitted two or three alternatives.
An example of one of the issues and the three choices is
listed below;   the item is excerpted from the section on curriculum and instruction in the April Working Draft ... (1970,
p. 2):

Issue: Educational Goals and Priorities

Central	Central/Regional	Regional
The central board shall adopt a state-	The central board shall adopt a state-	Each regional board shall adopt a state-

Issue: Educational Goals and Priorities (cont'd)

ment of its educa- tional goals and priorities annually for the School District of the City of Detroit	ment of its educational goals and priorities annually for the basic curriculum and the regional board shall do so for additional goals and priorities.	ment of its educational goals and priorities annually and the central board shall do the same for schools or programs under its direct administration.

A reaction sheet was provided to each person in the various groups to study the choices so they could indicate their preferences for each issue.   The choices provided the idea but not the exact language for the final document.   The day before the first set of ... Possible Guidelines ... were released, Public Act 244 was changed to Public Act 48. Actually, the two acts were similar and only four sections of the first act were changed.   The Text of Public Act 48 (1970) called for:

1. Creation of eight regional school districts by January 1, 1971 [As previously mentioned, the final outcome was that the numbers of schools within each region ranged between 29 and 54].

2. Establishment of regional school boards, consisting of five-elected members, for each region.   (The candidates must be a resident of the region and at least 21 years, later changed to 18 years, old.)

3. Expansion of the central school board from seven to 13 members.   (Five of these members were to be elected on a city-wide basis and the other eight were to come from the eight regions, one per region.)

4. Selection of the chairman of the regional school boards on the basis of the largest number of votes received, who in turn would serve on the central school board.

5. The central school board retaining all the powers and duties then possessed except for those given to the regional school boards under the provision of the Act or subsequently delegated by the central board.

6. The central school board performing all functions related to purchasing, pay roll, contract negotiations, property

maintenance, bonding, special education, and allocation
of funds to regional school boards and schools.

7. The regional school boards (a) employing a superintendent from a list of candidates submitted by the central
   school board, (b) employing, discharging, and promoting
   employees subject to the review if necessary of the central school board, (3) determining the curriculum and
   testing programs, (4) determining the budget based upon
   the allocation of funds received from the central school
   board, and (5) respecting the rights of retirement, tenure, and seniority of all employees transferred within
   and among the regions.

Returning to the Possible Guidelines, and now working
within the framework of Public Act 48, the Office of School
Decentralization involved three consultant groups--students,
parents, and school personnel--in eight meetings and also
conducted additional community meetings and sent approximately 1500 organizations and individuals questionnaires on
the guidelines. The results of the reaction to the possible
guidelines, coupled with some adjustments for the substituted
clauses of the new Act is the Public Reaction Draft of Decentralization Guidelines (1970). This draft represented what
seemed to be the majority or pluralistic viewpoint on all issues. As many as 3800 mimeographed copies were mailed
to interested people in August, to be returned on or before
September 4, 1970 with specific comments or suggestions,
as well as an overall reaction to each section and the entire
draft. According to the board of education, 84 percent of
the respondents agreed with overall draft. The school board
made a few additional modifications and issued on October 26,
1970, the Guidelines for Regional and Central Boards of Education of the School District of the City of Detroit. These
guidelines are in accord with Public Act 48 and specifically
state where the authority lies in curriculum, personnel, student policy, financing, etc. They were (and still are) the
rules for operation when the school system was decentralized
on January 1, 1971. In general, the regional school boards
have authority over:

Curriculum
Curriculum policies
Instructional services
Selecting textbooks (from an approved central list)
Program evaluation (but not for city-wide and
     standardized testing)
Elective and innovative programs

Personnel

Hiring teachers, administrators, and the superintendent
(from a list of eligibles supplied by the central office)

Developing its own procedures for promoting, transferring, and discharging personnel (but maintaining
the rights of retirement, tenure, collective bargaining procedures, etc.; appeals can be made to the
central school board)

Inservice training (but not preservice training)

Staff organizational patterns

Student Policy

Administering guidance, psychological, and health services

Keeping records

Dress codes, discipline, and suspensions (but appeals
can be made to the central school board)

Reporting student progress to parents

Requirements for student advancement (but not gradua-
tion from senior high school)

Assigning students in its boundaries (but boundaries and
schools within boundaries can be changed by the central school board)

Financing

Submitting requests for yearly budgets, including construction and maintenance costs (but the exact allocation of money is determined by the central school
board through a city-wide formula)

Deciding its own priorities and spending its allocated
money according to these needs

Developing its own special projects and securing funds
from sources other than governmental agencies

The central office provides special personnel and services to regions in order to help the regional school board
in the above areas. Keeping in mind that there are still a
few other minor items omitted above, the central school
board retains authority over all other matters. In addition,
it renders "the final decision on all questions related to interpretation of policies, programs, and these guidelines which
may arise between two or more Regional Boards or between
the Central Board and a Regional Board" (p. 2). At the
present, revisions and amendments to the Guidelines are being considered. Several regional school boards and black
citizen groups are demanding changes which will give the

regions more decision-making authority. Concurrently, several central school board members and white citizen groups
are demanding that decentralization be abolished, or that the
regions be made independent school systems and the central
school board be abolished (Detroit Information Officer, 1972).

The aftermath. Although the period since 1971 serves
only as a tentative basis for judgment, we will try to high-
light some of the events since the Detroit school system decentralized and implemented community control. The Summaries of Regional Board Meeting Minutes, from January
1971 to June 1972, report the usual discussion of school
events, including community drives, workshops and training
programs with universities, drug abuse programs, commen-
dations to students, community use of schools, acceptance of
gifts from local agencies, the formation of local advisory
councils [of the 300 schools, as many as 109 local advisory
councils had been formed as of March 1972], and the introduction of courses in black studies--the latter being required
for all high school students in history and English within Region 8 [in 1972, Region 8 comprised a 92 percent black student enrollment].

Some of the more controversial highlights which were
indicated in the summary minutes include the following: the
refusal of Region 1 to cooperate with the central school board
on several matters; the establishment by Regions 1 and 7 of
evaluative criteria for assessing teachers and administrators
which in turn led to grievances filed by the professional
teacher and administrative organizations; the establishment
by Regions 4 and 7 of quotas which favored the hiring of
black teachers and administrators; and the expression by
Region 4 of a need for security measures which involved
scooter patrol surveillance at the high schools, security
guards to issue tickets, students and staff to wear photo I. D.
cards on their apparel while in school, suspending students
found guilty of assault or extortion, and extra police to be
assigned to the high schools.

In addition, the newspapers (e. g. , Detroit News,
March 13, 1972) report that since decentralization and community control, there has been no indication of academic
gains for Detroit students; on state tests they continue to
average in the lowest (the 1st) percentile and on city tests
they fall more than one year below the norm. Both citizens
and regional board members have discovered that the real
power lies with the central school board--which at the present

is white and conservative but which is becoming more black
and more militant due to recent resignations and replacements.   Although the eight regional school board chairmen
constitute a voting majority on the 13-member central school
board, they seldom agree on issues.

   The first year for administrative decentralization and
community control cost the school system, which was already
in deep financial trouble, about an extra $5 million.   This
includes dollar costs for extra regional administrators and
members of the Office of School Decentralization, maintaining
regional offices, paying regional board members $20 per
meeting and central board members $30, with a limit in
each case of 52 meetings per year, vouchers for various
items to school board members (meals, mileage, baby-sit-
ting, out-of-town trips for "educational conferences," etc.),
and paying for eight automobiles assigned to central school
board members.   This also includes costs for paying the
salaries of six principals who were removed by regional
school boards under the pretext that the principals were unable to relate to the schools' predominantly black students;
these principals were given other "duties" in regional central
offices.   Still extra costs include, according to the Northeast
Detroiter (February 17, 1972), high sale prices (ranging from
$150,000 to $215,000) of buildings to some of the regional
school boards with high sales commissions (ranging from
$9000 to $12,000) to one realtor;   one of the partners of the
legal council for the realtor is George E. Bushnell, Jr., a
former attorney of the Detroit Board of Education.

   Educational reform seems to be a nonexistent priority,
although there is the constant rhetoric for reform, as politics
and related issues of race and ideology dominate the regional
school board meetings.   Region 8 seems to be the most political of all;   and for about half of 1972 it was unable to conduct school board business efficiently because of several community demonstrations, sometimes riotous conditions, and
the school audiences' trading racial insults (Detroit News,
March 23, March 28, 1972;   E. S. Shopper--Community News,
February 9, April 19, 1972;   Michigan Chronicle, April 22,
1972)--this last being due mainly to the regional school
board's refusal to accept the central school board's criteria
for filling two spots on the regional school board, where the
major qualifications for appointing them seemed to be their
blackness and their militancy (Detroit Free Press, March 26,
1972;   Detroit News, March 29, April 4, 1972;   E. S. Shop-
per--Community News, February 9, April 5, 1972).

In Regions 2 and 6 few parents bother to attend school meetings, and in Regions 2, 3, and 6 there have been charges by some segments of the community that regional school board members are insensitive to and do not represent the philosophy of the community (Michigan Chronicle, February 5, 1972; Redford Record, January 10, 1972). In Regions 4, 6, and 8, there is the continuous problem at regional school board meetings of determining which people represent the community on the local advisory councils; all the people tend to be voicing various political philosophies ranging through white segregationism, integration, and black power (Detroit News, March 14, 1972). The resignations of several school board members in Regions 4, 7, and 8 have led to unfilled positions for long time periods, the inability of the school boards sometimes to function properly, and methods of appointing replacements (mainly based on race) which have very little to do with the outcome of community votes (Detroit News, March 3, April 19, 1972; E. S. Shopper--Community News, April 12, May 3, 1972). Thus in January 1971 two out of 15 school board members in these three regions were black, but by December 1972 six out of 15 were black.

Along with Regions 4 and 7, previously mentioned, Region 3 also has established racial quotas in hiring teachers and administrators (Northeast Detroiter, April 20, 1972), and many unlicensed teachers not from the eligibility pool have been hired (Redford Record, January 10, 1972). Finally, in Regions 1 and 7 the teachers and administrators continue to question whether students and parents have in fact a real way to judge personnel and especially administrators (Detroit News, February 14, February 25, 1972). There are also the alleged statements by some white educators that certain evaluative instruments will be used against them as a means of ousting them from predominantly black schools. The major criterion in a person's evaluation may become his or her color.

Thus in the name of education, State Senator Coleman Young, Detroit Democrat, warned that the black community would "explode" unless citizens were given some control of the schools (Detroit News, June 13, 1971). Perhaps somewhat oversimplifiedly but nevertheless very visibly, the political and related racial and ideological situations can be summed up by the two statements below. According to the Detroit News (March 10, 1972), regional school board member Barbara Collins stated:

... [T]he Central Board [is] made up 'of mostly
whites, conservatives--and that to me means racists.'

... [T]he relationship between the Central Board and
Region 1 Board, with four of its five members black,
is one of 'confrontation or we just ignore each other.'

'The Central Board controls ... everything. What we
are trying to do in Region 1 is wrest some of that
control from the Central Board.' And they realize
it [p. 2-B].

As for the reorganization of the Detroit school system, Grant
(1971) wrote:

The issue was simply whether, as a practical matter,
community control is compatible with racial integration. And the unequivocal answer in Detroit was 'no'
[p. 1].

And elsewhere, Grant (1970) stated:

The blacks wanted regions that were all black so that
there could be black control of black schools. The
whites asked for all white regions for the same end.
Some groups even stated it quite bluntly: 'We don't
think the school system ought to be divided up. But
if it is, we want it done in such a way that we can
control the schools in our area.'

Few have talked about what decentralization might
mean for the quality of education in the schools [p. 2].

From community control to integration. It appears
that the only way to integrate most of the city school systems is to involve the surrounding suburbs, and to include
the bussing of the cities' predominantly black schools with
the nearly all-white schools of the surrounding suburbs. The
recent court orders involving Detroit and Richmond have both
aimed at this metropolitan procedure for promoting school
integration. [5] For our purposes, our discussion will be confined to Detroit and then end with a few words that have implications for the above two court decisions.

After Judge Stephen J. Roth ruled in Bradley vs.
Milliken in September 1971 that the Detroit school system
was segregated, he ruled in March 1972 that he had the

authority to develop a metropolitan plan for integrating the
schools (Detroit Free Press, April 6, September 28, 1971;
Detroit News, February 24, March 15, 1972; Phi Delta
Kappan, 1972a). The integration plan, ordered by Judge
Roth, involved the Detroit schools and the 52 surrounding
suburban school systems. In all it involved 290,000 Detroit
students, about 65 percent of whom were black, and another
450,000 suburban students, nearly all white. Of the 52 suburban
systems, 29 were all white and 16 were more than 95 percent
white. The aims were to redistribute the students so that
none of the schools would be more than 25 percent black and
to integrate the teaching and administrative staff in the city
and suburbs. Judge Roth also told the Detroit school system
to order 300 school buses and ruled that the state would be
required to pay the $3 million for them; this last ruling was
negated by the Sixth Circuit Court of Appeals on December 8,
1972.

        The judge's integration decision has created an emo-
tional furor, as was expected. It means that children of the
white middle class and the white wealthy in Bloomfield Hills,
Dearborn, Oak Park, and even Grosse Pointe would be bussed
into the inner-city neighborhoods of Detroit. According to
Serrin (1972), this was the "equivalent of requiring blacks
and whites to be bussed between Harlem and Scarsdale or
Chicago's South Side and Winnetka"[p. 13].

        Roth's order was appealed by the Detroit Board of
Education, the state department of education, and the suburbs.
According to the New York Times (June 18, 1972), Governor
William Milliken termed the order "disruptive" and "counter
productive," and former U.S. Commissioner of Education
Sidney Marland summed it up as "drastic" and "extreme."
The Detroit Free Press (March 24, 1972) pointed out that
even the U.S. Justice Department attempted to intervene to
stop the bussing--putting the federal government on the side
of the anti-integrationists--which is probably some kind of
first for the federal government since the Supreme Court's
1954 Brown decision. Roth ruled on May 9, 1972 that the
Justice Department had no legal right to intervene; however,
the appeal was heard by the Court of Appeals in Cincinnati;
the opinion was interpreted as follows: (1) both the State of
Michigan and the Detroit Board of Education are guilty of de
jure segregation; (2) these violations cannot be corrected by
a Detroit-only plan; (3) there will be a metropolitan plan
which includes the Detroit schools and the surrounding suburbs
(Detroit News, December 8, 9, 1972).

In the meantime, Serrin (1972) contends that Judge
Roth became "the most hated man in Michigan" in 1972
(p. 13). Bumper stickers and demonstrations expressed
hatred toward the judge; he was hanged in effigy in the
working-class suburb of Wyandotte, and was surely con-
demned in table talk throughout suburbia. The New York
Times (July 16, 1972) pointed out that some of the "fiercest
'nevers' " came from suburban liberals and teachers from
Detroit, as well as blacks who complained that integration
would relegate them to a minority without control of their
own schools.

The Roth decision asks a difficult thing from the white
parents: to place their children on a bus headed for the city
of Detroit that many worked hard to escape from so their
children could attend the better schools of the suburbs. Some
of the objections to bussing by whites are motivated by outright racism. But other reasons are linked with the white
parents' fear that the buses will bring the problems of the
ghetto to "their" schools and expose their children to assaults and exhortation and to the social ills that blacks have
had to cope with and which have turned many of their schools
into jungles. Some white parents also reject the idea that
some judge they did not elect may tell them they must send
their children into ghetto schools, especially when the judge
lives in a different area, as Judge Roth does (Flint, Michigan), or especially when he sends his children to a private
school which is in effect a segregated school, as does Judge
Merhige who decided the Richmond case.

The Roth decision was also difficult for blacks; they
have to send their children into communities which have made
it clear they do not want them or their children; in these
suburban schools, their children will be a minority. For
many blacks, meaningful educational reform can only come
about through community control of black schools.

A statement by the NAACP, which brought the suit
that led to Roth's order, asserts that equal educational opportunity can only come about through integration and what is
at stake is whether the U. S. Supreme Court's 1954 Brown decision will be upheld or made into a mockery (Serrin, 1972).
On the other hand, one might claim, as Ornstein (1972)
writes, "A new dimension of equal educational opportunity is
developing, the equal right to exercise control and make decisions concerning public education" (p. 146); this connotes
not integration but community control.

In order to bring the Roth decision into perspective
with nationwide events, one must understand that President
Nixon, who was overwhelmingly supported at the polls by
the white middle-class and suburban vote, has continuously
hinted that the interests of the country cannot be defined in
terms of the interests of a racial minority.   Writes Ornstein (1972):

> Mr. Nixon prefers compliance by 'good faith rather
> than by educational disruption'.... Before the 1971
> Supreme Court ruling [which supported bussing to re-
> move Southern state-imposed school segregation], he
> denounced bussing and other procedures that fit schools
> into a racial grid but were necessary to achieve de-
> segregation.   President Nixon ... insisted that educa-
> cation must come first and desegregation must be ac-
> commodated to the principle of 'neighborhood' schools.
> Similarly, he has distinguished between 'integration'
> and 'quality education,' contradicting the previous
> Supreme Court rulings [since 1954], and, rather than
> promoting integration, he has proposed to improve
> segregated schools [p. 107].

The above analysis was confirmed when President
Nixon signed the higher education bill in the Summer of 1972,
officially titled Educational Amendments of 1972.   The bill
directed $21.6 billion to education over a three-year period
and included a clause which stayed all school integration orders involving bussing or the transfer of students until all
appeals were exhausted.   (As of now, the bill does not apply
to the Detroit situation and State Superintendent John W. Por-
ter is at the time of this writing organizing an interim plan
to accomplish racial balance without changing the present administrative unit, to be followed by a long-range plan for
racial balance and change of the city-suburban administrative
units.)   The bussing provision of the bill becomes void after
December 31, 1973 and thus it permits Congress 18 months
to work out another approach (Phi Delta Kappan, 1972b).   In
the meantime, the New York Times (June 11, 1972, Section
4) wrote that the bill contained some of the strongest anti-
bussing language ever approved by Congress, thus fulfilling
Senator John Stennis' prediction in the late 1960s--when
Northerners are asked to integrate their schools, "you see
if Congress doesn't put its foot down" (p. 1).

At the time of this writing, there is no doubt that a
constitutional amendment will eventually be offered in

Congress.   In 1972, the anti-bussing amendment had passed
the House 282 to 102 but was filibustered to death in the
Senate.   The majority of senators were for its passage and
attempted to apply cloture, that is to cut off the delaying arguments, but were unable to get the two-thirds vote required
to stop the talk.   The amendment, if passed, would have for-
bidden bussing for school integration except as a last resort--
and then limited the bus ride to no further than the second
nearest school--and would have reopened previous bussing
orders (such as in Detroit) in line with the new limitations.

The bussing issue was one of the major issues in the
1972 election of President Nixon.   Mr. Nixon had taken a
rigid stand against bussing, and it was one of the reasons
why he was overwhelmingly elected, especially in the suburbs
where the people voted for him more than 3:1.   Similarly,
in many state elections, with Michigan the number-one state,
bussing was the chief political issue;   many representatives
and senators tried to prove they were more strongly opposed
to bussing than their opponents.   While the anti-bussing furor
in the nation is bound to come to a head in the heat of new
Congressional debates, we still must remember that congress-
men do not always keep their election promises and it still
takes two-thirds of the Senate to approve an amendment to
the Constitution.

It might be argued that the 1972 Higher Education bill
and the possibility of an amendment are both academic, that
implementation of the Detroit order, along with other bussing
orders of the 1970s already filed in Atlanta, Boston, Dayton,
Denver, Durham, N. C. , Grand Rapids, Mich. , Hartford,
Indianapolis, Louisville, Memphis, Richmond, and Wilming-
ton, may be overturned by the U. S. Supreme Court.   In the
Richmond case, the Court divided 4 to 4, with Justice Lewis
Powell, a former member of the Virginia State and Richmond
City Education Boards, having disqualified himself.   The dead-
locked vote left intact the decision of the next lowest court,
which had overturned the desegregation decision.   The other
cases also build new ground subject to review by the Supreme
Court, a Court that is becoming more conservative and whose
Nixon appointees have a known distaste for racial desegrega-
tion.

Since 1954, the Supreme Court has demanded an end
to de jure segregation of schools, a Southern problem, but
ignored de facto segregation, a Northern problem.   Most of
the Court's procedures for ending state-imposed segregated

schools could easily have been applied to the North, yet the focus of attention was the South.   Thus according to 1971 governmental statistics, 38 percent of black students in the South were attending integrated schools, but only 27 percent were in the North and West.   Events in Detroit, coupled with the growing number of court cases which have already reversed the bussing orders, and the increasing racial polarization within the country, suggest that we may soon see the beginning of a new national ebb tide on the issue of school desegregation.   Whether total school desegregation comes to Detroit, and some day to the rest of the country, may depend on nine high justices.   It is expected that a Supreme Court ruling will be made by 1974.

NEW YORK CITY

The discussion now turns to New York City.   This is one of the two school systems, along with Detroit, that provides a form of community control.   As with many other educational trends that started with the New York schools, it is here where the twin concepts of administrative decentralization and community control commingled and received their theoretical impetus.   The New York case is the most widely known because of the nationwide headlines over two related issues, the Ocean Hill-Brownsville experiment and the 1968 teachers' strike.   The discussion of these two controversial issues will be limited because they have been thoroughly examined in other books;   the focus of debate will be on the policy reports connected with these two issues.

According to Facts and Figures, 1972-72, the New York City school system consists of 964 schools, 110,000 professional personnel including 69,000 teachers, and 1,149,068 students.   The 1972 student racial composition was 36.4 percent white, 35.1 percent black, 23.2 percent Puerto Rican, 3.7 percent other Spanish surnamed, 1.6 percent Oriental, and less than .1 percent Indian.   The citywide board of education consists of seven members, five appointed by each of the five borough presidents and two by the mayor.   As a result of the 1969 School Decentralization law, the school superintendent is called the chancellor.

According to one New York Information Assistant (1972a) and one New York Information Officer (1972a) [these two school officials did not want to be quoted by name], the central administration is still being reorganized, basically because of retirement, "natural causes of events," and various forms of pressure, most of which is interpreted by this author to mean political factors and race and ideology. There are four executive directors of (1) business and administration, (2) personnel, (3) school buildings, and (4) instruction, as well as a lame duck deputy chancellor (equivalent to the deputy superintendent) of curriculum and instruction with dimished powers since curriculum and instruction are mainly developed by the local community school boards, all of whom are responsible to the chancellor. The four executive directors, the deputy chancellor, and the chancellor are appointed by the city-wide board of education.

According to the New York Times (January 16, 1972), former Chancellor Harvey Scribner and the city-wide school board were in favor of sweeping administrative changes because the central administration was not performing as effectively as it should; there was thorough confusion of roles and responsibilities as a result of administrative decentralization, widespread fragmentation, dissipation of innovative ideas, and waste of time and money on nonproductive programs; many of the administrators were unprepared to cope with their daily problems. A plan for reorganizing the central administration includes the creation of four deputy chancellors to strengthen the central management and provide greater services to the local community districts. The plan should be in operation by January 1974.

Conversations with the New York Information Officer (1972a) revealed that in the 1950s and 1960s the New York City school system contained between 24 and 54 school districts. Since the 1969 School Decentralization Law, the school system has been divided into 32 community school districts. The new educational law permits the eligible voters of the school districts to elect their own community school boards, comprising nine members who select their own community district superintendent. According to The Day Schools Register by School District ... (1971), the school districts each comprise approximately 20 to 25 schools and 20,000 to 30,000 students. [A more detailed analysis of the number of schools and students in each community school district will be discussed later in this chapter.]

The Summary of the Citywide Test Results for 1970-71 indicates that the reading achievement tests were administered in April 1972 for students from grades two to nine. The school system's medium score is below the national norm

for each grade, and the trend is for the difference to become
greater as students progress to higher grades (from second
grade with a -.2 norm-city difference to ninth grade with a
-1.4 norm-city difference). Facts and Figures, 1970-71
shows that for the school year the total budget was $1.9 bil-
lion, of which 51 percent was derived from city funds, 37
percent from state funds, 10 percent from federal funds,
and 2 percent from miscellaneous revenues. Instructional expenses per student was $777 for academic senior school high
students, $877 for junior high school students, and $608 for
elementary school students. However, The New York Information Assistant (1972b) points out that the average per student total cost based on average school attendance is $1,667.

Events and policy reports leading up to the 1969
School Decentralization Law. In 1965 the city-wide board of
education considered and rejected a plan by former Mayor
Wagner's task force for decentralizing the school system into
five districts, one in each of the city's boroughs. The plan
had been tried in the past and was considered a failure.
However, the school board took the first steps toward decentralization by enlarging the number of districts from 25 to
30 (thus reducing their sizes to make them presumably more
effective for administrative purposes) and increasing the responsibilities of the district superintendents.

Two years later the New York State Legislature passed
an educational bill, granting the city school system $54 mil-
lion in additional state aid if the school board would decentralize the schools into five districts. Again, the school
board rejected the idea of breaking down the school system
into five autonomous school districts, but it proceeded to set
forth its own Decentralization Statement of Policy (1967).
The policy statement maintained that "all members of [the]
Board [were] committed to the principles of decentralization"
and that it was "essential to have [increased] flexibility and
authority at the local level" (p. 1). The underlying principles
of the statement were the maintenance of 30 attendance school
districts, the increasing of the authority of the district superintendents, and strengthening of the role of the district school
boards.

With regard to personnel, the report suggested that
the district school boards recommend qualified candidates for
the position of district superintendent but the general superintendent would make the final selections. From a list of
eligibles, the district school board and district superintendents

were permitted to make recommendations for a principal
when a vacancy occurred. The final selection was considered
by the school superintendent; however, his decision could be
appealed by the district school board and district superintendent. Licensed teachers were assigned to the school districts rather than to the individual schools and the district
superintendents were given the power to assign the teachers
to the individual schools and decide on subsequent transfers.
Inservice training of teachers and supervisors was now considered the principals' responsibility. Although the curriculum remained centralized, the district school boards and
superintendents were granted the power to purchase books
from a recommended list, with room for local autonomy,
and the principals were given the responsibility for curriculum innovation and implementation. As for the budget, each
school district was allocated a lump sum by the city-wide
board of education, to be expanded by the district school
board and superintendent; the local school board and superintendent could also make recommendations concerning the
budget to the city-wide school board and general superintendent. The city-wide school board also reaffirmed its previous statements of October 1966 and February 1967, "to experiment with varying forms of decentralization and community involvement" (p. 5). It further recommended that a number of demonstration projects be organized, with its own local school board involving representatives from the parents,
community, and professional staff and with increased decision-making powers.

        The city-wide school board eventually designated four
demonstration districts: Upper West Side Manhattan, the
I. S. 201 complex in Harlem, Two Bridges in lower Manhattan
(between the Brooklyn Bridge and Manhattan Bridge), and
Ocean Hill-Brownsville in Brooklyn's Bedford-Stuyvesant area.
The first district declined to reorganize itself into a demonstration project; the other three districts proceeded to do
so. Here it is important to underscore the New York City
Board of Education's action in authorizing these experimental
districts; they were not produced by outside forces, although
they may have evolved from such pressure. Wrote Fantini
et al. (1970), "They [the three districts] emerged through the
legitimate channel of ... the school system" and had "official
authorization" from the Board (p. 144-45). The city-wide
school board's own initiative could be viewed as a real commitment toward experimenting with the idea of community
control at a time when most school boards across the country
were (and still are) permitting only advisory roles for

parental and community groups.   Yet one must also realize
that the experimental districts were established on a pilot
basis within the guidelines established by the "mother" system or city board of education.   They were supposed to
operate within the rules of the "mother" system and could
be dissolved by it.   When the three districts became too
controversial, especially the Ocean Hill-Brownsville district,
they were absorbed into larger school districts--resulting
from the 1969 School Decentralization Law.

In the meantime, the New York State Legislature provided temporary financial assistance to meet the school needs
of the city but by-passed the city-wide board of education
and requested former Mayor Lindsay to submit a decentralization and community participation plan.   The mayor organized a panel which was eventually headed by McGeorge Bundy,
who was then president of the Ford Foundation, and which
included Mario D. Fantini, a staff worker with the Foundation.   Thus the mayor's office and Ford Foundation entered
the arena, and these two groups would eventually ally with
the minority groups over the battle for school power during
the 1968 teacher strike and the numerous confrontations with
the school board.

In November 1967, the Mayor's Advisory Panel submitted its report, entitled Reconnection for Learning, or the
"Bundy report," after the chairman of the panel.   We have
already stated (see Chapter 1) that the report suggested that
(1) the schools be decentralized into 30 to 60 community
school districts, ranging in size from about 12,000 to 40,000
students, (2) the community school boards have broad powers
over personnel, curriculum, and the budget, (3) and the city-
wide board of education have powers over students transfers,
contract negotiations with the teachers, and school integration [this included the right to hire their own community superintendent, as well as the revision of criteria for appointments and promotions (in effect the elimination of competitive
examinations) to give the community greater freedom in hiring
teachers and administrators of their choice].   In addition, it
stated that (4) the community school districts would have authority over the elementary and secondary schools, (5) the
city-wide school board and state commissioner of education
should be responsible for maintaining standards, (6) the community school districts would be governed by local school
boards that would be selected in part by the mayor, (7) the
plan should go into effect beginning September 1969, and
(8) the state commissioner of education would be in charge

of the transition to the community school system.

The Bundy report was influential for several reasons:
the air of reform was widespread at the state level, the
mayor's office, and the board of education. City school systems, and especially the ghetto schools, seemed to be worsening, not only in New York City but across the nation, and
receiving even greater attention from educational critics. A
great deal of the criticism was voiced by liberal educators
and black militants, and their vocality was more forceful in
New York. In addition, the panel members were prominent
educators who would have to be taken seriously. (For a list
of the panel members, see Chapter 2.) The panel was legitimized by the state legislature, the state commissioner of
education, and the mayor's office. It also had input from
panel members and representative consultants of the minority
community. The panel members stated the urgency for reform had the original political backing of the state legislature
and the continuous political support from the mayor's office;
moreover, it has the economic support from Ford Foundation,
and community activist support from various civil rights organizations and city-affiliated community groups.

In March 1968, the New York City Board of Education
issued another administrative decentralization proposal, A
Plan for Educational Policy and Administrative Units (Further
Decentralization of the Public Schools). The proposal pointed
out that the major issue was money and "simply changing the
school structure" was not the answer to quality education
(p. 1). The school board reaffirmed the need for decentralization and district school boards, but rejected the concept of
complete community control, as would be the case with the
recommendations of the Bundy report. The school board
argued that the city was too complex and the "broader social
interests" of the schools should be assured "through centralized direction and control" (p. 2). Policies regarding the
merit system and promotions, cohesiveness rather than separation in society, and ultimately the quality of education was
best implemented on a city-wide basis from the central office.
The school board also contended that a drastic increase in
the number of school districts would lead to administrative
fragmentation and chaos; it concluded "that a massive [re-
organization] in the largest school system in the world in
one swoop ... would cause unnecessary and harmful disorganization" (p. 4).

The school board proposed to eliminate the "advisory"

restrictions of the district school boards. These boards
were to be granted power to hire their respective district
superintendents who would have responsibility over the elementary and junior high schools within his boundaries. Since
the high schools and special schools were organized around
an inter-district and inter-borough basis, it was considered
best that they remain administered from the central office.
The local school boards would have the power to grant or
deny tenure of employees on the recommendation of the district superintendent; in effect, this meant the district school
boards would have this power since they were given the
power to select their own district superintendent. Any person denied tenure could appeal to the city-wide board of education. The qualifying principal's examination was to continue, but the local boards could select their principals from
a list of eligibles. Teacher certification remained a function
of the central office and supervisory positions continued to
be based on merit and competitive examinations. [6] The district school boards were granted authority to determine their
own priorities, but the budget was still to be allocated by
the city-wide school board. While the plan encouraged curriculum innovation and implementation at the school level,
including the right of the local school board to offer elective
courses and adopt textbooks from a recommended list, it asserted that the central office would maintain responsibility
for evaluating and testing the effectiveness of the school programs. It was also recommended that the city-wide school
board be increased at that time from nine to 13 members so
as to ensure greater minority representation.

    To put the Bundy report and the school board's plan
in perspective, the reader must understand the times. Although the advocates of community control were both black
and white, the blacks who supported the idea at that time
were mainly militants who interpreted conflict as a legitimate
tactic and were even willing to use violence to achieve their
ends. The whites who supported the idea did not do it for segregationist reasons, as in Detroit, but mainly in the name of
the black cause. One must understand the middle- and upper-
class liberals that live in the city are not found elsewhere in
the country to the same extent or with the same influence.
This is especially true when we compare New York with Detroit, where most of the whites cannot economically afford
to be liberal. New York City liberals were caught up with
the rhetoric of reform and identified with the civil rights
movement of the early 1960s. Still thinking in terms of the
old liberal-black coalition, still thinking in the past, and

also because of their good intentions, many liberals today still refuse to admit to the excesses of community control and black power as it has developed.

Because those who supported the idea of community control did so in the name of the black cause, almost any-one who opposed it and was black was branded as a "Tom," and almost anyone who was white was considered as anti-black and denounced as a "racist." This strategy is still used today by many liberal-militant groups with great suc-cess; this extends beyond the schools and beyond New York. This is part of the "victim" strategy, explained by Moynihan (1972) and Sowell (1973), and used with great success in dealing with various social institutions in order to advance black demands.

On one side of the issue of community control was the mayor and his office. Mr. Lindsay had no extra money to satisfy the discontented; the schools were broke and still failing. Hence, he chose to give into demands for commu-nity control, since it did not require any investment of funds. Similarly, he established several "little city halls" around the city. It was alleged by union officials and many other voices that the city administration put on its payroll those who were community activists, who sometimes threatened to use violence. As Moynihan (1969) contends, many of these new bureaucrats were opportunists and hustlers, espousing a new political rhetoric which coincided with the times. Writes Feldman (1972), "The neighborhood school became as fertile for a shakedown as the neighborhood merchant, and it was all done ... on behalf of the 'poverty community' " (p. 2). The real problems of ghetto schools were ignored--say, im-proving the quality of education--while Lindsay rolled up his sleeves and walked through the streets of Harlem with his black aides who advocated "cool it." Mr. Lindsay looked very good on the tube, but he and his liberal allies now find it unsafe to walk through most of the black communities, much less the streets of New York in the evening; this needs little documentation for anyone who lives in New York.

Then there was the Ford Foundation, which provided the necessary money to the three experimental districts, thus coinciding with their liberal orientation, while ignoring the so-called "establishment" programs such as the More Effec-tive Schools (MES). The MES program had been started by the teacher union and was considered relatively successful. The union had hoped to expand the program to all elementary schools,

which involved the local school boards with shared power between the community and the professionals.   Along with the
Ford Foundation, there were several other liberal organizations, such as the Urban Coalition and the Public Education
Association, whose upper middle-class and wealthy members
were financially secure and who had no vested job interest
in the school system.   Caught up with the romanticism of
the black power struggle, supporting what they considered
was the avant-garde movement against the establishment,
they prated that the "oppressed" minority could and should
overthrow the yoke of the white "establishment," both teachers
and administrators.   Then there were the black militants and
the community action groups, who seemed to this author
rarely if ever to represent the actual community, voicing
anti-white sentiments--and with patronage at stake, described
by Feldman (1969, 1972), Kemble (1968), Mayer (1969), Moseley
(1972) and Shanker (1971b, 1972d).

On the other side of the issue were the integrationists
such as the teachers' union and League for Industrial Democracy who were ironically labelled as "racists" because they
viewed community control as a separatism movement that
would impede integration.   The labor unions also supported
the teachers' union, because the rights of the teachers as
individuals and as members of the union were continuously
violated by the black militants, despite the findings of black
Judge Francis E. Rivers, discussed below, the pledges of
Rhody McCoy who was the unit administrator of the Ocean
Hill-Brownsville demonstration district, and the repeated
declarations of the board of education.   The black teachers
were troubled, especially over the Ocean Hill controversy
and the subsequent teachers' strike.   The union was opposed
to outright community control with no safeguards for the
teachers, yet the union had been in the forefront of the civil
rights movement and had benefitted blacks personally by securing their jobs and improving their working conditions without discrimination.   In 1968 most of the black teachers supported the union and went out on strike throughout the city;
in doing so they were rejecting the black militants and open-
ing themselves to charges of "tomism" by the most militant.
Whether this split would happen today is debatable, for blacks
seem nowadays reluctant to criticize other "brothers" and
"sisters" in public.   This is related to the growing influence
of the militants and the rhetoric of the militant ideology.
Dissension is discouraged and considered as aiding whites.

The Puerto Rican community, comprising about 15

percent of the city's population, was divided; while they
were alienated by the white power structure, they did not
trust the black community and especially the militants. For
the greater part, the white community saw no real need for
control of the schools; their children were succeeding in
school, at least going on to college.   Only the conservative
white organization, the Parents and Taxpayers, and a few
other conservatives, supported community control; this implied white segregation in the schools and black control of
the schools in lieu of higher taxes.

The most vocal opposition to community control was
the teachers' union. To the union which had always favored
integration and was involved in many civil rights demonstrations, community control meant separatism. Most important,
it was interested in the rights of its members (rightfully so
since this is the function of a union). The union saw the
major issue centering around the 19 dismissed Ocean Hill-
Brownsville teachers and administrators, later increased
to more than 100 white educators, without notice and
without due process. Seemingly as a ploy by the liberal-
militant community for the purpose of ignoring union issues and radicalizing the black community, the union was
accused of defending the status quo and perpetuating racism,
even though there was considerable anti-white sentiment expressed by many militants from outside the Ocean Hill community toward the white teachers in the form of threats, anti-
white literature, racial epithets, pictures on bulletin boards,
auditorium demonstrations, classroom indoctrination in anti-
white attitudes, and violence in the Ocean Hill schools directed toward the white teachers and administrators (Donovan,
1968; Feldman, 1969,1972; Mayer, 1969; Moseley, 1972).

The union members were old-fashioned liberals, what
today is considered by some as conservatives. They wanted
to decentralize the system and reduce the bureaucracy, yet
still try to work within the system. They had brought about
many innovative and worthwhile changes not only in teacher
salaries and conditions but also in programs for the education of the students. To them, legalizing segregation through
community control and demanding all black or predominantly
black staffs in ghetto schools was racist. It was a new form
of "separate but equal," new in the sense that the blacks and
not the whites were advocating such a move. Both the supervisory association and the board of education tended to agree
with the teachers' union; the administrators and the city-
wide school board members were apprehensive toward the

concept of community control. The school board rejected
the idea because it not only meant an abdication of power
which no group willingly surrenders but is also implied separation and not cohesiveness, segregation and not the possibility of integration. The militants viewed separation as a
legitimate tactic and a necessary state in the quest for black
power; they also viewed integration as an unfilled, white
hoax. The administrators, like the teachers, were mainly
white (almost 90 percent) and at best envisioned their jobs
and subsequent promotions as in jeopardy, and even worse,
the possibility of "vigilante" groups harassing them, which,
according to Mayer (1969) and Shanker (1969), did occur.
For the militants, many of the white educators and especially
white administrators could not be tolerated. The events of
the Ocean Hill-Brownsville controversy and subsequent events,
where white teachers and administrators were (and still are)
forced out of their schools, seems to have corroborated
these fears (Bard, 1972; Mayer, 1969; Moseley, 1972). The
school board and professional educators envisioned chaos and
violence if community control was implemented; moreover,
they were afraid of the militants running the schools, possibly terrorizing the white teachers and administrators, and
forcing them to leave the black schools--which is now happening in some of the ghetto schools of the city, as well as
in some other large cities (but on a lesser scale). (Bard,
1972; Moseley, 1972).

     The school board and professional educators did not
think that the lay public were able effectively to run their own
schools--especially the poor and uneducated--for the city's
educational problems were considered too complex--much
more complex than a town or village in suburbia. According
to Shanker (n.d.) and Sizer (1968), this was a political tactic
to reduce the pressure from the black community and to shift
the blame for inevitable school failure from city and state officials to the poor and minority groups. On the other hand,
the black community no longer trusted the predominantly white
school board and professional educators; they were considered
symbolic of the white power structure and members of the
system which has in the past discriminated against blacks.
For militants the issue was clear: blacks needed to control
the schools so as to use it as a base for further power.
Thus Carmichael and Hamilton (1967) declared, "We must begin to think of the black community as a base of organization
to control institutions in that community. Control of the ghetto schools must be taken out of the hands of 'professionals'....
Black parents should seek as their goal the actual control of

the public schools in their community ... " (p. 166-67). The
fact that the schools had failed to educate blacks was used
as a supportive argument, but the real issue was (and still
is today) not education but politics and economics.   Although
the militants did not speak for the entire black community,
black people were beginning to stress black unity and power
and therefore became increasingly more reluctant to take issue in public with the black militants.   Indeed, the Kenneth
Clarks and Bayard Rustins--the black voices of moderation--
were overshadowed by the emotionalism and rhetoric of black
militancy, and the subsequent white reaction and fears to this
black ideology.

From its inception in 1967, the Ocean Hill-Brownsville demonstration district was plagued with racial hostilities.
The militants had gained control of the governing school board
and proceeded illegally to dismiss 13 teachers and six administrators without formal charges or a hearing.   The governing school board refused to submit the dispute to binding arbitration;   to submit it to arbitration could mean the end of
a confrontation that the governing school board wanted in order to mobilize the black community, which was becoming
disenchanted with the local school board.

Shanker (1969) points out that a Harris poll was taken
in the spring of 1968, a few months before the beginning of
the confrontation, and it found that the black community was
dissatisfied with the performance of the black unit administrator Rhody McCoy (44 percent of the responses were negative;   29 percent were positive;   the remainder undecided)
and the black governing school board (47 percent were negative and 38 percent were positive), and only 29 percent of
the respondents supported the decision to remove the 19 white
teachers and administrators.   Furthermore, during the summer of 1968, a petition signed by more than 2000 community
people demanded new elections for a local school board,
which was "twice as many people as had originally voted the
previous summer" for the members of the school board
(p. 457).

During the summer of 1968, Judge Francis E. Rivers
invalidated the dismissal charges against the 19 educators.
The Ocean Hill governing board refused to budge from their
position;   moreover, it added approximately 85 additional
teachers to the dismissal list.   The teachers' union viewed
this as a threat to its rights and security;   the union assembly voted (approximately 1900 to 250) to strike and the

membership followed suit (voting approximately 12,000 to
1800). According to Shanker (1969), the president of the
teachers' union, it was not the issue of administrative decentralization or community control but the rights of teachers
to return to the class and the future security of teachers
which led to the strike in September 1968, the violation of
the settlement (when teachers were reinstated, they were
given no classes to teach) which brought on the second strike,
and the continuous harassment and threats of violence and
even assault toward the union teachers that brought on the
third strike (Feldman, 1969,1972; Mayer, 1969).

When the strike began, the militants found the larger
black community divided and opposed to them. The NAACP
and other black integrationist organizations favored community control so long as it did not prevent integration. This
position left these organizations without a practical strategy
and they eventually fell into the background. A. Philip Ran-
dolph and Bayard Rustin and a large group of trade unionists
publically denounced community control. Assemblyman Sam-
uel Wright, a member of the governing board, repeatedly opposed the black militants; he eventually discharged them
when he became president of District 23 as a result of the
city-wide community control elections in 1970. As previously
mentioned, the majority of black teachers in the school system supported the union and went out on strike--in effect,
rejecting the black militants. And the residents of the Ocean
Hill-Brownsville community, afraid to come to meetings because of intimidation and violence, attempted without success
to enroll their children in other schools. Despite militant
threats against them, thousands of them signed a petition opposing the decision to remove the white teachers and administrators and they also demanded new elections.

Since the black militants could not rally support of
black community and most of the black teachers in the school
system, as pointed out by Feldman (1972), the governing
board successfully changed the real issue of the illegal dis-
missals of the teachers to one which they could gather the
most sympathizers: they were the "oppressed" minority trying to overthrow the white colonialists; they were the forces
of change fighting against the white establishment--teachers,
administrators, and the board of education. At that time,
the three most influential black militants were Herman Ferguson, who had been indicted and was later convicted for
conspiracy to murder civil rights leaders,[7] the Rev. Herbert
Oliver, chairman of the governing board, and Rhody McCoy,

the unit administrator of the experimental district, all of whom spoke about getting the yoke of the white oppressor off its back, about sophisticated forms of slavery, about the rape of the black community by the white teachers' union, and so on.   The race issue was played up by the media, too; it created sensationalism and sold papers.   When the black militants began to distribute anti-white literature, that issue was also emphasized by the media.   Even the mayor, who clearly was on the side of the governing board, in front of the television cameras denounced Albert Shanker, the president of the teachers' union and the entire union as "racist. "   Thus the question of due process for teachers and their rights as individuals and teachers, were set aside. Writes Feldman (1972): "The strike became in the public view, as had the community control issue, a struggle between whites and blacks, " and more precisely a struggle between the predominantly white UFT and the black community of Ocean Hill-Brownsville.   Anyone who opposed community control, depending on his race, was "accused of white racism or Uncle Tomism" (p. 2-3).   It is fascinating that the issue of race and the cry of white racism is still used today with great success by blacks, both militants and now some moderates, regarding other issues and other institutions in other cities.   The situation often boils down to black problems being defined in terms of "white racism" and the "sickness" of society, even when there are other factors to consider;   white problems are often defined in terms of their own "racism" and "rationalizations. "

The strike affected the entire school system.   The school administrators also saw their positions and security threatened and many of them walked off their jobs in support of the striking teachers.   With the exception of the three demonstration districts and a few other scattered schools, the giant school system was brought to a halt.   Together the three strikes totalled ten weeks over a four-month period. The racial violence which erupted, even with the presence of the police, only confirmed the white teachers' and administrators' fears of community control.   On the other hand, the militants seemed backed into a wall, and in their attempt to politicalize the community and gain complete control of the schools, violence may have been a normal procedure for the militants to follow.   In any event, the heightened racial tensions of the strike spread beyond the school gates throughout the city and the entire city became (and still is) racially polarized.   The polarization reached the point where Glazer and Moynihan (1970) were forced to revise their melting pot theory and conclude that it was unlikely to work between blacks and whites, at least in New York City.

In the spring of 1968, the state legislature met to discuss a decentralization bill, but partially because of the pending crisis in the Ocean Hill-Brownsville district it passed the Marchi bill that delayed a definite decision for a full year. However, the state legislature permitted the mayor to appoint four additional members (in addition to three vacancies to fill) to the city-wide board of education, giving him the opportunity to appoint a school board headed by the liberal John Doar and the Rev. Milton Galamison, Jr., both of whom seemed mainly responsible to a select group of community control advocates and who created continuous blunders--whose motives were political and not educational (Feldman, 1972). It also permitted the school board to devise a decentralization plan for the interim period.

In September 1968 the board of education, now enlarged from nine to 13 members, resolved, in the Delegation of Functions to Local School Boards, temporary powers and obligations of the 30 community school districts and three demonstration districts. The 33 community school boards (note the new term "community") were granted the power to hire their own community superintendents and direct the policies of the elementary and junior high schools within their respective boundaries. The community district superintendents would be responsible to the community school boards in the same way the general superintendent was responsible to the city-wide board of education. The community school board, in consultation with its superintendent, was allowed to hire its own school principal from a list of eligibles and to fill vacancies and recruit its own teachers from city-wide lists. The community school board could grant tenure, promote personnel, and discontinue the services of nontenured personnel (the latter with the approval of the general superintendent). The local school board was also permitted to proceed with charges against tenured personnel, but these people would be entitled to review procedures. With respect to curriculum, the local school boards were to follow the general course requirements, but they could make curriculum adaptation to meet local needs, develop additional courses beyond the mandated courses, and determine and order their own textbooks from approved lists established by the city-wide board of education. The community school boards were granted the power to prepare a budget and submit it to the general superintendent, who in turn took into account

individual local needs in relation to the city-wide budget and
then submitted his recommendation to the city-wide school
board for approval. The decision of the general superintendent could be appealed by any local school board to the city-
wide school board. Local school boards were also given the
authority to allocate available resources so long as it did not
conflict with union obligations or city-wide standards. In
general the new plan was similar to the decentralization proposal, A Plan for Educational Policy and Administrative
Units ..., which was then six months out of date; the new
plan, however, did grant slightly additional powers to the
community school boards.

The 1969 School Decentralization Law and its aftermath. In April 1969, the state legislature amended the educational law in An Act Directing the Board of Education of
the City of New York to Prepare for the Development of a
Community School District System.... The Act is commonly
called the School Decentralization Law; the wording in the
Act changed the name of the school superintendent to chancellor and referred to the school (local) districts as "community districts," the (local) district school boards as "community school boards," and the (local) district superintendents as "community superintendents."

The legislators agreed that the Doar-Galamison school
board was a divisive force and that they had to go. It was
stated that the city-wide board of education would consist of
five elected members, chosen by the voters of each of the
five boroughs, and two members appointed by the mayor, to
serve for four years. (The courts subsequently ruled that
this procedure was unconstitutional, because it violated the
one-man, one-vote principle.) The state legislature then extended the life of the interim school board and it was in operation until 1973 when the courts revised the ruling and permitted the seven-member board. An interim school board
was empowered to prepare a tentative district plan to define
the boundaries of the community districts by December 1969.
From 30 to 33 community districts would be established,
each consisting of "no ... less than twenty thousand pupils
in average daily attendance in the school under its jurisdic-
tion" (p. 7).

Each community district would be governed by a community board of education, consisting of from seven to 15
members elected for seven years by the registered voters
residing in the community boundaries and parents of the

children attending the schools within the community. The
New York Information Assistant (1972b) indicates that the
city-wide school board eventually decided on a nine-member
community board. The chancellor was responsible for conducting training sessions for the new community board members.

The community school boards could hire their own
community superintendents, and delegate to them its administrative powers and duties as it deemed appropriate and
modify or rescind any of its authority so delegated. The
community school boards' power over personnel, curriculum,
and the budget were similar to those proposed by the city-
wide board of education in September 1968, and they were
still limited to the elementary and junior high schools, not
to include the senior high and special schools. The board
of examiners were still permitted to administer examinations
to determine the merit and fitness of teachers, supervisors,
and principals; however, appeal procedures were adopted
which were mainly geared for minorities since they felt discrimination existed within the licensing procedures. Instead
of the community boards selecting personnel from eligible
lists, the chancellor would make the assignments to the community districts with the attempt to honor individual requests
and the community boards would assign the personnel to the
schools. An additional provision authorized the community
districts to take bids and issue contracts up to $250,000 for
annual repairs to schools within their respective boundaries.
The chancellor was granted the power to suspend a community board member or an entire community board, if deemed
necessary, to ensure compliance with the new educational law
and its rules and regulations; suspensions could be appealed
to the city-wide school board. In sum, the community school
boards were granted extensive powers over personnel and
curriculum and broad powers over the budget, including the
right to allocate funds as they deemed necessary; conditions
were established whereby the chancellor of city-wide board
of education might intervene.

The matter of hiring teachers and administrators was
perhaps the most controversial issue. A compromise between
the UFT and black community was reached. For those schools
whose students fell below the city's 45th percentile in reading, the community school boards could hire their own
teachers either out of rank order from eligibility lists or if
they had passed the National Teacher Examination, which is
considered by many New York educators to be easier than

the city examinations, for the latter requires a test in the
candidate's specialized area as well as an essay examination,
neither of which does the NTE include. It merely asks multiple choice questions related to education. The supervisory
examinations were also changed from competitive to qualifying testing procedures in order to make it easier for minorities to take and pass the examinations.

While the School Decentralization Law is considered
conservative in terms of the demand for community control
advocated by liberal educators, to black militants (who had
captured the initiative in organizing the black community in
New York City), the provisions were radical in comparison
to the extent of community control permitted in other school
systems. These provisions granted sufficient community
control so that the professionals seem now at the mercy of
a few individuals, nine members on a local school board,
who are supposed to speak for the community, but whose
representation and motives can nevertheless be questioned.

An interim board of education was established, as mentioned above, consisting of five members appointed by the five
borough presidents. In accordance with the School Decentralization Law, the school board issued in November 1969 a tentative
report, Proposed Plan for a Community School District System
in New York, establishing 30 community districts. "More than
80 percent of the [people queried] stated in effect, 'We do
not want any change,' while the bulk of the remainder spoke
in terms of relatively minor changes" (p. 5). Consequently
the school board implemented minimal boundary changes consistent with the new educational law.

The most heated issue centered around the three demonstration districts. The school board's report reiterated
that the School Decentralization Law did not permit "the re-
tention of the districts as community districts because of the
requirement that 'no community district shall contain less
than 20,000 pupils in average daily attendance' " (p. 6).
Since the average daily absentee rate in the city schools ex-
ceeded 10 percent, this meant that "the minimum register of
the ... schools in the district must generally be more than
22,000" (p. 6). Not one of the three demonstration districts
contained even half the number. It was agreed that each
demonstration district should remain together; however,
there was a split opinion on whether they should be merged
with nearby schools to meet the minimum prescribed number
of students in average daily attendance or continued to operate

as separate administrative units. The majority of school board members (3 out of 5) believed they did not have the power under the new educational law to continue the existing demonstration projects; the minority felt that it did.

Public hearings followed throughout the city and hundreds of written statements were analyzed. The boundary plans were finalized a month later in December 1969 in a report called the District Boundary Lines under the Community School District System. Although there were many requests to continue the demonstration districts, for reasons outlined in the tentative plan, the majority of the school board members still maintained that the School Decentralization Law did not permit such action. Thus the eight Ocean Hill-Brownsville schools were merged with 14 additional schools to form District 23 with a total register of more than 25,000 students. The five schools within the I.S. 201 complex were merged with 19 additional schools to form District 5 with 24,000 students. And in downtown Manhattan, the five schools in the Two Bridges area were merged with 18 schools to form District 3 with 22,000 students. Each of the three new districts comprised more than the minimum number of students in average daily attendance. A total of 30 districts were formed, with the borough of Richmond comprising one separate district. In February 1970 district 5 was split into two districts (5 and 6) to form 31 districts. In mid 1973 a District 32 was formed in Brooklyn. In addition, the high schools were formed into a separate District, 78, and the special schools were formed into still another District, 75, both run by the city-wide board of education and divided into five subunits to represent each borough with the special schools further divided according to their functions.

The Day Schools Register by School District on October 30, 1970, a report published by the Department of Educational Program Research and Statistics, shows the size of 31 of the 32 community districts; in theory, they seem large enough to offer a full range of educational services, yet small enough to be aware of the interests and needs of the community residents (see Table 4.1).

The School Decentralization Law, while not providing complete community control, has permitted more citizen participation than any other large school system. The movement toward community control seems to have led to adverse consequences and certainly has failed to achieve its goals,

Table 4.1

NEW YORK CITY COMMUNITY DISTRICTS
(Number of Schools, Number of Students)

District Number		No. of Schools Elem.	Jr. High/ Intermed. [a]	No. of Students Registered
M[b]	1	16	4	18,411
M	2	21	5	21,507
M	3	19	4	21,856
M	4	18	4	21,379
M	5	19	5	23,983
M	6	11	3	19,588
Bx	7	18	4	30,041
Bx	8	19	6	33,805
Bx	9	20	5	34,970
Bx	10	17	7	27,693
Bx	11	19	6	26,648
Bx	12	17	4	35,929
Br	13	18	4	25,633
Br	14	21	6	29,739
Br	15	20	5	26,459
Br	16	23	4	38,078
Br	17	13	4	25,737
Br	18	14	5	21,932
Br	19	22	7	37,468
Br	20	24	6	27,837
Br	21	23	6	29,003
Br	22	22	5	28,576
Br	23	19	4	25,489
Q	24	19	5	23,085
Q	25	22	6	26,390
Q	26	24	5	20,872
Q	27	27	4	30,479
Q	28	22	6	28,032
Q	29	22	4	25,713
Q	30	20	5	24,353
R	31	38	6	36,964

[a]Note that District 78, comprising the high schools, and District 75, comprising the special schools, are not included, since they are not community districts. In 1970 there were 94 high schools with 285,228 students and 56 special schools with 8198 students.

[b]M = Manhattan   Br = Brooklyn   R = Richmond
Bx = Bronx   Q = Queens

although the disaster that some opponents predicted has not
eventuated. The new educational law was designed with the
intentions, at least in the ideal sense, to fulfill the following
goals: greater (1) citizen participation, (2) representation
for minorities, (3) educational innovation, (4) community
unity and responsibility, (5) teacher accountability, (6) flexibility in hiring and promoting teachers and administrators,
(7) relevancy for students, and (8) achievement among students.

With regard to the first two goals, The New York
Times (August 15, 1971) reported that only 15 percent of the
eligible voters bothered to go to the polls in the first (1970)
school board election; furthermore, in District 23 (where
the Ocean Hill schools were merged), only 5 percent went
to the polls. Shanker (1971a) wrote that

> ... this small turnout occurred at a time when mem-
> ories of the 1968 school confrontation were still fresh
> in citizens' minds. Future elections, in a less heated
> atmosphere, may well attract fewer voters. Obviously,
> the advocates of community control had grossly exag-
> gerated the size of the demand for participatory de-
> mocracy [p. 11].

According to the Times (August 15, 1971), a large percentage of the voters had no children in school or their children
attended private or parochial schools. In the same vein,
Shanker (1971a) pointed out that most of those who voted were
members of organized groups: affiliated with churches, political organizations, labor unions, and anti-poverty agencies.

The same issue of the Times raised the question of
what constitutes a representative community school board.
In District 25 in Queens, a book about ghetto life, "Down
These Mean Streets," was removed from the school libraries
because of sexual descriptions. This led to an outcry that
the school board was not representative of the community.
In District 10 in the Bronx and District 20 in Brooklyn, Ro-
man Catholic priests were voted in as presidents. In District 3 located in Manhattan and Districts 13 and 15 located
in Brooklyn, community school boards with a white majority
were chosen to govern schools that were overwhelmingly
black and Puerto Rican. Wrote Shanker (1971a), "When the
votes were counted, parents and minority groups found themselves with less power in schools than ever before" (p. 11).
According to Boulton H. Demas, one of the original

proponents of community control and a member of the Institute for Community Studies at Queens College, "analysis of the results in the five boroughs reveals that local school boards, with very few exceptions, are dominated by [those] who have little or no commitment to public education, let alone community control" (p. 29). The Institute, which was financially helping to support the Ocean Hill-Brownsville experiment, termed the election "a disaster unparalleled in the history of the New York school system."

The second community school board elections were in 1973. The New York Times (May 2, 6, 1973) reported an even lower turnout than the 1970 elections. Only 11 percent of the eligible voters went to the polls, despite the fact that numerous organizations campaigned and urged people to vote. For the greater part, the 288 candidates that won community seats, not to speak of the 700 who ran for office, were almost completely unknown to their constituents; there were too many people running and the news media is city oriented, not community oriented. Indeed, one can raise the question if community control in New York City is really a concern of the people, or of a few liberal and militant voices. One can question whether community control is the most democratic method of running our schools.

The apparent indifference of most eligible voters toward community control of the schools also coincides with the apparent indifference to other community institutions. The result is, according to Moynihan (1969), that militants and activists often manage to gain control of community programs and these people often do not represent the majority of the residents, and sometimes they do not even live in the community itself. The same nonvoting pattern coincides with community action programs. For example, in 1967, at the time when community control and "maximum feasible participation" of minority and poor residents were being advocated, the voting turnout for these programs was 2.7 percent in Philadelphia, .7 percent in Los Angeles, 2.4 percent in Boston, 4.2 percent in Cleveland, and 5 percent in Kansas City, Mo. (Wall Street Journal, August 25, 1967). The result was that maximum feasible participation turned into organized militants gaining control of most of these programs, creating conflict for purpose of implementing change, and alienating local and federal governmental officials who were threatened by the conflict. In the end, these programs became a liability to the government and were eventually phased out. (Moynihan, 1969).

The third goal was educational innovation and the
fourth was community unity and responsibility. As for innovation, the advocates of administrative decentralization and
community control argued that the system had become too
rigid; there was the need to break down the system and
provide local autonomy to permit innovation and experimentation. Unfortunately it does not appear that such a change
has taken place; if anything, the system appears more rigid
than before reorganization.

Shanker (1972c) points out that outdated supervision
practices abandoned decades ago have been reinstated in many
community districts. One example is a standardized, mimeographed teacher rating form which includes such items as
(1) absenteeism, (2) lateness, (3) submitting records accu-
rately, (4) submitting them on time, (5) accounting for location during free periods and nonteaching assignments, (6) use
of students' progress charts, (7) monthly student examinations, (8) room upkeep, (9) classroom management, (10) attitude toward supervisors, etc. Teachers are also rated
through "quickie" observations by another form:

> 'Dear (Mr. , Mrs. , Miss) _____: Please explain
> why at this late date, _____, your pupils still
> (1) are without a loose-leaf notebook, (2) are without
> a spiral for foreign language, (3) do not write head-
> ings on their papers, (4) are not seated during morn-
> ing pre-session, (5) are not seated during lessons,
> (6) arrive late to class, (7) do not have a section to
> their notebooks for your subject area, (8) are still
> wearing hats and coats in class. ' Through the use
> of these forms, principals can show their superinten-
> dents that a huge amount of 'supervision' has been
> done, even though not a single teacher has been
> helped to correct any weakness or encouraged in
> areas of strength [p. 7].

The teachers are also required to submit monthly forms ex-
plaining how many times they have assigned book reports,
essays, special projects, homework, etc. , and checked students' notebooks. Another weekly form consists of a grid
which they fill in describing their whereabouts and activities
at all times outside of class. Still another bimonthly form
is for the teachers to project the percentage of students who
will pass the student examinations. Teachers are also requested to turn in a student progress chart in which every
student is listed and graded under headings such as

"outstanding work," "book reports," "condition of notebook," "homework," etc. Not only is this a return to the worst type of bureaucracy and rigidity, and lack of innovation and experimentation, but it also burdens the teachers with additional paperwork and unprofessional and petty details, thus distracting them from their real job of teaching. It also creates an enormous amount of data, both negative and positive, either aspect of which can be selected for political and ideological purposes. Teachers feel the need for supervisors who can provide genuine support and services, not those who serve as inspectors or treat them as cogs in a machine, or worse, who may seek to discharge them in the name of community control.

According to Kenneth B. Clark (1972a) a black psychologist and one of the original and moderate supporters of decentralization and community control, innovation has not been forthcoming. Most of the community school boards seem preoccupied with the question of politics and how to spend their allocated money. Asserts Clark (1972a):

> I do not see that we have kept--or the local boards have concentrated on--quality and methods for raising quality as much as they have concentrated on power [and] control of finances [p. 1].

And Shanker (1971a) declares:

> Many community board meetings have been marked by confrontations between rival local political forces vying for patronage. Discussion of educational innovation, when it does occur, has usually been in the form of pressure to dismantle innovative programs which cost more for each child than the regular program--the argument being that a fixed amount of money should be spent on each child throughout the district [p. 11].

Reports from many other community districts illustrate that the school boards' meetings have degenerated into ideological and racial debates. Many of the "moderate" community school board members in black communities have experienced threats or actual harassment, pressure, and assault from militant blacks and unrepresentative community activists; the outcome is that many of the moderates have resigned and the vacancies either have not been filled, making it difficult to function because of the lack of majorities on issues which are presented, or have been filled largely by militants. In the first year alone, 32 of the 279 elected community school board members resigned; only 18 of these vacancies were filled--many after protracted struggle (Clark, 1972a, 1972b; New York Times July 23, 1970, August 15, November 15, 1971, April 20, 1972; Scribner, 1971, 1972; Shanker, 1971b, 1972d). Hence, the wishes of the voters have been overridden in many cases by a small contrary group; the same situation has also occurred in Detroit.

Perhaps District 23 has been characterized by the most intense conflict. For three years, since 1970, several incidents of conflict and violence among blacks have been reported by the New York Times. The new black school board was composed of moderates who originally were denied access to the records of the Ocean Hill district; threats and beatings have been inflicted on several of them allegedly by supporters of the former governing school board; new school board members have resigned because of threats on and fear of their lives; the offices and homes of school board members have been ransacked; and several teachers and principals originally hired by the former governing school board have been dismissed by the new community school board.

The fifth goal was concerned with teacher accountability. Since the new educational law, the city-wide board of education has encouraged parent associations to serve in an advisory capacity to rate and evaluate personnel. Shanker (1972b) points out that the principal or superintendent, or both, are supposed to make the final decisions concerning the evaluation of personnel, but since their own jobs depend on evaluations by the same parent organizations the "advisory" role in effect becomes a crucial, if not, determining one.

Writes Shanker (1972b)

Still another problem facing the schools is a rising wave of vigilante-type activity by 'parent' and 'community' groups.

In one school, P. S. 12 Queens, the Parents Association mailed mimeographed letters to all the parents. The letters listed the names of all teachers in the school who were on probation and said: 'If your child had, or has had, any of the above teachers, or if you have any information concerning any of these teachers, please complete the attached form and mail it to the Parents Association in the enclosed envelope. All

information will be kept in strictest confidence. '
(... [T]he files on teachers which could result in
dismissal are kept in 'strictest confidence. ') The
letter then asks parents to fill out a full-page form
for rating the teacher on adequate lesson preparation,
interest of presentation, classroom control, satisfactory instruction. ...   Finally, the parent is asked,
'Do you feel your child has made adequate progress?'

In a number of districts, another procedure is being
followed: classroom observation by parent visitation
committees of anywhere from three to twenty.   These
committees then 'advise' the principal (whom they are
empowered to hire or fire) on which teachers should
be ousted.   One Community School Board (District 3)
acknowledges that 'sophistication' in these matters
varies from parent to parent ... [p. 9].

In a school atmosphere of politics and ideology, coupled with crime and violence (discussed below), it is questionable if the parents can rate teachers objectively, regardless if they have the expertise to do so.   The experts themselves (social scientists, educators, and teacher-behavior
researchers) find it difficult or more realistically impossible
to objectively rate and evaluate teachers (Jackson, 1968;
Popham, 1972).

Henry S. Dyer (1970), the former vice president of
Educational Testing Service and perhaps the foremost expert
on test construction, and the person commissioned by the
New York City school board to devise an accountability model,
points out that an accountability scheme that only focuses on
the teacher or administrator "is likely to do more harm than
good" and is misleading (p. 206).   The accountability model
must take into account the student himself, as well as conditions of the home, community, and school.   In a rush to hold
teachers accountable, the community school boards appear to
be making the sort of mistakes that Dyer cautions against.
For whatever reasons, some parent groups seem intent on
putting the total blame on a number of teachers while forget-
ing about the other variables--such as, for example, student's
family characteristics, motivations, and diets--that interact
with the teaching-learning process.   Chancellor Scribner's
response was simple: the community school boards have the
power to hire and fire their personnel.

At the present, many liberal and black militant groups

argue against tenure.   They tell us that they wish to do away
with tenure so as to rid the schools of incompetents and hold
teachers accountable.   Those who defend tenure tell us that
lack of tenure exposes educators to dismissal for holding un-
popular views or for being victimized by vigilante groups.
In fact, it is common knowledge that in many ghetto schools
a racial factor has evolved: white teachers and administrators are being harassed, threatened, assaulted and forced to
leave their positions under pressure (Bard, 1972; Moseley,
1972).

     The concept of black power and community control
connotes black solidarity, political ideology, and anti-white
sentiment.   For example, Carmichael and Hamilton (1967)
lump white educators together as being "dysfunctional and
at worst destructive" to black children (p. 166).   The authors argue that "race be taken into account in determining
policy" and that blacks be favored in personnel practices
(p. 167).   For Sizemore (1972), black power and community
control mean that blacks are able to maintain "solidarity
against oppression ... and produce ideologies that make liberation possible." She emphasizes the need to discharge
whites and overturn the white power structure so as to "enhance the myths, rites, and rituals which preserve [black]
solidarity" (p. 283).   And Billings (1972) states that the "conflict over community control ... of schools represents nothing more or less than a struggle for power between blacks
and whites" (p. 277).   When we link the issue of tenure or
accountability with black power and community control, white
teachers and administrators become increasingly afraid that
it will be used in the ghetto schools as weapons against them,
not for educational reasons.   Moreover, in predominantly
white schools only unqualified whites may be replaced because
it is politically unwise to replace unqualified blacks because
of existing militancy and quotas.   Tenure and accountability
qualifications may become increasingly based on hereditary
factors, not merit or competency; furthermore, these policies can easily be implemented along side affirmative-action
programs which already discriminate against whites. [8]

     With regard to the goal of flexible hiring and promo-
tion practices, the original intent, according to Fantini et al.
(1970), was to attract teachers and administrators with more
initiative and innovation but that "appointments and promotions
be competitive" and not spell "ethnic favoritism in hiring"
(p. 131).   In reality it is difficult to determine what is initiative and innovation; they have differing meanings.

Nevertheless, the NAACP went to court to block the use of
the objective examinations in New York City, and the chancellor refused to enter into a legal defense.   While the issue remains unsettled, the community school boards in the
ghetto areas hire their own teachers and "acting principals"
who are unlicensed.   Moseley (1972) makes the following com-
ment:

> The [eligible] lists, when published, have been ignored.
> In the high schools the examination system has become
> so attenuated that it would be difficult indeed to fail
> many of the examinations given.   In the case of ele-
> mentary and middle schools there have been instances
> of persons' literally being invited in off the streets by
> community boards to staff classrooms.   These people
> are without any vestige of official qualification either
> in the form of a license from the Board of Examiners
> or a certificate from the State Department of Educa-
> tion [p. 561].

Bard (1972) contends that with the nonenforcement of
eligible lists there is a strong possibility of buying and sell-
ing of jobs and hiring on ethnic basis, and the latter "is apparent already in the ethnic pattern behind [the] appointment
of 'acting principals' in low income areas ..." (p. 555).

Bard sums up the current situation in New York:

> What is at stake here, of course, is the question of
> granting to the [32] New York boards the right to make
> the same mistakes and exercise the same prejudices
> as, shall we say, as a Cicero or a Scarsdale....
> There are signs they are exercising these preroga-
> tives.   The NAACP said that some acting principals
> have been chosen by community boards 'on (the basis
> of) their ability to do the job' rather than through the
> testing apparatus.   The examiners' rejoinder was that
> they were chosen on the basis of 'unprofessional, sub-
> jective, and invalidated judgment' of an elected board,
> and: 'It may be that even the applicant's race plays
> a part in that judgment.'   Additionally, there has been
> testimony that some community boards ask the ques-
> tion, 'Where did you stand during the Ocean Hill
> strike?' when interviewing candidates for supervisory
> jobs.   They are doing, in other words, the same sort
> of things that politically conservative school districts
> do in screening out potential 'troublemakers.'   They
> are seeking conformance [p. 557-58].

Shanker (1972a) points out that as a result of Mayor
Lindsay's Executive Order No. 49, quotas favoring minorities, rather than individual merit and qualifications, are being employed in the New York City agencies and the board
of education. He illustrates where the interpretation of ethnic quotas borders on or can degenerate into reverse racism.

> Last November, a group calling itself the Concerned
> Parents Union of Junior High School 56 Complex, Man-
> hattan, distributed to children outside the school a
> newsletter addressed to the parents. The newsletter
> said 'Chinese, Blacks, and Puerto Ricans MUST unite
> to demand ... a qualified, good Black principal in
> JHS 56.' A few weeks later the acting principal of
> the school wrote to Human Rights Commissioner
> Eleanor Holmes Norton protesting that: 'They do not
> say why they do not want a good Chinese ... [or]
> Puerto Rican principal. They do not say why they do
> not want a good White principal....' Please note that
> the ethnic balance of the school is 21.3% Black,
> 51.8% Puerto Rican, 14.6% Chinese, 1% other Spanish,
> and 11.3% White; yet, the 'Concerned Parents Union'
> calls for a Black principal. Why? [p. 9].

(The acting principal went on to claim that the parent group
was violating state and federal laws pertaining to discrimination in hiring based on race and that as a white person his
human rights were being violated. Commissioner Norton re-
plied that the parent group had the right under the First
Amendment to express its opinion.)

In the meantime, Districts 1 and 3 have already openly
announced quotas in the hiring of personnel, and it is common
knowledge in New York that many of the other districts are
engaging in the same practice without publically admitting it.
The chancellor of the school system has remained silent;
only two of the five city-wide school board members at the
time publically opposed this practice. The events in District
1 especially seem unstable. The community district superintendent resigned in 1972 because of increased conflict and
violence in the District (New York Times, August 8, 1972).
The original 1970 community control vote in District 1 resulted in the election of seven "moderates" and two "militant"
advocates. Because of pressure one moderate switched philosophy, two resigned, and still another moderate was harassed, threatened, and her business property vandalized to
the point that she no longer attended the community school

board meetings.   The militants in the community--a parent
group consisting of approximately 15 members--managed to
intimidate the other parents into not coming to the local
board meetings and managed to appoint community control to
replace the moderates on the local school board.

The new community superintendent is Luis Fuentes,
a former principal in the Ocean Hill-Brownsville demonstration district who was appointed by the militant governing
board but dismissed as incompetent when the moderates took
control as a result of the 1970 elections.   Shanker (1972e)
points out that because of the experimental nature of the
demonstration district, he was permitted to serve in the
position without meeting eligibility requirements.   Although
Fuentes was originally rejected as a candidate for the position of community superintendent, when it was found that his
major letter of reference was a forgery and that he had de-
faulted on a loan in 1958 and that six of his teacher colleagues who served as co-signers had to pay the balance of
nearly $2000, he was reconsidered and appointed when the
militants took control of the district.

The New York Times (August 8, 1972), the UFT,
and several civil rights organizations also raised questions
about his personal and professional conduct, which included
the introduction of corporal punishment and documented ut-
terances of a great number of ethnic insults aimed at a wide
variety of religious, racial, and national groups during the
time he was principal.   He declared that the Jews passed
the supervisory examination in large numbers because it is
"written in Yiddish."   When reminded that the names of
those taking the tests were unknown to the examiners and
were coded to prevent bias, he remarked "Maybe I should
put a star on my examination paper."   He has gone on record in claiming that blacks express "themselves physically
because they cannot do so verbally."   He has referred to
Puerto Rican parents who disagreed with his procedures as
"all garbage."   He referred to his Italian assistant principals as "wops" and "guineas" and as probably having "Mafia"
connections in order to pass the supervisory examination.
He dubbed Catholics at a nearby Catholic university that refused to send student teachers to his school as "ignorant"
people.

Nevertheless, District 1 supported Fuentes' character
and the chancellor and the state educational commissioner
dropped an investigation of Fuentes.   Also, the liberal mayor

and the Ford Foundation, and the black Human Rights Commissioner, remained silent on his appointment. Only one city-school board member, Joseph Monserrat, the president and himself a leading spokesman for the Puerto Rican community, publically objected--in part illustrating how officials are hesitant to oppose an individual or group who belongs to a minority group or claims to represent the group. Few people are willing to oppose someone like Fuentes for fear of being denounced as a "racist. "

Similar hiring trends are affecting most major cities across the nation. Minority groups and whites both know it, no matter what kind of guarded language is employed. These new trends may reflect in part a law of sociology: the rise of one ethnic group and the decline of another group in matters related to the control of the city school systems.

Certainly there is mass failure in the ghetto schools. The reasons can be debated; the research is unclear, but as mentioned in Chapter 2 it points to family characteristics as the primary variable affecting the students' education (Coleman et al. , 1966; Jencks et al. , 1972; U. S. Commission on Civil Rights, 1967; Whiteman & Deutsch, 1968). To the knowledge of this author, there is no research that shows a cause-effect variable related to the ethnicity or color of the school principal and student achievement. In Southern ghetto schools, the black principals have not significantly effected student achievement rates. If there is any significant difference, it is that Northern black students have higher achievement rates than Southern blacks (Clark, 1965; Coleman et al. , 1966; Light & Smith, 1969), and the former black student group has in the past attended more schools with a white principal than the latter (Southern black) group. In Northern city school systems such as Gary, Philadelphia, St. Louis, and Washington, which have a majority of black principals and assistant principals, and in Baltimore, Chicago, Newark, and Oakland, which have a large percentage (around 30 to 50 percent) of black principals and assistant principals, the ghetto students are achieving just as low as in New York City, and in some cases even lower.

The quota system can also be used for purposes of curtailing school desegregation, and a recent incident in New York City illustrates the problem. A six-week controversy in 1972 between blacks and whites--involving Junior High School 211 and seven other area schools of District 18-- erupted in Canarsie, the southern section of Brooklyn. The

conflict was related to the bussing of 32 black and Puerto
Rican students into J. H. S. 211. The clash included police
barricades, racial insults among the parents across the barricades, racial clashes between youth gangs, a three-day
sit-in by the white parents of JHS 211, and a two-week boy-
cott of the schools in the community district, which reduced
attendance to about 10 percent.

Junior High School 211 is already overcrowded and
30 percent nonwhite as a result of the school's being situated
near two low-income housing projects. The white parents
claimed the school was "naturally" integrated and there was
no need to bus students from outside its area. They also
feared that additional students would "tip" the neighborhood
by causing white parents to sell out and move elsewhere to
educate their children. The reader can claim this is sheer
racism, but the social history of our city neighborhoods and
schools indicate a tipping as we go beyond the 70:30 ratio.
In Canarsie there was the additional bitterness that nearby
Junior High School 68, about one mile away, was 97 percent
white. Although it is more overcrowded than JHS 211, the
white parents claimed that the new students should have been
bussed into this other school--even if it meant bussing 32
white students into Canarsie to avoid additional overcrowding
of JHS 68. The chancellor accepted the idea of bussing the
black and Puerto Rican students to JHS 68, but the black
parents rejected it and the city-wide school board rescinded
the chancellor's ruling--thus embarrassing him--apparently
in a bow to the demands of the black community. The most
interesting aspect of the controversy is that the decentralized,
community-controlled system was established in order to
mollify black demands for local autonomy. They got it, and
now for the first time whites in New York City wanted to exercise their local autonomy on a major issue. Whites were
vetoed by the city-wide school board, again apparently influenced mainly by pressure from the black community, or
so it seems to the white parents of Canarsie (Chicago Tribune, November 8, 1972; New York Times, October 10, 25,
November 5, 12, 1972).

With regard to the seventh goal, there has been little
student relevancy, but rather an increase in student crime
and violence, including dope peddling, bombings, rape, and
even killings. The victims have been both students and
teachers. Vincent Baker (1972), the Coordinator of Anti-
Crime Activities for the NAACP in the New York metropolitan area, asserts:

Crime and violence have made many schools jungles
in which neither teaching nor learning can be a continuing process. Mugging, rape, extortion, dope peddling, vandalism and simple disruption have become
the order of the day [p. 9].

Teachers and principals are reluctant to act, according to Baker. When they do, the courts or community advocates see to it that the students are returned, "with the
principal and the complaining teacher fearing for their very
lives" (p. 9). Baker then sets down some realistic guidelines:

Education is to be planned and carried out by educators, not by students, not by well-meaning but unqualified adults. All students are entitled to equality
of opportunity, none to special privileges or dispensa-
tions. Standards of performance and excellence are
indispensable to education in today's world.... Crime
and violence in schools must be ended now--by expul-
sion and procecutions [p. 9].

Writing about big-city teachers in general, Ornstein (1972)
stated:

The teachers have increasingly become the victims of
student assaults, which many supervisors and administrators are reluctant to report, since it may be misconstrued as a blot on their records.... Furthermore, many colleagues and supervisors do not support
the victimized teacher, even during the immediate crisis, since the staff members are sometimes divided
along racial and political lines ... [p. 36].

White teachers in ghetto schools have increasingly become
the victims of assaults. The author continues:

... [I]f the principal wishes to take action himself,
he is often powerless to suspend the student for more
than a few days.... If the principal takes sterner action, he often risks conflict with student and community groups. Thus, students are learning that their
actions are going unpunished, even encouraged by militant student and community groups [p. 56-57].

The relations between white teachers and black students and the black community in general have

continued to worsen since the [Ocean Hill controversy
and teacher] strike, which in turn has intensified the
black-white polarization of the city and the decline of
'liberal' support for the black social revolution. This
trend is reflected in part by the steady increase in
school violence--ranging from stabbings and rapings
of teachers to the use of Mace and Molotov cocktails.
The violence steadily drives more white teachers out
of the schools and brings in more police, a vicious
cycle ... which has [recently] snowballed in New York
City ... [p. 150].

Moseley (1972) indicates that the community control
advocates utilize violence in order to gain control over the
community and use the students for their own political ends.
The violence committed by the community activists and students goes unpunished:

To march into a public school with a small group of
determined militants and ... to keep it open or shut
it down, to use its students for one's own political
purposes, to stand in the schoolhouse door and bar
entrance to others, to seize the principal and hold
him prisoner, to ... vandalize its property, occasionally even to burn it to the ground--all these are illegal actions. But ... they go generally unpunished
and sometimes unremarked ... because of fear on the
part of school and public officials that they will suffer
a loss of popularity, of political acceptability, if they
act otherwise than they do [p. 560].

The author continues:

Pupils are not disruptive because they are not well
taught. They are disruptive because superintendents
of schools and boards of education have taught them
to be disruptive.... They do not beat teachers because they are irrated by the irrelevance of the curriculum; they do not engage in narcotics traffic only
as some symptomatic outgrowth of a deeper psychological urge. Those who do these things do them because
those in the highest positions in our school systems
often encourage them [p. 563].

Much of the school violence is never reported to large
city central boards of education, and rarely makes the newspapers or is frankly discussed in college classrooms.

However, the editors of Saturday Review (February 5, 1973) indicated that in the 1972-73 school year New York City school officials reported more than 5000 "acts of violence and disruption," including rape, holdups, gambling, assault, bomb scares, even murder. For the first two months of the 1972-73 school year, the New York Times (November 5, 15, 1972) reported that the school board records showed that 75 teachers, mostly white, were mugged, held up, or assaulted in ghetto schools. The Times (November 5, 1972) reported several additional incidents of violence that were not recorded by the city-wide school board, thus suggesting that many other incidents may not be recorded by the school board; even worse, the records show that more than twice the number of students were the victims of assaults, and there is the strong possibility, the Times continued, that fewer of the assaults on students are reported than those on teachers.

To combat this rising school violence, a number of suggestions have been offered, ranging from walkie-talkie parent patrols, hiring off-duty police to moonlight and serve as school security guards, and providing each teacher and administrator with a pen-sized electronic alarm device (New York Times, October 25, November 15, 1972). In the meantime, the UFT asked for 5000 to 6000 "well trained men" to patrol the schools and has announced a $5000 reward to any person who provides information leading to apprehension and conviction of a person who assaults a teacher. In this crisis, even Mayor Lindsay agreed with the union, and the New York Times (January 14, 1973) reports that he had announced plans to help bring "a sense of peace and stability" to the city schools. Quality education was no longer the mayor's most important school priority, but it was eliminating fear so that education could proceed. The mayor allocated an extra $5 million for the 1973-74 school budget to pay for extra guards and school aides to help the police and 500 school guards that had already been assigned to selected schools.

The rise of school violence may reflect in part the ills of urban society. Nevertheless, we cannot ignore the fact that community control advocates are encouraged to use violence as a political tactic (Barbour, 1968; Carmichael & Hamilton, 1967; Moseley, 1972; Moynihan, 1969). In the same vein, community control advocates are spurred on by papers like the Black Panther and Black Liberation and the educational ideas of Barbour (1968), Carmichael and Hamilton (1967), and Sizemore (1972). Furthermore, the

community control advocates and the students have a battery
of lawyers provided gratis by community action programs
(federal money), the American Civil Liberties Union, and
other liberal and students' rights organizations.

With regard to the last and most important goal, student achievement, the data by Ravitch (1972) have already
been mentioned (see Chapter 2).   Although the reading scores
in Ocean Hill-Brownsville declined, it is unfair to make any
generalizations about community control from this.   The
Ocean Hill project was atypical and constantly under political
pressure.   In this connection, Gittell (1971) argues that "one
must in the final analysis beg the question" concerning the
effects of community control on educational achievement.   It
would be unwise "to attempt a full scale evaluation of the
educational achievement of an experimental program in a few
short years" (p. 110).   However, the continuous decline in
reading ability of the students in the city after two and a half
years of community control indicates to some extent that the
advocates of community control were wrong about improving
the quality of education.   The advocates did not mention the
real reasons for seeking community control--reasons which
had very little, if anything, to do with the students' educational achievement.

In only 25 percent of the system's 632 elementary
schools and 158 of its intermediate and junior high schools
were at least 50 percent of the students reading on grade
level, according to the New York Times (November 19, 1972).
District 23, which now includes the Ocean Hill-Brownsville
schools was the lowest district in terms of reading scores,
with a median percentile of 21.8 and a 27.5 to 17.1 range.
Sharing lowest honors with District 23 were District 1, which
now comprises the Two Bridges experimental schools and
which had a 17.5 median percentile and a 29.5 to 9.6 range,
and District 5, which now comprises the I.S. 201 complex
and which had a 23.2 median percentile and a 45.3 to 7.1
range.   In an "average" school, decentralized district, or
system, the students would score at the 50th percentile.

A tentative appraisal of administrative decentralization
and community control was summed up by Clark (1972a), one
of the original advocates of community control.   He said:
"My assessment of the consequences of decentralization" has
changed from my original views three years ago "when we
were fighting for it."   There is no evidence, he said, that
it has resulted in improving the quality of education for

students.   Those involved in decentralization have ignored
the original purpose.   "The purpose was not a struggle for
power or control [but] to improve" education (p. 1).   What
has actually occurred, he continues, is the people now
"squabble and fight ... and neglect the children" (p. 26).
Elsewhere Clark (1972b) reported in private testimony that
decentralization "had been a 'disastrous' experience" in
which the children suffered and "selfish forces ... and racial politics" plagued local school boards (p. 7).

SUMMARY AND CONCLUSION

[Perhaps the one best summary statement that pulls
together the above analysis and forms a whole picture is
Shanker's (1972d) synopsis, following.]

"Dr. Kenneth Clark, an early and ardent supporter of
school decentralization, has now pronounced decentralization
a failure, saying, 'I personally do not see evidence that decentralization has resulted in an increased quality of education for children in the schools.'   Dr. Clark's statement, as
well as Paul Parker's extensive news coverage on WINS and
recent articles in the New York Times, Daily News and the
Post, have made a start at providing a picture to the public
of how our schools are faring under decentralization.   Here
are some of the picture's highlights:

"District 1 on Manhattan's lower East Side is still
without a functioning community board.   Its board meetings
have been the scene of conflict and violence.   Its superintendent has decided to retire.

"District 6's community board sent a one-sentence
memorandum to 'Parents, Community Organizations and
Friends of the Community' on April 21 stating, 'Because of
the climate of violence which has been attendant at Public
Meetings, we are forced to cancel the meeting of April 24,
1972 which was scheduled at JHS 143.'   This was followed
by a fuller statement on April 25: 'Community School Board
District 6's Public Meetings have consistently been disrupted
by special interest groups.   As a result of the most recent
disruption, no federally funded Summer Programs for the
children of this district have been approved.   To maintain
viable public meetings, Community School Board 6 has again
and again requested adequate police presence and these requests have been refused.   Physical attacks against Board

Members have taken place. . . . ' CSB 6 charged that the violence
was caused by an organization called NEGRO which had sent
two busloads of demonstrators to the meeting.   NEGRO, led
by Dr. Thomas Matthew, is a federally funded program which
has recently received large increases in funding from the
Nixon Administration.

"In East Harlem's District 4, a recent Times editorial
charges: '. . . the increasing chaos . . . involved, in addition
to deliberate disregard of rules and procedures, the flagrant
violation of personal rights of parents and the professional
rights of administrators.   Community members and their
children have been threatened.   Public board meetings have
been disrupted and coerced by special interest groups.   The
district superintendent, after being denied the right to speak
despite the parent's overwhelming demand that he be heard,
last week was physically assaulted and had to be escorted by
police to safety. . . .   The board's policy-making functions are
being undermined by improper pressures from outside groups
. . . .   Members of the East Harlem Community Corporation,
an antipoverty agency, have brazenly intimidated the community board during its public meetings. '

"To these highlights must be added other elements of
the emerging picture: The misspending of hundreds of thousands of dollars has been charged to District 23. . . . In District 9, a trip to Puerto Rico by certain members of the
community has been planned at a cost to the local school
board of $60,000.   (When Chancellor Scribner was informed
of the junket, his response was that the 'community' could
spend its money any way it wanted.) . . . Another board used
school moneys to send some of its members to the Black
Power conference in Gary, Indiana. . . . In yet another district, assistant health coordinator Ilene Biggs resigned her
$18,000 a year job following her refusal to sign time sheets
which would have authorized salary payments to employees
who had not shown up for their jobs.

"To round out the picture: While over 10,000 regularly licensed teachers, most of them graduates of our City
and State Universities, are waiting for jobs, 10,000 others,
not regularly licensed, have been assigned to schools.   With
10,000 New Yorkers waiting for teaching jobs, some community boards are spending badly needed school funds in efforts
to recruit new college graduates from the South--strictly on
a racial basis.   To make the picture worse, with thousands
of experienced supervisors leaving the system, there is the

prospect of greater conflict over the question of who will fill
the openings.

"What the schools are coming to is painfully clear.
The Times on April 20 reported, 'the observation among
many parents and residents in District 5 that, as the influence of the old political clubs has waned because of a lack
of money and jobs and because money that once flowed into
the antipoverty program has slowed to a trickle, available
money and jobs have shifted to the local school districts....
A general attitude among parents that squabbles over money,
power and influence have overshadowed the real educational
needs of the students. '

"What conclusion can be drawn from all this? What
is to be done? Predictably, advocates of total community
control, like David Seely, of the Public Education Association, and Marilyn Gittell, who channelled Ford Foundation
funds into the original demonstration districts, argue with
their usual incomprehensible logic that these problems would
disappear if communities were given complete power and
were not subject to controls by a central board and a Chancellor, or by licensing standards and union contracts. That's
roughly equivalent to arguing that the most effective way to
rid the world of crime is to abolish all police forces.

"On the other hand, Dr. Clark has been as quick to
reject decentralization as originally to embrace it. He seems
to be dismayed because political and administrative school
changes have not resulted in educational improvements. But
that should hardly have surprised him; surely he is aware
that educational improvements will be made on the basis of
educational programs rather than political and administrative
ones.

"Neither centralization nor decentralization is an educational solution. Nevertheless, New York City schools are
decentralized, and it will be hard to put Humpty Dumpty together again. Meanwhile, decentralization can work much
better than it has thus far--but only if Dr. Scribner and the
Board of Education do their jobs. They must be strict in
the area of fiscal controls, for the taxpayer must know that
his money is being spent on education and not on political
giveaways. Furthermore, they must support civil service
employment policies which will put an end to the violent push
for patronage jobs at the local level and hiring on a discriminatory basis" [p. 9].

The way the reader reacts to Shanker's summary statement above and to the chapter in general will in the main reflect
his own bias. Those who oppose community control will
have found ample data to coincide with and perhaps harden
their original views. Those who have advocated community
control for educational reasons, like myself at one time,
may change or at least start rethinking their ideas. Those
who still purport the virtues of community control are mainly
speaking from an ideological slant, and it is doubtful if they
are going to alter their opinions. If anything, they may most
likely question the author's motives and accuse him of nasty
"isms," a ploy used with great success when the subject is
race. In effect, a person who is denounced as a "racist" is
put on the defensive, and the real issues and problems become secondary or are temporarily ignored.

Indeed, it is boring to hear the accusation of "racism"
applied almost whenever a response or description may be
construed as unfavorable to the black cause. Blacks and
others who characterize contrary viewpoints as a burst of
racist backlash or sheer bigotry oversimplify the problems.
When educational chaos grips a large city school system,
when student crime and violence snowball, when quotas replace competency and anyone who objects to them is accused
as an "elitist" or "racist," when teachers and administrators
are harassed, assaulted, and even killed on the job, when
school board members threaten each other and literally fight
among themselves, when public officials and educators look
the other way at disruptive and violent acts because of fear
or loss of unpopularity, when politics is intensified and re-
places education in the schools, when the tune to the new
bandwagon movement is one of ideology, when the opponent
is always wrong and there can be little or no compromise,
when the schools become battlefields, and when the most influential and liberal city in the country is divided by an un-
bridgeable abyss across which understanding no longer seems
possible, then I think people are justified in objecting to a
movement that seems to create or aggravate divisiveness.
My original views (Ornstein, 1970, 1971, 1972), like Clark's,
were favorable toward community control, but my analysis
has changed.

It is important to remember how little we know. A
concept such as community control is only a premise--that
if X is done Y will occur--and it is often difficult to know in
advance whether a premise in social sciences is valid or
what will really happen when human variables interact in

real situations. One hopes that the future advocates and designers of community control and the related trend toward
administrative decentralization will learn to examine their
premises more carefully, conduct some experiments on a
more modest scale before mass implementation, learn through
systematic collection of data, and implement change according to evidence. Once social change or legislative policy is
enacted, it is difficult to rescind.

NOTES

1. It was unclear whether this person wanted to be quoted
   by name. His cooperation was invaluable, having provided the author with several newspaper clippings of
   events from 1969-73.

2. The disparity between city and suburban school revenues
   are common throughout the nation and had led to the
   famous Serrano v Priest (1971) California court case
   which concluded that the state's method of financing
   school systems denied students equal educational opportunity guaranteed under the Fourteenth Amendment,
   because it results in substantial disparities among
   school districts in the amount of revenue for education. For example, based on 1968-69 figures, the
   Beverly Hills school district of Los Angeles spent
   $1232 per student, while Baldwin Park school district,
   in the same county of Los Angeles, allocated $577 for
   each student. The main reason for this inequality was
   the difference in local assessed property valuation per
   student. In Beverly Hills, the amount was $50,885
   per student and in Baldwin Park it was $3706 per stu-
   dent--a ratio of 13:1 (Serrano v Priest, 1971).
   Or, another example, across the nation: New York
   City in the 1967-68 school year received $170 less
   per student than average from the state but raised
   $325 more per student at the local level than the
   state average. Overall total revenues including federal sources) in New York City was $55 above the
   state average--meaning that the city residents were
   heavily taxed to absorb the differences between state
   and local funds. A similar story was repeated in
   Detroit; the city received $71 less per student than
   the state average. Total revenue sources including
   local, state, and federal monies was $111 below the
   state average, and the gap was wider with the

wealthier suburbs (<u>Finances of Large-City School Systems</u>, 1971). In Oklahoma, the richest school district spent $2566 per student in 1969-70; the poorest spent $342 (<u>New York Times</u>, November 12, 1972).

In 1973 the <u>Serrano</u> interpretation was reversed by the U. S. Supreme Court.

3. Quoted in Grant (1971, p. 2). The editor of the <u>Michigan Chronicle</u> wrote to the author (November 21, 1971) pointing out that the original source requested was not on file.

4. According to the newsletter <u>Detroit's Schools ...</u> (1970), the number of school board candidates totaled 136 and in each region ranged from 15 (in Region 8) to 38 (in Region 4). With so many candidates, it is hard to believe that the voters knew the qualifications or platforms of most of the persons running or elected to the school boards.

5. The first metropolitan desegregation plan to make headlines across the nation was submitted to Congress in 1971 by U. S. Senator Abraham Ribicoff of Connecticut. The bill, defeated in Congress, would have required that all schools in a metropolitan area have a percentage of minority students at least equal to half the percentage of minority students in an entire area. Thus, if 50 percent of the students in a metropolitan area were black, 25 percent of the students in each school in the city and surrounding suburbs would have to be black. The bill would have given the school systems 12 years to achieve this level of integration but required substantial progress each year if the schools were not to lose their federal funds (Ornstein, 1972).

6. The New York City's supervisory examinations are being contested by an NAACP lawsuit. Regardless of the outcome in court, city school systems across the country are attenuating these tests, in part to increase the minority proportion in school executive positions.

7. Kemble (1968) points out that Ferguson was appointed as one of the principals of the schools in the Ocean Hill-Brownsville district by the governing board; the city-wide board of education vetoed the appointment.

8. While we only briefly discuss the issue of quotas in the
    New York City schools, there is a large amount of
    data on the rise of quotas and reverse discrimination
    throughout the job sector.   See Abrams (1972), Glazer
    (1971), San Francisco Chronicle, November 2, 1972,
    Seabury (1972), and Seligman (1973).

REFERENCES

Aberbach, Joel D. and Walker, Jack L.   "Citizen Desires,
    Policy Outcomes, and Community Control." Paper Pre-
    sented at the Annual American Political Science Associa-
    tion.   Chicago, September 1971.

_____ and _____.   Race and the Urban Political Com-
    munity.   Boston: Little, Brown, 1972.

Abrams, Elliott.   "The Quota System." Commentary, Octo-
    ber 1972, 54-57.

An Act Directing the Board of Education of the City of New
    York to Prepare for the Development of a Community
    School District System.   State of New York, Senate
    5690, Assembly 7175, April 30, 1969.   Albany: State
    of New York Senate-Assembly, 1969.

Baker, Vincent.   Quoted in Albert Shanker, "A Time for
    Action Against Disruption in the Schools." New York
    Times, March 26, 1972, Section 4, p. 9.

Bakke, Birger.   "Detroit Schools: Mirror of a City." Na-
    tional Association of Secondary School Principals, 1971,
    55, 124-38.

Barbour, Floyd B. (ed.).   The Black Power Revolt.   New
    York: Macmillan, 1968.

Bard, Bernard.   "The Battle for School Jobs: New York's
    Newest Agony." Phi Delta Kappan, 1972, 53, 553-58.

Billings, Charles.   "Community Control of the School and
    the Quest for Power." Phi Delta Kappan, 1972, 53,
    277-78.

Carmichael, Stokeley and Hamilton, Charles V.   Black Power.
    New York: Random House, 1967.   (Vintage ed.)

Central Administrative Structure of Detroit Schools.   Detroit:
    Office of School Decentralization, Board of Education of
    the City of Detroit, September 1971.

Chicago Tribune, November 8, 1972.

Clark, Kenneth B.   Dark Ghetto.   New York: Harper &
    Row, 1965.

_____.   News article in the New York Times, May 8,
    1972(a), p. 1, 26.

_____.   Quoted in the New York Times, December 3,
    1972(b), p. 7.

Coleman, James S. et al.   Equality of Educational Opportu-
    nity.   Washington, D. C. :   Government Printing Office,
    1966.

The Day Schools Register by School District on October 30,
    1970.   New York: Department of Educational Program,
    Research and Statistics, Board of Education of the City
    of New York, April 1971.

Decentralization Statement of Policy.   Adapted at a Public
    Meeting.   New York: Board of Education, April 19, 1967.

Delegation of Functions to Local School Boards.   Special
    Committee on Development of a Community School Dis-
    trict Plan.   New York: Board of Education, Septem-
    ber 4, 11, 1968.

Demas, Boulton H.   The School Elections: A Critique of
    the 1969 City School Decentralization.   New York: Insti-
    tute for Community Studies, Queens College of the City
    University of New York, 1971.

Detroit Free Press, Aug. 5, 1970;   Nov. 7, 1970;   April 6,
    1971; Sept. 28, 1971; March 24, 1972; March 26, 1972.

Detroit Information Officer.   Periodical Letters to the Au-
    thor, 1972-73.

Detroit News, June 13, 1971; Feb. 14, 1972; Feb. 24; Feb. 25;
    March 3; March 10; March 13; March 14; March 15;
    March 23, March 28; March 29; April 4; April 19; Dec. 8;
    Dec. 9, 1972.

Detroit Public Schools Directory, 1971-72. Detroit: Office
     of School Decentralization, Board of Education, 1972.

Detroit's Schools Make History with Decentralization. De-
     troit: Office of School Decentralization, Board of Edu-
     cation, October 1970.

District Boundary Lines under the Community School District
     System. Special Committee on Decentralization (Commit-
     tee of the Whole). New York: Board of Education,
     December 22, 1969.

Donovan, Barnard E. Superintendent's Report to Members
     of the Board of Education of the City of New York,
     October 14, 1968.

Dyer, Henry S. "Toward Objective Criteria of Professional
     Accountability in the Schools of New York." Phi Delta
     Kappan, 1970, 52, 206-11.

E. S. Shopper--Community News, February 9, 1972; April 5;
     April 12; April 19; May 3, 1972.

Facts and Figures, 1970-71. New York: Office of Education
     Information Services and Public Relations, Board of Edu-
     cation, May 1971.

Facts and Figures, 1971-72. New York: Office of Educa-
     tion Information Services and Public Relations, Board
     of Education, May 1972.

Facts with Figures, Detroit Public Schools 1971. Detroit:
     Office of School Decentralization, Board of Education,
     1971.

Fantini, Mario D., Gittell, Marilyn, and Magat, Richard.
     Community Control and the Urban School. New York:
     Praeger, 1970.

Feldman, Sandra. The Burden of Blame-Placing. New
     York: United Federation of Teachers, 1969.

_____. "The UFT and the School Conflict." United
     Teacher, April 23, 1972, 1-8.

Finances of Large-City School Systems: A Comparative
     Analysis. Prepared by L. H. Fox and G. E. Hurd,

National Center for Educational Statistics.   Washington, D. C. : Government Printing Office, 1971.

Gittell, Marilyn.   Demonstration for Social Change.   New York: Institute for Community Studies, Queens College of the City University of New York, 1971.

_____ and Hevesi, Alan G. (eds.).   The Politics of Urban Education.   New York: Praeger, 1969.

Glazer, Nathan.   "A Breakdown in Civil Rights Enforcement?" Public Interest, No. 23, 1971, 106-15.

_____ and Moynihan, Daniel P.   Beyond the Melting Pot (2nd ed.).   Cambridge, Mass. : M. I. T. Press, 1970.

Grant, William R.   "School Decentralization in Detroit: A Review of a Confusing Issue. " Unpublished paper, June 27, 1970.

_____.   "Community Control vs School Integration--the Case of Detroit. " United Teacher, November 7, 1971, 1-4.

Guidelines for Regional and Central Board of Education of the School District of the City of Detroit.   Adopted in Accordance with Public Act No. 48 of 1970 State of Michigan.   Detroit: Board of Education, October 26, 1970.

Jackson, Philip W.   Life in Classrooms.   New York: Holt, 1968.

Jencks, Christopher et al.   Inequality: A Reassessment of the Effect of Familiy and Schooling in America.   New York: Basic Books, 1972.

Kemble, Eugene (ed.).   New York's Experiments in School Decentralization.   New York: United Federation of Teachers, 1968.

Light, Richard J. and Smith, Paul V.   "Social Allocation Models of Intelligence: A Methodological Inquiry. " Harvard Educational Review, 1969, 39, 484-510.

Mayer, Martin.   The Teachers' Strike.   New York: Harper & Row, 1969.

Mayor's Advisory Panel on Decentralization of the New York
    City Schools. Reconnection for Learning: A Community
    School System for New York City. New York: Ford
    Foundation, 1967.

Michigan Chronicle, Aug. 15, 1970; Feb. 5, 1972; April 22,
    1972.

Model Regional Organization Chart. Detroit: Office of School
    Decentralization, Board of Education of the City of De-
    troit, (n. d.).

Moseley, Francis S. "The Urban Secondary School: Too
    Late for Mere Change." Phi Delta Kappan, 1972, 53,
    559-64.

Moynihan, Daniel P. Maximum Feasible Misunderstanding.
    New York: Free Press, 1969.

_____. "The Schism in the Black Family." Public In-
    terest, No. 27, 1972, 3-24.

National Advisory Commission on Civil Disorders. U.S.
    Riot Commission Report. New York: Bantam, 1968.

New York City Information Assistant. Letter to the Author,
    March 10, 1972(a).

_____. Letter to the Author, April 28, 1972(b).

New York City Information Officer. Telephone Conversation
    with the Author, July 3, 1972(a).

_____. Letter to the Author, July 3, 1972(b).

New York Times, July 23, 1970; Aug. 15, 1971; Nov. 15,
    1971; Jan. 16, 1972; April 20; June 4; June 11;
    June 18; July 16; Aug. 8; Sept. 24; Oct. 10; Oct. 25;
    Nov. 5; Nov. 12; Nov. 19, 1972; Jan. 14, 1973;
    May 2; May 6, 1973.

Northeast Detroiter, Feb. 17, 1972; March 23; March 28;
    April 20, 1972.

Ornstein, Allan C. "Decentralization: Problems and Pros-
    pects. " Negro Educational Review, 1970, 21, 24-29.

_____. "Decentralizing Urban Schools. " Journal of
    Secondary Education, 1971, 46, 83-91.

_____. Urban Education: Student Unrest, Teacher Be-
    haviors, and Black Power. Columbus, Ohio: Merrill,
    1972.

Phi Delta Kappan. "News Notes. " 1972, 54, p. 73. (a)

_____. "Washington Report. " 1972, 54, p. 69-70. (b)

A Plan for Educational Policy and Administrative Units (Fur-
    ther Decentralization of the Public Schools). New York:
    Board of Education, March 7, 1968.

Popham, W. James. "Found: A Practical Procedure to
    Appraise Teacher Achievement in the Classroom. "
    Nation's Schools, 1972, 89, 59-60.

Proposed Plan for a Community School District in New York
    City. Special Committee on Decentralization (Committee
    on the Whole). New York: Board of Education, Nov-
    ember 17, 1969.

Public Reaction Draft of Decentralization Guidelines. De-
    troit: Office of School Decentralization, Board of Edu-
    cation, August 1970.

Quamby, Lucille. Coordinator of Information Services, De-
    troit Public Schools. Letter to the Author, February 1,
    1972.

Ravitch, Diane. "Community Control Revisited. " Commen-
    tary, February 1973, 70-74.

Redford Record, January 10, 1972.

San Francisco Chronicle, November 2, 1972.

Saturday Review. (The Editors) February 5, 1973.

Scribner, Harvey B. Chancellor of the New York Public
    Schools. Letter to the Members of Community School
    Board District 1, November 29, 1971.

_____. News article in the New York Times, May 8,
1972, p. 26.

Seabury, Paul. "HEW & the Universities." Commentary,
February 1972, 38-44.

Seligman, Daniel. "How 'Equal Opportunity' Turned Into
Employment Quotas." Fortune, March 1973, 160-68.

Serrano v Priest, 1971. Text of the Court Case, Adapted
by Arthur Wise, "The California Doctrine." Saturday
Review, November 20, 1971, 78-79, 82-83.

Serrin, William. "The Most Hated Man in Michigan."
Saturday Review, August 26, 1972, 13-15.

Shanker, Albert. "UFT Statement on Decentralization," The
Federation, (n. d.).

_____. "The Real Meaning of the New York City Teachers'
Strike." Phi Delta Kappan, 1969, 50, 434-41.

_____. "Decentralization II: The New York Experience."
New York Times, August 15, 1971(a), Section 4, p. 11.

_____. "Decentralization: Have the Claims Proved Valid."
New York Times, November 28, 1971(b), Section 4, p. 9.

_____. "A Threat to Human Rights Confronts Us Once
Again: Ethnic Quotas vs. Individual Merit." New York
Times, February 20, 1972(a), Section 4, p. 9.

_____. "A Time for Action Against Disruptions in the
Schools." New York Times, March 26, 1972(b), Section 4, p. 9.

_____. "19th-Century Rigidities Return as the New Look."
New York Times, August 20, 1972(c), Section 4, p. 7.

_____. "School Decentralization: A Troubled Picture
Emerges." New York Times, May 14, 1972(d), Section 4, p. 9.

_____. "The Outrageous Appointment of Luis Fuentes."
New York Times, July 30, 1972(e), Section 4, p. 9.

Sizemore, Barabara A. "Is There a Case for Separate

Schools?" Phi Delta Kappan, 1973, 53, 281-84.

Sizer, Theodore. "Report Analysis: Reconnection for Learning." Harvard Educational Review, 1968, 38, 176-84.

Sowell, Thomas. Black Education: Myths and Tragedies.
New York: McKay, 1973.

Summaries of Regional Board Meeting Minutes. Detroit:
Office of School Decentralization, Board of Education of
the City of Detroit, January 1971-June 1972.

Summary of Citywide Reading Test Results for 1970-71. New
York: Bureau of Educational Research, Board of Education of the City of New York, January 1972.

Text of Public Act 48. An Act to Amend the Title and Sections 4, 5, 6, and 7 of Act No. 244 of the Public Acts
of 1969. East Lansing: State of Michigan--75 Legisla-
ture--Regular Session of 1970.

U. S. Commission on Civil Rights. Racial Isolation in the
Public Schools. Washington, D. C.: Government Printing Office, 1967.

Wall Street Journal, August 25, 1967.

Whiteman, Martin and Deutsch, Martin. "Social Disadvan-
tage as Related to Intellective and Language." In: M.
Deutsch, I. Katz, and A. R. Jensen (eds.), Social Class,
Race, and Psychological Development. New York: Holt,
1968; p. 86-114.

Working Draft of Possible Guidelines for Implementation of
Public Act 244, 2 vols. Detroit: Office of School De-
centralization, Board of Education of the City of Detroit,
April, May 1970.

Zwerdling, A. L. Speech Presented to the Research Council
of the Great City Schools. Washington, D. C., November 12, 1969. Reported in the Detroit Free Press, November 14, 1969(a), p. 3A.

_____. Speech to the Detroit League of Voters. Detroit,
November 14, 1969(b).

_____. Quoted in the Detroit Free Press, January 18,
1970, p. 3A.

INDEX OF NAMES

INDEX OF SCHOOL SYSTEMS

INDEX OF SUBJECTS